HOME FREE

Betty Pruden

7/26/97

*To Janette,
my dear Hopewell
school mate!
Love,
Betty Pruden*

E.M. Press, Inc.
Manassas, VA

This is an original work of literature.

ISBN: 1-880664-20-8
Library of Congress Catalog Card Number: 96-48124

E.M. Press, Inc.
P.O. Box 4057
Manassas, VA   20108

DEDICATION

To my Sister, Beverly E. Wilkins, and to
the Fight Against Child Abuse and Neglect

ACKNOWLEDGMENTS

I wish to thank every person who encouraged me to write this story, especially my long-time friends, Sheila Thomas, Rosie Thrasher, Saundra Keller, Tamieson Cranor, Lynn Carter, Clyde Jones, Gerrie Gallagher, Helen Franklin, Dawn Gill, Brenda Shepherd and Rennie Snow.

For my sister, I am forever grateful. Without her, my book would have no spark.

And to my husband, Peter, I shall be indebted always.

I thank Social Services for its far-reaching and endless work in caring for the unfortunate. In my heart, I know that my path into adulthood would have been a destructive one without the good lessons and moral standards I learned in foster care.

Also, I thank the Child Abuse Prevention Council for their very vital work, and, along with my sister, I dedicate this book to them and to Social Services.

The Author

PREFACE

My purpose in writing *Home Free* is to help in the fight against child abuse and neglect. I feel that this writing will also be an inspiration to teenagers who need encouragement and strength to believe in themselves and to cling to uplifting values.

This book is based on my childhood from the years three to fourteen.

And so, dear friend, read the book and help a child along the way.

CHAPTER 1

Inside Out

Matthew Lucas walked quickly on a brisk January morning in 1937. He always walked fast during the cold winter days in upstate New York. Tall and slender, he took long, even strides up the familiar road, his heavy wool army coat slapping at his black arctics as he plunged each boot into the newly-fallen snow.

New York winters began with the first snowfalls in late October, and many a year the residents of the rural areas and small towns did not see the brown earth until the April thaws. There were snowfalls upon snowfalls, and there were blizzards that caused whiteouts that made visibility impossible more than a foot or two ahead or behind. Some less intense storms picked up small swirls of the powder, danced them around the surface of shimmering whiteness, and then dropped them into whatever corners, hollows or crevices they found.

But the day that Matthew Lucas walked up the main road of Gallaway, the night's snowfall lay undisturbed on rooftops, trees, and road as the dawning light spread hues of pink and purple over the boundless landscape. No tracks were seen on the vast mounds before him, and he had heard no sounds of morning coming from the low bungalows behind the stores on Main Street. It was seven o'clock, and the stores stood dusty, white and still, awaiting wake-up calls from their owners.

Matthew paused a moment to catch his breath. He'd been walking steadily since he'd left his home a half hour earlier.

"Old ticker ain't as strong as she used to be," he mumbled. "And this dang hill gets longer every day."

He squinted in the sunny brightness of the hour and looked to the top of the hill at his friend's pipe and tobacco store.

"Lou'll be waiting for me," he puffed, and the fog of his breath distanced the little shop from his view.

"Yeah, he'll be there, for sure, and want me to help stock the shelves," he chuckled. "Works from sunup to sundown. Don't guess he ever goes home."

He laughed and shocked himself with his loudness. "I'll be waking up the whole town if I'm not careful," he whispered, and feeling revived and eager to get out of the harsh coldness, he lifted his foot and placed its print in the smooth snow ahead of him. Before he could take another step, however, his ears picked up a sound that made him tremble in disbelief. He froze in his tracks, almost not daring to breathe so he could hear better. Now, it was clear—a baby crying.

"Baby crying," he shouted, "where, where?" He raised his gloved hand to his forehead to shadow his eyes from the blinding glare, and he looked ahead of him up the hill to a sight he would never forget.

"It's a carriage outside Lou's door—a carriage with a crying baby in it. Gotta hurry now," he puffed and pulled the ends of his thick wool muffler tighter around his neck, all the time moving quickly up the hill in an awkward stumbling trot.

When he neared the carriage, he grabbed the handle and stopped, huffing and trying desperately to get his breath. He reached under the hood of the carriage and pulled the blanket back, and there lay the red-faced crying baby. As he lifted the small bundle up close to his chest, he heard a scream and felt a tugging at his coat and soft kicks on his leg. He turned to see the tear-filled eyes of a little girl in a blue snowsuit.

"Don't t-t-take m-m-my sis—ter," she cried. "P-p-ple-e-ese, Mis-ter M-M-Man—d-d-don—t-t-take her..."

And so begins Mary Elizabeth Easley's story.

*   *   *

I was just three years old, and Millie was almost one when our world was turned inside out. I felt inside out because we were not in our home anymore. We were out in the world.

Mommy took us to the pipe store because our house was right behind it. She dressed us in our snowsuits and said she was taking us to the store to get Daddy a new pipe. But when we got to the front door, it was locked, so she said she'd have to go get Daddy to help.

"You stay right here, Mary," she said, "and you watch your baby sister. Don't you let anyone take you away."

That's why I was so afraid of Matthew. I thought he'd steal us, and then Mommy would never find us. But Matthew was a nice man and took us inside the store to get us warm. We waited there a long time, but Mommy never returned. Finally, Matthew took us across the road to the courthouse, and when we got inside the big doors, he asked to see Miss Warring.

"Who's Miss Warring?" I asked.

"She's the social worker, and she'll know what to do," said Matthew.

I listened to them talking.

"I found these babies on the street," said Matthew, "and Lou and I think they're Easleys. Mary, here, says her mommy left them and was coming back to get them."

"Not likely," said Miss Warring. "The Easleys are poor and no one ever knows what Mrs. Easley will do, even leave her children on the street."

That meant Mommy was bad, and I didn't like to hear that. Matthew asked Miss Warring what she would do.

"Oh, I'll do the usual and put them in a home," she said.

"I'd rather have them myself," Matthew said.

"Well, you can't," said Miss Warring. "You don't have a wife, and we'd be breaking the rules if they don't have a mother."

But we did have a mother, and I couldn't imagine what had happened to her. I thought somebody took *her* away.

Miss Warring took us to her house, and then I asked her, "Where's my mommy?"

"I don't know, Mary. Nobody knows. Everybody is looking, so don't worry. We'll find your mommy."

Millie and I stayed at Miss Warring's house for a lot of days. I don't know how many. Millie cried a lot, and Miss Warring said it was because Millie's toes and fingers had been frozen.

"Can't you make them better?"

"Only time will do that," she said.

Every day, I asked Miss Warring if Mommy would come to get us pretty soon, and she said she hoped so.

One night after supper, Miss Warring carried Millie and said we'd go in the living room to talk. She didn't smile when she said it, so I thought something bad had happened to Mommy and Daddy, and I started to cry.

"It's all right, Mary. You're going to be fine," she said.

Miss Warring pulled me up on her lap beside Millie and said, "Mary, I want you to listen to everything I say."

"Is Mommy dead?" I asked, and I felt my mouth go closed like it did when I was going to cry.

"No, no, your mommy's not dead. But, she's been found, as has your daddy. They're fine, but they don't have enough money to feed their three children, so we'll have to let you and Millie live with somebody else for awhile. Your older brother, Billy, will stay with them for now, but he'll go to another home, too, when we find one for him."

"C-c-can we live with you?" I asked.

"No, you have to live with a lady who has a husband, so you can have a mommy *and* daddy like children are supposed to have. I've found a good home for you and Millie with the Sinks."

"Where do they live, and what are their other names?"

"They don't live very far from my house, so you can come to visit me sometimes. How's that?"

"I don't know," I said. "What are their other names?"

"The mother's name is Esther, and the father's name is Charles, and why do you want to know?"

"Because they won't be Mommy and Daddy, and I have to know what to call them."

I looked into Miss Warring's face and she smiled at me, but I didn't want to smile back. I wanted to live with Mommy and Daddy. So I cried, and when Millie heard me, she cried, and we didn't stop until Miss Warring put us in our beds and we went to sleep.

The next morning after breakfast, I helped pack Millie's and my boxes with clothes that Miss Warring had bought at the store. She threw out our old ones because she said they were too small and ragged. I didn't want them to be thrown away, but she said they weren't any good to us. I asked her if I could keep my blue mittens, even if they did have holes, and she said that would be all right.

"They are my very fav'rit mittens, 'cause they keep my hands very warm," I said. "I will wear 'um under my new mittens, an' the red ones will hide the holes in the blue ones. How's that?"

"Good idea, Mary. You're a smart little girl, aren't you?"

"Uh, huh. Daddy said so. Will I see him at my new house?"

"You might."

"That's good. I'll show him all my mittens—one, two, free, four of 'um."

She dressed us in our new snowsuits, boots and hats and carried us to her black car where she put us in the back seat. I had to hold Millie's arm so she wouldn't roll off onto the floor as Miss Warring drove over the snowy roads to the Sink's house. I couldn't see out the window because it was too high, but we didn't ride very long before Miss Warring stopped her car.

"Here we are, girls," she said. "That wasn't far, was it?"

"No, but I don't know the way to your house," I said.

"Esther will show you. Don't worry. She'll probably bring you to see me in a few days."

She carried Millie inside first and then came to get me.

"I want to walk in the snow in my new boots," I said.

"You'll fall and get all snowy and wet," said Miss Warring.

"No, I won't fall down. I wanna walk."

"All right, but I'll have to hold your hand."

And so I walked in the snow with all my new clothes on, and I felt very warm and happy. I looked up at the open front door and saw Mrs. Sink standing there in her red dress and red lipstick.

I looked up at Miss Warring. "She's pretty," I said. "Is she a nice lady, too, like you?"

"She's a very nice lady, and you will be happy with her. Let's hurry, so she won't get cold there in the doorway."

*   *   *

I called them Esther and Charles, and I remember the happy times we had with them. Sometimes I thought their house was better than mine. It was warm, and it had pretty curtains. We had good beef and ham and spaghetti to eat and lots of milk to drink. And sometimes we had cocoa with marshmallows.

"You're beginning to look like little roly-polys," Esther said one night when she was giving us a bath in the sink.

"What's a roly-poly?" I asked.

"It's something round and fat and happy," she said. "You are such pretty little girls."

"Will you read us a story tonight?" I asked.

"I think Charles will read tonight. I'm a little tired. Is that all right with you? I'm sure he'll let you choose. Which one do you think Millie would like?"

"Millie likes what I like, and I like *Cinderella.*"

*   *   *

When summer came, Charles and Esther took us to a lake to swim, and then we had a picnic and fed the ducks the bread crusts. Charles tried to teach me to swim, but I was afraid to put my head in the water.

"Oh well, we'll just try next summer," he said. "No hurry. You have lots of time to learn."

When we were riding back home, I heard Charles tell Esther he would make a swing for us in the big oak tree. She said that would be nice, and maybe he could fix a seat to fit in it for Millie.

"Why not make two swings," I said, "one for me and one for Millie. Then we could swing together like in the park by our house, and I wouldn't have to wait for Millie to get out of my swing."

"Good idea," said Charles. "That's just what I'll do—put one on each side of the tree!"

I was so excited about having my own swing. "And you get yours, Millie. How's that?" I asked, tickling her under her chin to make her laugh.

A few days later, when Esther was pushing us at the oak tree, I saw Charles go into the garage with wood under his arm.

"Whatcha doin'?" I called.

"It's a surprise," he shouted.

"What's he doin', Esther?"

"He didn't tell me, either, so I don't know who's getting the surprise. Maybe it's for me, but it may be for you and Millie."

"When will we know?"

"Let's see, it's October now. You know, Mary, he may be working on a Christmas present, and maybe it is for me. What do you think?"

"I think it's for you 'cause Santa Claus brings Millie's surprises and mine. Will he be mad if you know?"

"We won't tell him what we think. We'll just be surprised."

In December, I turned four and Esther made a blue birthday cake for me because that was my favorite color. I asked her if she'd make one for Millie when it was her birthday.

"Yes," she said. "What color should Millie's be?"

"Millie's will be red 'cause that's her favorite color."

"And just how do you know her color?" asked Esther laughing.

"I show Millie a blue block and a red block and she always takes the red one, so I know that's the color she likes best."

"What will you do if she takes the blue block sometime?"

"She can take the blue block, but she can't have my blue cake. How's that?"

"Perfect!" said Esther.

On Christmas Eve, Santa Claus brought me a rag doll dressed in blue and my own *Cinderella* book. He brought Millie a teddy bear with a red ribbon around its neck and a book of nursery rhymes, and he filled our stockings with candy, nuts and oranges. But I didn't see a wood surprise for Esther, and I was afraid she'd be sad if he didn't give her that present. He gave her a watch and white sweater, but where was the wood present?

Finally, I couldn't wait any longer, and I quietly went to Charles.

"Where's Esther's wood surprise?" I asked.

"How do you know about that?" he laughed. "You ladies come to the back room with me."

Esther picked up Millie and I took Charles' hand. When we got to the back room door, he pushed it open and shouted, "SURPRISE!"

"Oh, Charles, how beautiful," Esther said.

"FOR US!" I exclaimed.

"Yes, ladies, it's a playhouse with three rooms. You can take it outside in the summer and have a great old time. What do you think?"

Esther ran to Charles with Millie in her arms and hugged him so tight Millie squealed from being squashed. I hugged him around his legs.

"Oh, thank you," I said as I looked up and saw his smile.

"You like it, huh?"

"It's the most wonderfullest present of all. And you can play in it, too. How's that?"

CHAPTER 2

Ups and Downs

Millie's birthday came on February second, Ground Hog Day, but we didn't call her that name. She was too pretty, with all her curls, to be called any kind of a hog. She had her cake with pink frosting, not red, because she told Esther that pink was her "favor cawere." I didn't like watching her eat that cake, though, because Esther let her eat with her hands and I thought she looked funny. She looked awful, especially with pink curls!

Millie and I looked out the window every day so we'd know when the snow went away, and we could take our playhouse out to the backyard near the swings. But we all went to church Easter Sunday, and the snow was still on the ground, and it was almost time for May Day before it melted and ran down the driveway like a little creek. We stood at the window squealing with delight when the last white patches disappeared along the gravel road.

"Now we can take the playhouse outside, Millie. Hooray for spring!" I shouted.

"Not so fast," said Charles. "Look at the water in the yard. You'd have to swim in your little house. When you don't see any more puddles, and when the sun comes out full force and makes the day bright and warm, we'll move the house out under the oak trees."

We went to church many more Sundays, and they were happy days. Esther dressed Millie and me in our pretty dresses and long stockings and curled our hair. Charles called us his little princess girls. Millie and I went to Sunday school together where we learned words from the Bible and sang songs about Jesus. I didn't understand much, but I liked to hear things like "God loves you" and "He will take care of you." Miss Ella Curtis was our teacher, and she said God did take care of Millie and me when he sent Matthew Lucas to find us.

"What a friend God is," she said, "and He will never leave you."

I didn't see Him anywhere, so I wasn't sure what she meant when she said He'd never leave me.

Sometime in May, when the water was all gone from the ground and the sun made the day warm, Charles carried the playhouse out to the trees, just like he said he would. He's grand, I thought, to build this big surprise for us, and that's what I told him just as soon as he put it under the largest oak near the kitchen window.

"You're the nicest man in the whole, wide world, Charles," I said, hugging him around his legs and looking up at his face.

"I'm glad you think so, Mary, and I think you're about the best kid in the whole world," he said as he picked me up and put his arms around me tight.

I pushed away from him and looked right into his blue eyes. Then drawing up my shoulders, I took a deep breath, gave him my biggest smile and let the breath back out.

"How's that?"

"Just wonderful," he laughed, standing me back on the ground. "Go have fun. I'll see all of you when I get home from work."

We did have fun in our house all day, except at nap time. Esther said she was tired out, and she knew Millie and I must be, too.

"Not me," I said. "I'm going to stay here all day."

"No, Mary. You have to come in and take a nap along with Millie and me. You may play again when we get up."

I didn't want to sleep, so I stuck out my lip and said I'd just play. Esther gave me a whack on my bottom and told me to get along inside. I did, but I cried a lot and I made Millie cry.

We had to sit in the corner until we stopped, and then we had dinner and went to bed.

After napping, I played outside and waited for Charles to come home. When it was time for him to drive in, Esther came out with Millie.

"We'll wait out here for him," she said.

We waited for a long time.

"It's six, and he's not here," said Esther. "Hmmm. Guess I'll call the foundry and see if he's left yet."

And because I felt a little scared, I followed her into the kitchen. Her lips were pursed, and she didn't look at us when she talked, so I knew she was worried. It made me feel like shaking all over, even though I didn't know what could have happened to Charles.

She turned the crank on the phone to call the number—two long turns and three short ones.

"Hello, Tom. This is Esther. Is Charles there? He did? Hmmm—he's not here yet. Yes, I'll call you when he gets here."

We waited until seven o'clock, but Charles didn't come in the driveway. Esther picked up Millie and put Millie down, and in a few minutes, she picked up Millie again.

"Esther, did Charles get hurt?" I asked.

"Oh, dear, I don't know, Mary. He should be home."

The phone rang—one long ring and one short ring.

"That's our ring," I said. "Maybe Charles is calling you."

Esther carried Millie, and I hurried behind her into the kitchen where Esther grabbed the receiver and put it to her ear.

"Hello, hello," she said, almost shouting. There was a long pause. "Yes, yes, this is Esther Sink." Pause. "Oh—oh—no—no. Y-Y-Yes, I-I-I'll c-c-all my m-m-moth—er. B-B-Bye," she whispered and hung up.

I felt very frightened when Esther started crying and screaming, "No, no, no, it c-c-c-an't be." She pulled the receiver to her ear again and turned the crank—three long and one short. She was crying so hard, I didn't think she could talk, but she did.

"M-M-Mother come quick. Charles was in wreck. He's at the hospital. I have to go." She put the receiver back.

"Charles was in a wreck?" I said. "Will he die? Can I go with you? I don't want him to die."

Esther looked at me and reached down to pick up Millie. She went to a drawer near the sink and took out two handkerchieves, put one in her apron pocket and blew her nose with the other, and then walked over and sat in a chair near the kitchen table.

"Come right here, Mary," she said, patting a chair near her.

I sat down. "I'm scared. I don't want Charles to die, and if he was in a wreck, he will, won't he?"

"Where Chawers is?" asked Millie. "He home now?"

"No, Millie, not yet. Mary, I don't think he will die, but he's—he's hurt really bad. I have to, have to go to him. Granny will come and keep you and Millie until I get back."

"Will Charles come back with you today?"

"He'll have to stay where he—he is for awhile."

Esther sat Millie in her high chair and went to the stove.

"I'll fix your plates and you eat your supper like good girls. Granny will put you to bed, and I'll see you in the morning. I want you to be brave and do just what Granny tells you."

"B-B—But I want to see Charles, too," I said, feeling sad.

"Children aren't allowed in the hospital; it's not safe for them, so you help Granny take care of Millie like a good girl. That will make Charles happy, too. Will you do that for me and for Charles, Mary, and we'll all say our prayers and ask God to help him."

"I'll be good and help Granny, and I won't let anything happen to my baby sister, either. I know how to take care of her, don't I?"

"Yes, you do, and I'm proud of you."

"And I know how to say a prayer, too, 'cause Miss Curtis told us. We just say, 'Dear God, take care of Charles, please. Amen.'"

"That's right, Mary, and thank you," said Esther, and she picked me right up and squeezed me tight.

Granny took care of us for a lot of days until Charles came home from the hospital. He came in an ambulance, and the men wheeled him into the living room on a bed.

"Don't you go causing your pretty wife any trouble, Old Sport," they said as they told him good-bye.

"Nah," said Charles in a strange, low voice.

I wanted him to get off that high bed with the metal legs and come and pick me up and hug me, but he just stayed there with his eyes closed and his chest going up and down as he breathed.

I turned to Esther, who had come from upstairs with two pillows. She placed one gently under Charles' knees and then, very slowly, she lifted his head and pulled the fat, white pillow beneath it. He opened his eyes, looked at her face close to his and kissed her on her cheek.

"Thank you," he whispered.

"I love you," she said softly.

I felt left out, and I was mad at Charles for getting sick.

"Will he get better and get out of bed?" I asked loudly.

"Of course he will, Mary. Why don't you and Millie come into the kitchen and we'll have some dinner. I'll bet you're both hungry."

"No," I said stubbornly. "I won't go unless he gets up and goes, too. Get him up. What's the matter with him?"

I screamed and then I cried. Esther came quickly from the bed, took Millie's and my hands and led us to the kitchen where we sat around the table. By this time, Millie was crying, too.

"You'll both have to stop crying so I can talk to you," Esther said gently. "I'll get you a little chocolate milk. That will make you feel better."

She set the two blue Shirley Temple glasses in front of us, and Millie and I, still sniffling, took a drink as Esther tried to explain about Charles. She said he'd get better, but that he'd never walk again because his legs were paralyzed.

"But I will take care of him the very best I can, and I'll take care of you, but I'll need your help. I think we can have fun helping each other, but you must remember that things won't be the same."

"What things?" I asked, feeling frightened about something bad happening to Millie and me.

"You'll have to play alone more, and we won't go for rides in the car as often. We'll have to be quiet when Charles is resting. Mary, you'll have to watch Millie closely so she doesn't get hurt. But both of you must remember, too, that we'll do everything we can to keep you with us."

"That's good," I said. "Isn't that good, Millie? We can stay right here and help take care of Charles, and you an' I'll play good together. I'll watch you so you won't get hurt. How's that?"

"No, no, no," protested my sister, grabbing my hand and shaking it. "I hewp an' take cahr of Mawee, an' she won't get hoort. Me big goowl."

Esther and I laughed at Millie. But I didn't want things to be different. I wanted everything to be happy, and I knew they would be sad because Charles was sick.

"I-I th-th-ink Charles w-w-will die," I whispered, and before I could get out of my chair and go to my room, tears began to fall. I put my face in my hands and cried. I felt very, very sad all over.

"Esther, I did say a prayer every day and ask God to take care of Charles, but He didn't. Why didn't He?" I quietly asked.

Esther came to sit beside me and put her arm around me.

"Oh, but Mary, God did take care of Charles. It's a miracle that Charles is alive. A man who had been drinking drove his car into the side of our car where Charles was sitting. So we don't blame God for what happened, because He tells us to do what is right. And when we do something wrong, we hurt ourselves and other people. God can't control everything we do, because lots of times we make the wrong decisions. Do you understand?"

"I understand a little, but I wish the drunk man had not hit Charles."

After that day, home was just like Esther had said it would be. She took care of Charles when he ate and when he had to go to the bathroom, when it was his bath time and when he had to get dressed and undressed. Every morning after breakfast, she sat by his bed and read the newspaper to him. When we were upstairs at night, and after she had read stories to us, I heard her reading downstairs to Charles.

Millie and I played with blocks and dolls and puzzles. We looked at pictures in our books about Peter Rabbit, Uncle Remus, and Cinderella, and I pretended I could read and made up stories for Millie.

It wasn't long before the Fourth of July arrived with its loud firecrackers and bright sparklers. Esther, Millie, and I sat on the front steps at night and watched the colors in the sky.

The day after that was very hot. Millie stayed inside because of her sore throat and said, "Too hot out dere for Miwwee" when I asked her to come and play with me. I spent the morning in an old tire swing that hung from a half-dead maple tree in the field behind our house. After a long time in the sun, my face was burned and my throat was dry and scratchy, so I wandered barefoot, dodging the honey bees through the cool clover back to the house where I got some water. I saw Esther sitting at the table with her head on her arms. She was crying, crying so hard that it scared me. Had Charles died? I stood by her for a minute and wondered if I should say something or go back outside. I got another drink and again stood beside Esther.

"What's the m-m-matter?" I asked, gently shaking her arm.

She sat up and wiped her eyes with her old apron. Then she looked at me and held out her arms. "Come here, Mary," she whispered. She pulled me up on her lap, put her arms around me and held me tight, so tight that I could smell the pink soap from the bathroom on her hands.

"Charles is very, very sick now, Mary. He's so sick that I will have to be his nurse every day and every night. I won't be able to keep you and Millie any longer." She cried again, and said over and over, "I'm so sorry."

I thought I should get out of her lap. "Maybe I'm too heavy," I said to her as I wiggled to get down.

"My mommy left us on the street. Are you going to put Millie and me on the street, too?"

"Oh, no, Mary," she said as she held me closer. "No, Miss Warring will find another home for you and Millie." I saw her take a blue hanky out of her apron pocket, and I watched as she blew her nose and wiped her eyes.

"We all have to do things sometimes that we don't want to

do, things that hurt us so bad we almost can't stand it. But I have no choice. Miss Warring said the welfare department demands that children have a normal home situation. They think I'll have to spend so much time with Charles that I won't care for you as I should. And even though I pleaded with them, I got nowhere. Do you understand, Mary?"

"No, I won't go. I don't want another house. I don't want another mommy and daddy. I want to stay right here with you and Charles forever and ever. Please let me stay and Millie, too," I begged, turning her face to mine and holding it so I could look at her and I'd know she could hear me. "Please!"

"Oh, Mary," she whispered as she took my hands from her face. "I love you and Millie like you were my own babies. I wish you could stay with me always. Charles says our lives will be so empty without you little ones, and I know it's true."

I leaned back against her and wished I didn't have to go.

Miss Warring came for us the next afternoon. Esther stood with Millie and me as we told Charles good-bye at his bedside.

"We'll miss you little girls more than you'll ever know, won't we, Charles?"

"Yes, yes, we will," he said, and I saw a tear fall on his pillow.

He looked scary to me there in his bed. He was skinny and he didn't look like Charles anymore; he looked like a very old man.

"Come, girls," called Miss Warring. "We have to go."

With her hands on our shoulders, Esther steered us to the living room where we saw our boxes of clothes and toys at the front door.

"Take Millie's hand, Mary, and Miss Warring and I will carry the boxes."

As we stepped out the door, Millie and I both started crying and saying we didn't want to go, but Miss Warring, as she put us in the back seat of her car, told us to stop being such babies and behave ourselves. I tried to stop, but when I looked out the car window, I saw Esther in the yard holding her face in her hands with a handkerchief. I knew she was crying just like we were. She was being a baby, too.

When Millie and I were quiet again, Miss Warring told us to count the cows in the fields on our way to our new home.

"One, two, three, four, five"...on and on I counted, and Millie tried to count.

"Un, toooo, free, foah, fiii," said Millie after me.

There were too many cows: brown ones, white and brown ones, black and white ones that I couldn't count anymore. I was too scared about going to a new place to live, and I was mad at Miss Warring for taking us away from Esther and Charles. I stood up from my seat so I could see out the windshield as we drove along. I wanted Miss Warring to turn around and go back to the Sinks, so I leaned forward to see her face. She looked straight ahead, squinting her eyes and wrinkling her forehead. She looked mad, so I sat back down and watched trees going by the windows on both sides of the car. They moved back and forth in the wind while little green leaves hung on tight so they wouldn't fall. I thought about all the happy days with Esther and Charles and how everything was changed.

I took Millie's hand and we sat quietly, riding along to our new home, afraid to talk and afraid to cry.

CHAPTER 3

We Meet the Pittses

"Here we are, girls," Miss Warring called out, slowing the car to turn a corner into a long driveway. She drove over holes and little stones, and Millie and I bumped up and down on the back seat. I saw big green trees out of Millie's car window, and then Miss Warring stopped by an old wooden house with a porch on the front and side of it. The side porch had a screen door, and I saw a big lady open it and come out. She had short, gray hair and a big nose and teeth. She wasn't pretty like Esther. She wasn't pretty at all, and even though she smiled, she looked mad.

"Stay here," said Miss Warring, "while I go talk to Mrs. Pitts."

I didn't want to sit in the car, especially since Millie had started crying again. I wanted to cry, too, but then both Miss Warring and Mrs. Pitts would call us babies. So, I pulled up hard on the door handle, got the door opened and jumped out. I used both hands to close it, but that made Millie cry harder. She was screaming because she wanted to get out, too. I went around to Millie's half-open window.

"Don't cry," I said. "I'll tell Miss Warring to let you out."

Mrs. Pitts was helping Miss Warring get the two boxes out of the trunk. She didn't scold when she saw I was out of the car. She just looked down and shook her head and then let Millie out. Mrs. Pitts took Millie's hand and gave it a couple of jerks.

"Don't cry," she shouted above the noise. "You're out now."

Millie tried to stop, but she sniffled while the two of them walked with Miss Warring to the porch and up the steps as I followed. When we were in the kitchen, Mrs. Pitts said we should go in the living room so she could get acquainted with "her girls."

I didn't want to hear that we were her girls. I didn't want to be anybody's girl anymore.

Mrs. Pitts took a dish of cookies off the table and asked Miss Warring to carry the tray with milk and tea.

"Why don't we just sit here in the kitchen?" suggested Miss Warring. "The girls can sit at the table and have their snacks."

Mrs. Pitts said that would be fine, but they didn't ask Millie and me if we wanted snacks. I didn't feel like eating anything, and I knew Millie didn't either. Mrs. Pitts held Millie on her lap, but I knew my sister would rather sit by me, so I got in the chair beside her and took her hand.

Mrs. Pitts talked loud and fast. I was afraid of her. She was big up, down, and around. Her face was round and red, and she had little, squinty eyes. Her hands were big like a man's, and I didn't like her shoes that tied up high and looked like boots with big heels. And her kitchen wasn't cool and clean like Esther's. It was hot and had a wooden floor with dirt between the cracks.

After we had eaten a cookie and finished our milk, the four of us went out of the kitchen through a swinging door, down a dark hallway, and into the living room where Mrs. Pitts showed Miss Warring the tall piano and an old sewing machine. The two ladies walked over to the window and were looking out as they talked in low voices. I didn't hear what they said, and I didn't want to stay in the room while they talked.

"Come on, Millie," I whispered as I took her hand. "Let's go. I think somebody went in the kitchen 'cause I heard the screen door slam. I think it might be kids talking out there."

I pulled my sister behind me down the hallway and through the swinging door into the kitchen.

"Did so," said a girl.

"Did not," said a boy.

I stood looking at the big kids. The girl was pretty, but the boy was not pretty anywhere on his bumpy face.

"Hi, I'm fourteen, and my name is Lana," said the girl, grabbing her long blond braid. She pointed with her thumb. "And that's my brother, Walter. He's twelve, and he's a big pest."

She walked barefoot across the rough, wooden floor, and I wondered why she didn't get slivers. She opened the oven door on the black and silver wood stove.

"Pies ain't done yet," she moaned as she slammed the door and latched it. She fanned her face with a ragged oven mitt.

"It's too darn hot in this kitchen. I wish them pies would hurry up," she said as she threw the mitt on the table and walked over to the screen door. "Get outta here," she said, banging on the screen to make the flies go.

"You better behave here," she said as she turned around and shook her finger at us, "or you'll get to sit in the cellarway."

"Yeah, where the rats can eatcha," sneered Walter with his face close to mine.

"Get out of here, Walter," said Lana as she raised her fist. "Go out and ride your bike. Leave us alone."

"Aw, who wants to be with ugly girls?" he grumbled. "That's all we need around here—more girls." He went out the door beside the stove.

I was glad he went because I thought he was mean to Lana, and I wondered why a brother would be that way. I remembered Billy, and he was never mean to me.

"Well, he's gone," said Lana. "What are your names?"

"I'm Mary and I'm four, and this is Millie and she's two."

"Me two," said Millie, as she leaned her shoulder against me.

"Well, you are pretty," said Lana, "both of you, and I'm glad you came to live with us. Will Millie cry if I pick her up?"

"No, she'll be all right, because I'm here with her," I said.

Just then Miss Warring and Mrs. Pitts came back into the kitchen.

"I have to go now," said Miss Warring. "I'll be back to see you before long. You do what you're told, and you'll be fine."

She went over to the screen door and opened it just a little. Then she let it bang closed, and all the flies that were stuck on it flew away again. She opened the door wide and went out and down the steps to her car. I watched out the door until her car was gone, and I wished I could be with her. I didn't want to live here with Mrs. Pitts, but I couldn't tell her that 'cause she'd be mad at me. And I didn't even have a chance to tell Miss Warring that I didn't like this very old house that was dark inside and didn't smell good.

"Well, girls," said Mrs. Pitts in her loud voice, "I see you've met Lana, and I guess you met Walter, too."

"Yes, and Walter, too," I said, turning from the door. "But where is Lana's daddy?"

"He's out working in the hay field today. He'll be in for supper and you can meet him then. But let's take your boxes up to your beds. Lana, you carry one and I'll take one."

We left the kitchen and went down the hall, past the living room and up the stairs. When we turned the corner at the top of the stairs, I saw two canvas cots in the hallway. Mrs. Pitts stood beside the first one near a window. "This is your bed, Mary," she said, and as she pointed to the one along the wall, I knew she'd say it was Millie's.

"Lana, put the box you have under Mary's cot, and I'll put mine under Millie's. Their clothes are in here, and I guess some books. I'll bring that old chest from the cellar up here tomorrow and we'll put their things in it. Let's go back downstairs now. I have to get supper and I know that pie is done by now. Come on, all of you, follow me back down because I want some help."

When we got back to the kitchen, Mrs. Pitts pointed to the door by the stove.

"Out there's the back room where we hang our coats and hats and take off our boots," she said. "I also do my washing out there. Sit at the table now, and Lana, go down to the cellar and get the potatoes."

Lana opened the cellar door and went down, and I looked around the kitchen while Millie and I sat at the table. The sink didn't look right. There were no faucets, just a funny thing with a handle. I wondered how Millie and I would get a drink or wash our hands.

"That sink is too high for us, Mrs. Pitts," I said.

"You will call me 'Mother,'" she said. "And don't worry about the sink. I'll get a wooden box for you to stand on."

"Can we go out and play?" I asked.

"Yes, go under the trees in the front yard where it's shady. If you have to go to the toilet, it's around the back of the house. You better go before supper. Take Millie so she won't wet her pants."

Millie and I found the outhouse, and coming back from it we saw Mr. Pitts coming up across the yard from the barn.

"Are you Lana's daddy?" I called to him.

"Yep. Are you Mary, and is that Millie?" he asked.

"Yes, we are," I said.

"Well, it's good to see you. Are you ready for supper?"

"I'm ready," I said.

"Me weddy," said Millie.

Mr. Pitts got between us and took our hands and we walked into the kitchen together.

"Wash your hands girls," said Mrs. Pitts. "There's the wooden box to stand on. I have your plates at your table for you."

"Aren't they eating in the dining room with us?" asked Mr. Pitts.

"No room, and they'll mess up everything. They shouldn't be eating with the family anyway. They're not family," said Mrs. Pitts.

"Seems a shame they have to eat here alone. Let's see. There's you and me, Walter, Lana and Helen, if she comes home. Johnny'll be in shortly, as he's been helping me all day..."

"See, John, there's not room."

She gave us each a glass of milk. "Don't spill it," she said.

I think she's the witch in the Hansel and Gretel book, I thought. She talks like one, but Charles told me there's no such thing as a witch, so I guess she's not.

After she left, I got out of my chair and helped Millie hold her glass, and I showed her how to use her fork. She always used a spoon at Esther's house. She jabbed her face a couple times, but then she was all right with the fork.

*   *   *

Not many days passed before I knew what the cellarway looked like. But before I got in trouble, Millie wet her pants and had to hold them over the hot stove until they dried. Then she had to wear them so she'd stink and not wet them again. That's what Mrs. Pitts said, but Millie wet her pants lots of times after that. Sometimes, she got spankings along with having to hold them up to dry. I knew Millie couldn't help having accidents, but I guess Mrs. Pitts didn't know that.

My trouble started when I spilled my milk at the supper table. I was jabbing peas with my fork when my plate tipped and bumped my glass. Millie had been sad all day, and I was trying to make her happy.

"Muvver," called Millie, "Mawee pill mulk." Mrs. Pitts looked like she was flying when she came through the door from the dining room. She grabbed my arm and led me toward the cellar.

"Open the door and get in there," she said, and when I got in, she slammed the door closed. "You can just stay all night for all I care," she yelled.

I stood in the black dark and couldn't see a thing, but after I was in there a few minutes, I could see shapes, like the steps, so I sat on the top one. I'm not even scared in here, I thought. I could see the walls along the steps, but that was all. I looked hard at where the bottom of the steps should be, but I couldn't see anything, so I just sat there and waited to get out.

I hope she doesn't forget me because I don't want to stay here all night, I thought, as I put my face in my hands on my knees. After a long time, Mrs. Pitts opened the door.

"Get out here," she said. "And don't ever spill your milk again, or next time you'll get a whippin', too. Go to the toilet and then go on up to bed."

I was so happy to get out of the dark that I didn't care if I did have to go to bed. I knew Millie would be in her bed already.

Many things happened at the Pitts, and it seemed like most of them were bad. Walter was mean to Millie and me every time we went outside to play. He'd always be where we wanted to be, and I hated him for throwing stones at us, trying to ride his bike over us, and chasing us with snakes and frogs. Even if I said I wasn't afraid of him, he'd do all those things anyway. Sometimes his father saw him throwing walnuts or stones at us, and he made him help with the chores. But most of the time, nobody saw him. I tried to catch him and beat him up with my fists or kick his legs. Sometimes I was so mad when he hurt my sister that I wanted to hurt him, too.

"You're nothin' but a big baby. You couldn't hurt a flea," he'd say and laugh and run away.

Lana was like Millie and me, because she hated Walter, too. But the sad thing about Lana was her mother gave her whippings with a razor strap. It was awful to hear Lana crying and screaming. I wanted to run away and not listen, but I also wanted to be sure Lana was all right when it was over.

"You ain't my kid," Mrs. Pitts shouted when she was hitting Lana. And Lana screamed. I thought maybe Mrs. Pitts would kill her, and I didn't know why Mr. Pitts didn't hear Lana and come and help her. I wanted to help her, but I was so afraid of Mrs. Pitts, I couldn't think of what to do.

One day, after Lana got a beating, she showed me puffy red stripes on her legs and arms and back.

"I'm going to run away," she said, "just like my two big sisters did, and I won't ever come back."

"Where will you go?" I asked.

"I got a boyfriend who wants to marry me someday. He said I could live with his folks."

"I will miss you, Lana," I said sadly as I walked over to the swing in the big oak tree.

"I'll push you," she said. "Hold on tight. And don't worry. I won't leave for awhile 'cause Dad needs me to help him with the chores. My big brother, John, is getting married, so he won't be here to help, and Walter's no good about working. So, I'm the only one Daddy has."

*   *   *

I went to kindergarten in the fall, but I didn't like to leave

Millie home with Mrs. Pitts. I think Mrs. Pitts hurt my sister when I wasn't there, but Millie wouldn't tell me what they did every day.

Winter came and I was five in December. I pretended my birthday was Christmas, because it was a happy day.

"I don't know what day your birthday is," Mrs. Pitts said, "but it doesn't matter. You were born in December. That's all I know."

When I didn't have to be in school, Millie and I played in the snow with an old sled that Mr. Pitts found in the barn. We went out to the apple orchard on the hill behind the house. There weren't many trees left, so there was lots of room to slide down the hill.

When we didn't play with the sled, we sometimes tried to make a snowman, but Walter always came and ruined everything. So, I told Millie we just wouldn't make anything else for that old bully to break.

She and I played fox and geese, and we pretended that we had our own house under the evergreen trees in the front yard. Nobody could be there but the two of us, and we didn't have a cellar or a razor strap in our house.

The snow began to melt away from the ground and the days got warmer. Just before Easter, Miss Warring came to take us to buy new clothes. When we were riding to town with her, she asked us if we were happy, and I said we were. I remembered that Mrs. Pitts had warned me that if I ever said anything to anybody about what went on in her house, she would give me a licking like she gives Lana. So, I pretended that everything was all right. I didn't think Miss Warring had another house where we could live, anyway. Sometimes, I wished we could live with her, because I didn't think she'd put us in the cellar or make us eat alone in the kitchen while she ate in the dining room.

We got our new clothes for summer and went back home, and when Miss Warring drove away, I felt sad that I couldn't go away from the Pitts' house like she could.

Millie was happy in the summertime when I was home with her.

"Muvver won't hit me if you home, Mawee," she said.

"Why does Mother hit you, Millie?" I asked.

"I cwy if you go," she said.

"Well, I'm not going for a long time now, so we'll play and we won't go in till dinner. How's that? Good thing?"

"Good fing," she said, laughing and running down the hill. "Mawee can't ketch me," she called, all the time knowing that her big sister could catch her. And that's just what I did.

CHAPTER 4

We Lose a Friend

One summer day in 1938, when Millie and I were playing on the swing, I saw Mr. Pitts walk out of the barn and go across the backyard to the porch. He walked some steps and then he stood still and then walked some more. I watched him until he went up on the porch and into the house.

"C'mon, Millie," I said. "Let's go see what's the matter with Dad." I took her by the hand and ran with her to the porch and up the steps. I looked through the screen door and saw Mr. Pitts sitting in a chair at the kitchen table.

"What's wrong with you," screamed Mrs. Pitts as she shook his shoulder. "Answer me, John," she said. "Is it your heart? What should I do for you?" She walked to the door, and Millie and I went down the steps away from her. She came out on the porch and shouted.

"Wall—ter, Wall—ter, come, come quick. Your dad is sick." She turned and ran back in the house.

Millie and I tiptoed back up the steps so we could hear the voices in the kitchen.

I saw Mrs. Pitts shake Dad again, and he raised his head.

"I'm all right now," he said in a shaky voice. "Just felt kinda sick out there—couldn't get my breath. That's all."

"Well, let me help you to the couch, and you stay there for awhile. Here, lean on me, I'll hold you up." She put her arm around his back and side, and it looked to me like she could have carried him because she was a lot bigger than he was.

A minute later Walter came running across the yard and up the steps of the porch.

"Get outta the way, you dopey girls," he shouted. "Mother, what's wrong?" he called as the screen door slammed behind him.

"We're here in the living room," she answered.

I couldn't hear anymore.

"C'mon, Millie," I said. "We'll go back to that big tree and play on the swing some more."

*   *   *

Mr. Pitts didn't die that day like I thought he would. I knew how things died because our big yellow cat got hit by a car in the road, and I saw it lying there. It didn't ever move again, and Walter said he buried her in the ground.

Mr. Pitts spent the summer just walking around the yard and the vegetable garden. He was thin and his hair was almost gone. It laid in long strings from his forehead to the back of his head. Now when he walked, he wobbled, even when he had his cane. I thought he might fall, but if he did, I knew I could help him up.

On the warm summer nights, Mr. Pitts sat in his old rocking chair on the porch and smoked. His pipe looked like the dipper in the water pail, so I called it his dipper pipe.

Lana and I sat on the top step, and sometimes she talked to him, but I didn't because I didn't know what he wanted me to say. Lana talked about the cows and pigs and chickens she took care of for him. She asked why she had to help with the milking when Walter and Mr. Howard, the neighbor farmer, were both there.

"Walter calls me a dumb girl, and Mr. Howard calls me 'Bean Pole' and that's not my name. Why can't they do their own milking, Dad?"

"I'll talk to Bruce tomorrow," said Mr. Pitts.

The three of us often sat there until almost dark, or until Lana said she was going over to her friend Martha's house.

"Get back before bedtime," her father said. "You know how mad your Ma can get when you stay out too late."

"I'll get back," Lana said and then ran down the steps, down the driveway and up the road. She ran so fast, "like a deer," her dad said as we watched her go.

It was just Mr. Pitts and me after Lana left. And then all he said to me was "watch sunset" or "getting dark" or "going to bed."

I turned to watch Mr. Pitts smoking and looking at things. He looked up at the sky or down at his barn. He looked at the oak tree that had a million acorns on the ground around it, and he looked down the gravel road that went into town. He rocked and looked and rocked and looked, and sometimes he coughed. He coughed so hard that he could hardly get his breath, and I thought he would die right there in his rocking chair.

"Dammit," he said, "can't get rid of it."

He wasn't really talking to me, so I didn't say anything. When he stopped coughing, he looked out over the farm again and at the sky.

"Watch sunset," he said in his raspy voice, and I watched the sun making pretty colors in the sky and all around us as it was going down.

When it was almost dark, Mr. Pitts put his thumb on the bowl of his pipe and held it there until there was no more smoke. Then he put the pipe in his bib overall pocket, got up from his chair and walked slowly down the steps and around the house. I thought he was going to the outhouse because it was bedtime, so I waited for him to come back to the porch and go inside. I went down the path then before I went up to sleep in my cot.

Mr. Pitts just got thinner and thinner in his overalls all through the summer until September, when the corn was harvested and the five-pound sweets fell from the two biggest trees in the orchard. School started again and I was in first grade. That was when Mr. Pitts died. They said he had a stroke, but I think he coughed so hard that he lost his breath and never got it back.

The day after he died, I was in the side yard and could

hear Mrs. Pitts talking through the open window in the living
room. She was telling Lana that they were fixing John so
people could come and see him.

"He will be in the downstairs bedroom, so you kids stay
outside and don't come in when company's here," she said.

Then she cried and cried, and it sounded like hoo, hoo, oh,
ooo, hoo, ooo, hoo. I wished she would stop, but she didn't, so I
went with Millie way out in the orchard where I couldn't hear
her. I didn't know Mrs. Pitts could cry. I didn't cry when Mr.
Pitts died. Lana did, though, and so did Walter. I guess they
really liked him a lot. I liked him, too, but I didn't feel like
crying, even though I thought maybe I should.

For the next two days, Millie and I sat on the porch and
watched the people go in and out of the house. They got quiet
when they came up the driveway, and they looked down at the
ground. They walked up the steps of the porch past Millie and
then past me, where I was sitting in Mr. Pitts' rocking chair,
but they didn't say anything to us. They just opened the screen
door and went in. When they came back out, the ladies were
crying, but the men weren't. "Poor Helland," those ladies would
say. "What's she gonna do without a man to work the farm?
And she's got all these kids, too. Poor thing. The poor, poor
thing."

In the afternoon when things got quiet and Millie was
taking a nap, I got out of the rocking chair. I was glad Millie
wasn't with me, because I decided I was going to see Mr. Pitts
being dead. I thought it might scare Millie too much, but it
wouldn't scare me because I was big. I opened and closed the
screen door quietly and tiptoed into the kitchen and down the
hall. The bedroom door where he was supposed to be was open,
so I went in. My feet were quiet on the floor because they didn't
have shoes on them. Mrs. Pitts wouldn't hear me anyway because she was upstairs sleeping. When Lana came to get Millie
for her nap, Lana said Mrs. Pitts had taken a pill and had gone
to bed.

I looked around the room, which was sort of dark because
all the green window shades were pulled down. I looked for Mr.
Pitts, but he wasn't in any of the chairs that were in a circle

around the room. Maybe he's just a ghost, I thought. I saw a
high, fancy box in the middle of the room with flowers on it, so
I picked up a small wooden chair, carried it over to the box, set
it down, and climbed up on it to see the flowers better. But
when I stood on the chair, I looked down right into Mr. Pitts'
face. His eyes were closed, and he was very white. He looked
funny because he had on a white shirt and a tie and a black
suit. He would look better in his bib overalls, I thought. I never
saw him wear a black suit. I stood looking at him, and he
didn't move at all, just like that yellow cat didn't move in the
road. Where would they put him now, I wondered. He couldn't
just stay in the bedroom forever.

I decided I should get out of the room, so I got down from
the chair and put it back where I had gotten it. I went back
down the hall, through the kitchen, and out to the porch, but I
didn't feel like sitting in Mr. Pitts' rocking chair again. If I did,
I thought I might die, too, and dying was the most terrible
thing that could happen to a person or anything. But I still
didn't want to cry.

The next day, I was under the evergreens in the front yard
and Millie was in the living room with her blocks and books
when Mrs. Pitts called for us.

"Mary and Millie, come here."

I went into the kitchen where she was.

"Go wash your hands and go find Millie," she said. Her
eyes were red, and her face was, too. I watched her take out a
big blue and white handkerchief from her dress pocket and
blow her nose.

"Just get your sister," she shouted. "Don't stand there gawking."

I hurried from the room and went to Millie.

"Come here, Millie," I said. "You have to wash your hands
for supper."

"Don't wanna," said Millie, as she placed another block on
her tower. "I wanna pway."

"Well, you can't right now. Come with me or Mother will
whip us both. I think she's mad at us. She looks awful, and she
yelled at me, and I didn't do anything. I'll help you put away
your toys."

"Muvver mad?" asked Millie.

"I think so. Come on, let's get our hands clean."

When we got back to the kitchen, Walter and Lana were there.

"You and Millie sit at your table here, and I'll give you your supper," said Lana. She gave us our plates with ham, potatoes, and corn on them and a slice of bread and butter. She put a glass of milk at each place for us. Then she went with Mrs. Pitts and Walter into the dining room with their supper.

Our meal was late that night, so when we had finished eating, Mrs. Pitts said we had to go to bed. She walked into the kitchen and sat at the table looking out the window.

"I'm tired, funeral's tomorrow," she said. "I have to go to bed, so I...I...c-c-can..." She held her head in her hands and cried.

"Come on, Millie," said Lana, as she scooped my sister up into her arms. "I'll take you to the outhouse and then get you ready for bed. Mary, you and Walter carry the dirty dishes to the sink."

"I ain't helpin' no ugly girl with dishes, 'cuz I..." began Walter.

"Be quiet," said Lana. "We have to help Mother."

Walter and I cleared the tables, and after Mrs. Pitts walked into the living room, Walter followed her to the dining room where he grabbed up the tablecloth and took it out on the porch to shake out the crumbs. As he walked back into the house, he shouted at me.

"Get outta here, you creepy girl, and go to bed. I hate girls."

"And I hate boys," I shot back and hurried out the door. I sat down on the top step and watched the sun go down. I saw everything fade away, first the red barn, then the driveway and front yard. The evergreen trees were like shadows, but the oak tree just went away and took the swing with it. Then the outdoors was empty.

I went down the steps, around the house and down the path I knew so well. Lana had already put Millie to bed. As I walked, the wind blew my hair, and I heard tree toads down in the marsh near the woods. I liked to hear the happy toads sing.

When I got to the outhouse, I lifted the metal latch, opened the door and went inside. There I hooked the small lock before I prepared to sit on one of the three round holes. I liked an end one so I could lean against the wall and wouldn't be afraid of falling down the hole.

As I sat there, I thought about Mr. Pitts being dead and I felt scared. I might die, too, I thought. I might die right here, and I would be in a big box. Where will Mr. Pitts go in his box, I wondered. I was afraid to die because I didn't know what happened to someone who died. Walter had told me, "The boogiemen will take you away, and I'll never have to look at you again."

I jumped off the seat, pulled up my pants, and lifted the hook on the door to go out. But when I opened the door and looked down the dark path, I slammed the door shut, locked it, and sat on a board that covered the round holes. I was so frightened that I could hardly move, and I sat there for a long time, for such a long time that I fell asleep.

Suddenly, I heard a banging on the door. "Mary, Mary, are you in here?"

It was Lana's voice.

"Yeah, I'm here," I answered sleepily. "And I'm never, never coming out." I remembered how afraid I was of the dark.

"Yeeshooo are." I could tell Lana was talking through her teeth, and that meant she was mad. "It's late, and you have to be in bed."

"I don't care what you say, I'm not coming out."

"Maarree," she said sweetly. "You'll get...a...lickin' if you don't come out here." She wasn't really nice, though. Mad again, I could tell.

I was more afraid of a lickin' from Mrs. Pitts than I was of the boogiemen getting me, so I unlocked the door and held my hand out for Lana to take it. She grabbed it and half-dragged me back down the path.

"I never saw such a fraidy-cat," she sputtered. "There's nothing going to get you. I suppose I'll have to drag you back and forth like this every night now. Well, you'll just have to go alone. You're too big to be scared anyway."

"I'm only five," I said, hoping Lana would understand that I was smaller than she was and wouldn't be mad at me anymore.

"It's all right, Mary, I know how you feel," she said, and she let my arm go. "You don't have to be afraid, though. Nothing has ever gotten me, and I'm fifteen."

I was glad when I was safe on my cot in the upstairs hall. Millie and I usually whispered to each other, but she was asleep.

The next night, Lana walked to the outhouse with both Millie and me, and that's when she told us about the funeral.

"They put Daddy in the ground," she said. "I'll never see him again, and I can't bear the thought. Didn't help to have Mother crying all day long, either. She told me that she was mad at all of us because her husband was gone, and she wished she could go with him."

Lana was crying when we started back down the path.

"You...take Millie," she said in a shaky voice. "I'm going to my room." She ran, disappearing in the darkness. I was scared, but Millie couldn't know.

"Don't worry, Millie," I said taking her hand. "I'm right here, and I won't let any boogiemen get you. You just hang on to my hand."

"What boogie?" asked Millie.

"You're little," I said. "When you're big like me, I'll tell you."

"We wun," said Millie. "We wun fass. No boogie fine us."

"All right. We'll run into the house and up to our cots, and then nothing can ever get us, huh, Millie?"

"Wight," she said, and away we went.

CHAPTER 5

Weathering Storms

After Mr. Pitts died, Mr. Howard did not work the farm. Walter had to do the milking alone, and his mother told him she would find somebody to come each day and do the heavy work.

A week later, on Monday morning before I left for school, there was a knock at the kitchen door. I jumped down from my stool and ran to the door. When I opened it, there stood someone I knew.

"I'm the hired man," he said.

"You are Matt, and you found Millie and me in front of Lou's store," I said. "And you are the hired man?"

"Yes, I am, and where's your mother?"

I ran to get Mrs. Pitts in the dining room and told her the hired man had arrived, but I didn't tell her that I knew him. I wanted to have a secret.

* * *

During the winter of 1939, Millie and I got whooping cough, and since there was no bathroom in the house, Mrs. Pitts told us we had to go outside to throw up. "I don't want you puking all over the house, so when you have to cough, you do it outdoors."

We coughed a lot, and we went outdoors, but we came back

in as soon as we could so we wouldn't freeze like a snowman. No matter how hard we tried not to cough and choke, it happened anyway.

After we were better, I noticed that Lana and Mrs. Pitts got into fights whenever they were in the kitchen together. One warm spring morning, I came through the kitchen with a slop pail that I was taking outside to empty and wash. My job every morning was emptying and cleaning the pots everyone had used during the night. I lined them up, the first one having warm, soapy water in it, and then I took the old rag and scrubbed around in the warm water and emptied it into the next pot. On down the line I went until the four were clean. I felt proud of the clean pails, and I was happy to put them back in their places under the beds. That meant I was finished for another day.

But on this Saturday as I came through the kitchen, Lana was screaming, and Mrs. Pitts was holding Lana's hair with one hand and reaching for the razor strap with the other. I stood there with my pot and stared at Mrs. Pitts. Her face was red with sweat all over it, and her short gray hair was all mixed up on her head. Her eyes were squinted, almost closed. Her mouth was wide open, and she was swearing and yelling at Lana.

"Damn you, damn you, causing me all this trouble. Why do you think you can stay out all night? You're just no good. I'll fix you! I'll kill you for doing this to me."

"I was at Marsha's 'cause I didn't want to be here with you," screamed Lana. "Don't hit me. I didn't do anything wrong."

Mrs. Pitts let go of Lana's hair and swung the black strap across Lana's back. Lana screamed so loud, I thought maybe Matthew would hear and come and help.

"You hit me again, and you'll never see me," shouted Lana as tears fell on her dress.

"You got it comin'," said Mrs. Pitts as she swung the strap again, but Lana jumped out of the way.

"Mother, stop it. Stop it," Lana shouted. "You're crazy."

Just then, Lana jumped at Mrs. Pitts and jerked the strap out of her mother's hand. She ran with it, right past me and out the door. Mrs. Pitts started after Lana, so I quickly put my pail down and ran out the door behind them. I hid behind the rocking chair on the porch and watched Mrs. Pitts run, but I knew she'd never catch Lana, who was already out in the road and running up the hill toward Marsha's house.

Run, Lana, run, I said to myself, and don't ever come back to this mean old witch.

Mrs. Pitts just stood in the yard for a minute with her hands on her hips. Then she lifted one hand and pushed her hair from her face. She turned and walked past me into the house.

After awhile, I looked through the screen and saw Mrs. Pitts busy at the end of the kitchen by the cellar door, so I went in and down the hall to the living room where Millie was playing.

"Where Lana go?" asked Millie.

"I don't know, but don't say anything about it, 'cause Mother will get mad if you do," I said.

"I'm 'fraid of Muvver," said Millie.

"Me, too," I said, "but we will have to be as good as we can so she won't hurt us. I'll be here, and I won't let her hurt you. Now, let's go see Matt because he probably needs us to help him with the chores."

Millie and I had happy times with Matthew. We helped him throw the chicken feed in troughs, and we gave the garbage to the pigs. He let us visit the new calves, and we put our arms around their necks. He showed us where the kittens were so we could hold them.

I couldn't wait to tell Matt that Lana had run away after Mrs. Pitts had whipped her and that I'd never have to hear her being hurt again.

"Which way did she go?" asked Matt.

"Up the hill as fast as she could run," I told him. "And I bet she won't ever come back. I'll miss her, but I don't want her to get any more terrible lickins."

"She'll come back when she gets hungry," said Matt.

"Unh, uh," I argued. "She's got a friend named Marsha, and that's right where she'll live, at Marsha's house. She told

me once that her two big sisters ran away, and they won't come
back. I think Mother was mean to her, and she's mean to Millie
and me, but not Walter. How come she's not mean to Walter,
Matt?"

"Guess he's her favorite," said Matt, as he picked up the
corn bucket he had just emptied for the chickens.

"Not my favitt," said Millie, "cause he pull my coorls."

"And he throws those old walnuts at us, tries to run over
us, hits us. He just does everything he can to make us mad," I
added. "He's just the biggest dope in the world. I wish he would
run away."

"I'll take care of Walter," said Matt. "There's plenty of
work around here for the two of us; don't need anyone carrying
on with such foolishness."

I thought about how it would be with Lana gone. She
wouldn't be around to get Millie and me out of the house when
she knew Mother was mad and might hit us. She had done that
sometimes. She'd run into the living room and whisper loud to
us, "Hey, you two, come with me. Mother's on the war path
again." And she'd grab our hands and take us out the back door
of the living room and run with us to the orchard. "My mother's
a crazy person," she'd say.

Now Lana was gone, and I thought it would be even worse
living with Mrs. Pitts. I'd have to help with all the work because I was the oldest girl: clear the table, dry the dishes, dust
the furniture, wash the pots. Suddenly, I was so afraid of her
that I felt like crying, but I didn't. Instead, I told Matt.

"I'm so scared, Matt, that I will spill the pots when I carry
them down the steps. If I do, I know Mother'll give me a terrible lickin' like she gave Lana, and..."

"You clean them pots," roared Matt, opening the hen house
door.

"Sure I do." Now I was afraid of him because he was talking so loud. "It's all right. I'll just get Millie to help me. She's
four now, so she's big enough."

"I too widdle to cawee pots," mumbled Millie.

"Ain't neither one of you going to carry pots, unless they're
empty," said Matt. "You'll have to find some other way to help.

Huh! The idea!" He plunked three eggs into the straw-lined basket hanging on his arm.

"Why, Matt? What will you do?" I asked, tugging at his basket arm.

He swung his free arm and swished a hen off her nest. "You just never mind. I'll take care of it."

Oh, boy, I thought. I'm really in trouble now. She'll call me a tattletale, and I don't know what she'll do to me.

"But Matt, Mother will get mad at me for telling," I whimpered just as the hen went flying past me through the air.

"Chicken fwying," giggled Millie. "Do it agin, Maffoo."

"Nope, all through. Got all the eggs, Millie," said Matt. He took her hand and told me to close the door. "And don't you worry. I'll take care of it, and Helland won't say a word to you. All right, girlie?"

"Uh huh," I nodded, somewhat relieved. But I didn't believe all of what he said.

I took Millie and we went out to the garden to see what was there. It was spring, so I knew Matt would probably be planting the garden soon. But now there were dead things in the dirt like vines from tomatoes, squash, and cucumbers, and pieces of potato plants. Little baby weeds were growing everywhere and dandelions bloomed. They were pretty, and I made believe they were tiny suns shining up at me, so I picked some and held them up to my face. But there was gooey white stuff coming out of the stems that didn't smell good, and it got my hands all sticky. I don't like this dirty stuff on my hands, I thought, but when I wiped them in the grass, my hands were green and dirtier.

"Let's go to the pump, Millie," I said, "so I can wash this off. If Mother sees me, she'll hit me in the face for being such a mess."

"Muvver will not hit you. No, she won't 'cuz Maffoo gonna take care of it. He said so."

"And I'm taking care of me," I said, pumping the cold water on one green hand and then another. "I don't know what Matt thinks *he* can do, but I *know* what she can do. She's the boss of us all!"

Millie didn't agree with me, not for a minute.

"She can't hurt Maffoo," she said, stomping her foot in the puddle of water under the pump. And then, stepping up close and looking up at me with her big blue eyes and her lower lip stuck out, she pressed her little fists into the waist of her dress and told me: "He's a vewy big man, Mawwee, an' he will help us, you jus' wait an' see. He will. I know he will!"

CHAPTER 6

Rescued

"Gotta go," said Millie.

"Hurry up, then," I said, grabbing her hand and pulling her behind me. I thought about her standing over that hot stove holding her pants to get them dry, and I was so worried about it that I was dragging her down the path to the outhouse like Lana had dragged me.

"Don't," screamed Millie, "you hurding me. I will faw down."

I slowed and let her hand go, and my thoughts continued as I remembered Millie by the stove. Sometimes I was afraid she'd get tired and fall right on top of the hot area and get burned badly, so I stayed in the kitchen with her, even though Mrs. Pitts told me to get out. I argued and said I had to stay with my sister so I could help her put on her pants when they were dry.

Through the summer, Millie and I played outside, but when it rained, we went to the barn to play with the cats and walk around with Matt. Walter wasn't at home much, except when it was time to do chores with Matt. He worked on the farm next to ours, where Marsha lived, so he could earn some money for the car he wanted. Millie and I were glad Walter wasn't around. Our troubles with Mrs. Pitts were enough. We couldn't please her, and we were always reminded of her angry feelings.

"You girls get in this house and help with this work. You're too noisy and always messing up everything. Keep your clothes clean, stay out of that damn barn," were commands hollered at us daily.

And if we didn't make up our cots or pick up our clothes or come when she called, she'd be waiting for us with a stick from the yard.

"Stand right there," she'd say in a raspy voice, "and put your hands out in front of you, palms up!"

That hurt more than anything, when she beat our hands with a rough old stick. I would rather she had hit me with the razor strap or slapped my face, but I never wanted her to hit Millie. She did, though, and the bad feeling in my stomach moved up to my throat. I wished so much I was big enough to knock her down on the floor. One of the worst things I ever heard was my little sister crying when she was being punished.

And just when I thought I knew every way Mrs. Pitts could hurt us, she'd add another.

On a Saturday morning in September, when Millie was four and I was six and had started second grade, we were sitting on our stools at our kitchen table. We had just finished a bowl of oatmeal, as we did every morning. And, as usual, we still felt hungry. A bowl of oatmeal just wasn't enough.

"I'm not full yet," I told Mrs. Pitts, who was washing dishes.

"I not eever," said Millie.

Mrs. Pitts threw her dishrag into the water and turned toward us from the sink. Her face was redder than I had ever seen it, sweat was dripping off her nose, her eyes bulged out, and she almost screamed.

"I'm sick and tired of you two always being hungry, so I'll just fix the both of you, and you won't ever be hungry again! You sit right where you are—you're gonna be *full* this time!"

I watched her go to the cupboard and pull out a deep, round blue enamel pot, fill it with water at the sink and drop it down on the hot stove. She grabbed a couple pieces of wood from the barrel behind the stove, lifted the large front griddle and poked the wood down into the leaping flames. Then she moved the water over the large griddle. I didn't know what she was going to do with that big pot of hot water—pour it on us? After awhile, as we sat on our stools afraid to move, she took down the tall, round box of oatmeal and dumped its contents into the pan of water. She stirred vigorously with a large wooden spoon and grunted. She banged her free arm on her hip.

"You'll eat all of it," she screamed.

She reminded me again of that witch in the story of *Hansel and Gretel,* and I wondered if she would try to kill us. I knew she would do something terrible to us.

When the oatmeal was done, she scooped the hot cereal into our bowls until they were full.

"Eat, eat, eat all day," she screamed. She put the pan on the stove and came back over to our table. With her hands on her hips, she bumped us with her stomach while we ate.

When we finished the helping, she ran to the stove, picked up the blue pot, brought it to the table and filled our bowls again.

"Now, eat, eat, eat and eat some more," she shouted. "Eat until you bust. See if you ever, ever tell me you're hungry again."

"Can't eat more, gotta frow up."

I looked at Millie's white face and was so scared my hands shook.

"Don't...you...dare," said Mrs. Pitts with her teeth closed together.

Just then Millie threw up in her bowl.

"All right, you filthy thing, eat it," yelled Mrs. Pitts.

I could not believe what she was saying, or what Millie was doing—filling her spoon.

"No," I shouted, "no, she..."

"Shut up, or you'll eat it, too," she said.

Millie put her spoon in the bowl. She was crying. "Don' wan it."

"I said eat it, now," said Mrs. Pitts bending down and looking into Millie's face. "Eat it or I'll stuff it down ya."

Millie put her spoon in the bowl to fill it and, with her hand shaking, put the spoon in her mouth, and took the spoon out. She swallowed.

"No, no, no," I screamed, jumping off my stool and running around the table to get hold of Mrs. Pitts. "She can't eat that.

I won't let her. You can't do this...I hate you," I screamed as I pulled at Mrs. Pitts' dress.

She grabbed Millie's hair and was pulling her from the table. I knew she'd hit Millie in the face, and I couldn't let her do it. I kicked her legs, and pulled Millie's arm, trying to free her.

"Stop that kicking, you little fool," Mrs. Pitts shouted at me. She let Millie go and began boxing my ears and hitting me in the face and screaming, just screaming like the devil was after her.

"You damn kids are drivin' me crazy. I'll teach ya to mind me..."

"Run, Millie, run," I shouted. "Go 'way; go outdoors. Go. Go. Run. Go...get....Matt. Run fast."

Mrs. Pitts was hitting me and trying to catch Millie at the same time, but I kept screaming, kicking her legs, and pulling on her dress. When her arm was near my mouth, I bit her. She grabbed her injured arm, and I got away from her and ran out the door behind Millie. I didn't look back, I just caught up with Millie and pulled her with me by her dress.

We ran, panting and crying, into the barn hoping Matt would be there. He saw us from the hayloft and hurried down the old rickety ladder. We cried louder when he came and put his arms around us, but he just held us until we were calm enough to tell him what had happened.

After he heard the account, he reached for the pitchfork that was leaning against the wall next to him and threw it with all his might across the floor. He stood very still for a few minutes, looking out the door toward the house. Then he turned to us and said we should go back inside so we wouldn't catch pneumonia in the cold with no coats.

We did as Matt said, going very quietly through the kitchen door, down the hall and upstairs to our cots. We didn't see Mrs. Pitts anywhere, so I thought she must be in the outhouse.

In our hallway room, we sat on Millie's cot, and I tried to make her stop crying.

"Don't cry," I pleaded. "She'll hear you, and we'll be in trouble again. Matt will help us, Millie. Remember when you told me he'd help us?"

"Uh, h-h-huh, b-but Muvver...is...bad," sobbed Millie.

"I think she must be a witch," I said. "But listen, Matt must have found her. They're in the kitchen? Sh-h-h-h."

I never heard such noise coming from Matt and Mrs. Pitts. I thought Matt might hit her; he sounded so furious, and that would be all right with me. I wished he could do something to her so she'd never hurt us again. The racket stopped, and I heard the kitchen door slam, so I knew Matt had gone back outside.

That night, Millie and I had to go to bed without supper because we had tattled. But that was all right, because we didn't have any appetite. But we didn't like the rest of our punishment.

"You're going to eat oatmeal for breakfast and fried oatmeal for supper from now on," she said. "And if you dare tell Mr. Lucas, I'll make you live in the cellar and you'll never come out!"

She did what she said, and my sister and I got skinnier and skinnier, and we didn't feel good most of the time. We were hungry, always, we were hungry. I had a butter sandwich for my school lunch, and Millie said that's what she had at home. We just felt worse and worse, until one day, one very wonderful day, help came.

It was a Sunday afternoon, and Millie and I were sitting on the living room floor looking at books when we heard someone knock on the kitchen door. Then there were voices in the kitchen—Mrs. Pitts and a man.

"C'mon, Millie, let's go see who's here." We hurried down the hall and when I swung open the kitchen door, I looked right into the face of an old man who was dressed in a suit and tie and wearing glasses.

"Hello there, girlies," he called, smiling at me and then Millie.

Mrs. Pitts turned in her chair to look at us. "Go back in the living room and stay..."

"No, no, Helland. Let them come in here. I want to see them," said the man, walking around the table in his fancy clothes and standing in front of us. He knelt down, took my hand, and looked at my face and then Millie's. He stood up and looked at us from the top of our heads to our feet.

"Hmmm. Hmmm. What are your names?"

"I'm Mary, and this is my sister, Millie," I said, looking at him and then at Mrs. Pitts, who was scowling and had her lips pursed.

She glared at me, squinted, and shook her head.

"What've you been eating, girls?" asked the man. He waited for me to answer.

I was afraid to answer because Mrs. Pitts looked mean, but Millie said, "Oatmeal."

"Anything else?" he asked.

"Bwead and buttuh at noon."

"Anything else?"

"No."

"What to drink?" he asked.

"Mulk for breakfast, watuh noon and night."

"Mary, is that right?"

I was afraid to answer because I didn't want to live in the cellar.

He knelt down again and put one arm around me and the other around Millie.

"I'm Dr. Goodman," he said. "Why don't you go back in the other room, and I'll see you again soon." He turned us to the door and pushed it open.

We walked a few steps from the door and stopped to listen to Dr. Goodman and Mrs. Pitts.

"You're starving these children," he said in a low voice. "They're thin and have that awful pallor, and they're very unhappy. What in hell are you trying to do, kill them? I should go to the authorities tomorrow and report this..."

"Now, wait a minute, Frank," said Mrs. Pitts. "You can't do that. I need the money. They're all right. They have plenty to eat for kids...they..."

"*You* wait a minute. I'll be here tomorrow with vitamin shots for them, and I want to see improvement immediately or they go!"

Millie and I went to the living room, but we knew we had

a new friend, somebody else, along with Matt, on our side.

Life was calmer after that. The doctor gave us shots in our legs once a week, and we had cod liver oil, a whole tablespoon full, every morning before breakfast. And we had such good things to eat—potatoes, meat, vegetables, milk and dessert. For breakfast, we had oatmeal most of the time, but sometimes we had poached eggs on toast or pancakes. And I think we grew taller and stronger.

CHAPTER 7

Matt's Last Stand

The calm days didn't last long, and even though we had enough to eat, Mrs. Pitts just got meaner and meaner. It seemed that every day was worse than the day already past. Millie and I had no control over our bladders, and our cots were wet almost every morning. We woke up with cold bottoms, but not for long, because they were quickly warmed by the razor strap. I thought maybe if I stayed awake all night, my cot would be dry in the morning. But I got sleepy and just couldn't help not waking up to sit on the pot. And since we didn't have any way to wash the smell off without Mrs. Pitts knowing, I'd have to go to school "stinking like a skunk," as Mrs. Pitts would say.

"Let everyone know how nasty and dirty you are," she'd tell me. "Let them see how you stink. And when you come home, come in through the washroom, and I'll put you in the tub of rinse water to clean you."

That's what she did. Millie said she got "cleaned" in the morning while I was at school, but Mrs. Pitts was at the back door waiting for me to come home. She took off my snowsuit and school clothes. I stood naked and shivering, and she picked me up and put me into that cold rinse water, sloshed it over my body and then dunked my head. I didn't know why she did that; the odor wasn't on my face and head. I kept thinking she should rinse me off before I went to school, and then all the kids wouldn't call me Betsy-Wetsy.

We'd be in the school yard, and I'd hear shouts of "Betsy-Wetsy" and "Pee-Pot" and "stinkweed" from all the kids. I got tired of it, but I didn't know what I could do to help myself, so one day I went inside to tell my teacher.

"Oh, get back outside," she said, "and stop being a tattle-tale."

So out I went, feeling like the worst kid in the school, and I didn't know which was worse, being sloshed in the tub or being in the school yard with my second-grade class.

One day, though, something good happened after my sloshing. I was out of the tub and standing in the back room, feeling like one of the icicles on the barn. Mrs. Pitts threw me a towel and said, "Here's your clean clothes, too. Get them on and come and set the table for supper."

Just then, Matthew came into the back room, bringing with him a gust of snowy wind.

"Eeeek," I squealed and covered myself with my dress.

"Get outta here," shouted Mrs. Pitts to Matt.

"Come in the kitchen with me," he ordered, walking right past me without looking. The two of them pounded their feet on the floor, so I knew I was about to hear some noise. I dressed and listened to the argument behind the closed door.

"You've got to stop mistreating these little girls," Matt shouted. "You can't be putting that child in ice cold water in the winter. Where'd you ever learn such things?"

"None o' your business," said Mrs. Pitts, "I know what I'm doing. I've brought up five already, and these two have to learn to be civilized."

"You call what you just did civilized? Listen to me, Helland Pitts, and listen good. I want you to stop hitting them with the razor strap and with sticks, and stop putting them in that ice water when they wet the bed. Did you ever think that if you'd be better to them, they might not have problems? Just remember that I know everything that's going on, and I won't let it go unanswered. You *will* be reported."

Yippee, I thought, good old Matt. Go ahead and report her and get us out of this terrible place.

I was so cold I had goosebumps, but I was afraid to leave

the back room and go into the kitchen until I heard Matt walk
across the floor in his heavy boots and go outdoors. The kitchen
door banged and I knew he was gone, so I went quickly into the
warm room and sat by Millie at the table.

I watched Mrs. Pitts at the stove talking to the soup she
was stirring.

"That damned old fool," she said. "I'll fire the miserable
old cuss." She turned and saw Millie and me.

"And what are you doin' gawkin' at me. Git outta here. I'm
sick of you two. Go to bed. You don't get any supper tonight for
wetting your beds."

"But we're hungry," I said.

"Get outta my sight, or you'll spend the night in the cellar,
both of you. That old man ain't gonna tell me how to raise kids."

We left the room, went to the outhouse, and then upstairs
to our cots, hoping that Matt would report her and we'd live
somewhere else.

On Saturday, Millie and I were sitting at the kitchen
table playing with a puzzle, and Mrs. Pitts was making a cake.

Millie said her stomach hurt, and Mrs. Pitts told her to
shut her mouth. That made Millie cry. I looked up at Mrs. Pitts
and saw her face begin to get red. I patted Millie's hand to
quiet her, but Mrs. Pitts suddenly ran over to Millie, picked
her up by the arm and carried her over to the sink.

"No, no, no. No watuh on face," screamed Millie through
her tears.

"I'll shut that crying up," shouted Mrs. Pitts, and she put
Millie's face under the pump spout. She made the pump handle
go up and down, up and down, up and down, and the water was
pouring out into Millie's face.

My sister was choking and gurgling, and I knew Mrs.
Pitts would kill her, so I screamed as loud as I could, and I
grabbed Mrs. Pitts' dress and pulled to get her away from the
sink. I put my arms around her legs to pull her away, but I
couldn't make her move at all. Finally, I tried to reach her arm
that was pumping the water, and I got it when it came back
down with the pump handle. I just climbed right on it with my
two arms so she couldn't raise the handle.

"Get away from me, you little fool," she yelled.

"You're drowning my sister," I shouted, and I screamed long and loud as I hung there on her arm.

Just then, in all that commotion, the door opened and banged against the wall and there stood Matt. In two quick strides he was at the sink, where he pushed Mrs. Pitts, with me still attached to her, and reached to pick up Millie who was gasping for breath.

Mrs. Pitts hit me on the head and told me to let go, but I wanted to hold her until Matt could put Millie down. He held Millie over the sink and slapped her on the back several times. Mrs. Pitts was trying to pry my hands from her arm, but she couldn't do both hands at the same time.

"Spit it out, girlie," Matt told Millie. "You'll be all right."

"Is she gonna die?" I asked, more frightened than I'd ever been for my little Millie.

"Nope, I'll hold her for a minute. Mary, let go of Helland's arm, and go to the washroom and get a couple of towels. Then take Millie upstairs with you. I think she's all right now."

"Get outta my kitchen, you damn fool," shouted Mrs. Pitts, reaching for Millie. "Give her here to me. This is my business, and you keep your nose out."

I hurried to get the towels and when I came back in the kitchen, I saw Matt holding Mrs. Pitts by her wrist. He was very tall, but she was bigger around. I wondered if she could hurt Matt.

He stood Millie on the floor, and I took my sister's hand and left the room.

When we were walking up the stairs, I heard Matt shouting to Mrs. Pitts, so I put the towels around Millie and we stood very still and listened for the magic words from Matt.

"This is the last time you'll hurt those children," he said. "I'm going right now to the welfare office. The girls will be out of here before you know it."

"Get outta here," she shouted, "and don't ever come back. I don't need you working for me anymore."

Mrs. Pitts must have gotten hold of a broom because I heard Matt tell her to put it away.

"No broom is gonna help you now. I think you've lost your mind," he said.

I got Millie dry and put another dress on her, and then we went down to the living room. Mrs. Pitts was standing by the front window and turned around when she heard us come into the room.

"Come over here, girls," she whispered. "We can watch from the window."

We stood with her, looking out. I saw Matt at the end of the driveway. He really was going away. I knew because he carried a pack on his back, and I thought it must hold all his belongings.

"You don't want them to take you away, do you?" said Mrs. Pitts. "The old fool. He hasn't got a car, and it's cold and blowing snow. He can't walk all the way to town in this weather. He's old. He'll freeze. How does he think he can get across those fields, over those drifts? He doesn't know how far...they'll find him...dead. The old fool."

We stood there, Mrs. Pitts with me beside her and Millie beside me, watching Matthew Lucas on that very cold January day in 1940.

He was dressed in his old long army coat with a brown scarf wrapped tightly around his neck, a red and black wool cap with flaps over his ears and thick brown mittens covered his hands.

Matt crossed the road and walked into the open field, where the blowing snow stacked drifts along a snow fence. He trudged slowly, lifting one black boot and then the other. He brought his feet together and stopped, slightly bent over.

Had he changed his mind? Was he coming back? No, no, Matt, I thought, you can't come back. Keep going. I said a prayer in my mind, like I learned to do in Sunday school when I lived with Charles and Esther. "Please, God, help Matthew get there."

I thought he must have heard me, because he pulled himself up very straight and tall and turned to look back at the house.

Here we are, Matt, waiting for you to help us. Please

keep going, please get there. You can do it, please go. I wished that I could have said those words to him. Maybe he could see us at the window. I hoped so. He'd know that I was praying he would *get us away from this terrible place.*

Just then a strong wind blew the snow into swirls, and we couldn't see him anymore.

"The old fool," said Mrs. Pitts, turning from the window. "Let's go now, girls. I have to call Walter and get him back here to do chores."

CHAPTER 8

Home Three

For two days after Matthew left, Mrs. Pitts was kind and quiet. Her face was not red when she talked to us about what might happen.

"Now, if Miss Warring comes here and asks you if you're happy with me, you say yes." There was no threat this time about what might be if we didn't do as she said. I think she was afraid she'd lose us. I remembered one day in the summer when I had heard Walter ask her why she had to keep stinky girls, she'd said it was because she needed the money.

I went to school on Monday morning and knew that Millie would be all right, because Mrs. Pitts was being good. She did not shout at us or get mad about anything all weekend, and she even let us eat in the dining room with her and Walter on Sunday.

In school, I was working at my desk when my teacher came and stood beside me.

"Come with me, Mary," she said quietly. "There's someone here to see you."

I stood up and followed my teacher to the coatroom, where I saw Miss Warring dressed in her fur hat, red coat, and boots.

"Is Millie sick?" I asked.

"No, she's fine," she said. "Please get your pencils and papers from your desk because I'm going to take you to a new home and a new school. You may go back into the room, Mary,

and tell your friends good-bye because you won't see them anymore."

I was so happy my lip was quivering, and I could feel the
tears coming in my eyes. "Where will we go?" I asked.

"You'll see," she said quietly, taking my hand and holding
it in hers. "Everything will be fine. I'll talk to you more when
we're in the car. Go get your things."

I wasn't one bit sad about leaving these "Betsy-Wetsy"
people. In fact, I was glad I wouldn't have to see them anymore.
I got my things out of my desk and went back to Miss Warring
in the coatroom.

As we walked to the car, she told me she was taking Millie
and me away from Mrs. Pitts' house.

"You will never have to see her again," she said.

"Are you getting Millie now?" I squealed, jumping up and
down. "I don't want her to be there without me. Did Matt find
you and tell you about us?"

"Yes, Matt came to my house late Saturday," she said.

I thought about Matt, walking in the cold and all that
snow, and I knew he'd found Miss Warring just like he'd said. I
was so happy that Matt didn't freeze to death like Mrs. Pitts
thought he would. I wondered if he'd stopped in at houses along
his way to get warm.

"Can we see Matt and tell him thank you?" I asked, as
Miss Warring opened the car door for me.

"I'm sorry, Mary," she said when she got in the car. "I have
something sad to tell you. Matthew had a heart attack yesterday and died at the hospital last night."

I started to cry, and she put her arm around me.

"I know you're sad, Mary. Matthew Lucas was the best
friend you had, and he cared so much about you and Millie.
Think of him as God's helper who watched out for you and
Millie. Now, he's safe and happy in heaven. Does that make you
feel better?"

I wiped my nose on the handkerchief Miss Warring gave
me and said I felt better.

"But, I'll really miss Matthew," I said.

"I know you will. And, Mary, when you and Millie are

alone tonight in your bedroom, you can tell her about Matthew like I told you."

"I will," I said, "and Millie will cry, too."

"Yes, she will, and speaking of Millie, we'd better get over to that place and get her, hadn't we?"

Thinking about leaving the Pitts' house was a happy thought, but losing Matthew was very sad. But, I had to be happy now, because we were getting my sister away from Mrs. Pitts.

When we got to the house, Miss Warring told me to stay in the car.

"I'm going to get Millie and bring her out. I'll come back later for your clothes, so don't you get out of the car. Just wait for me."

It seemed a long time before Miss Warring came out with Millie in her arms. I had worried that Mrs. Pitts would argue and not let Millie go. As Miss Warring ran to the car with my sister, I looked past her and saw that the kitchen door was still open. I wondered if Mrs. Pitts would come out shouting. When Miss Warring opened the car door to put Millie beside me, I asked her where Mrs. Pitts was.

"In the living room by the window. See her looking out?"

"You didn't close the door," I said.

"Couldn't. Had my hands full. Had to leave fast because Mrs. Pitts is very angry."

She closed the back car door and opened the front. As she got in, she asked me why I didn't let her know how bad things were. I told her because I was afraid of what Mrs. Pitts would do to Millie and me.

The drive to our new home was wonderful. We hadn't gone for a ride in a long time, and we both sat looking out our windows at the sparkling snow and pretty houses. I hoped the mother and father in our new home would be just like Esther and Charles Sink.

"Look girls, there's your brother, Billy, sliding downhill. See him? Do you remember him, Mary?"

"Yes," I said. "He lived with us at Mommy's and Daddy's, and he's bigger than we are, and one time he hit me in the mouth with a rake."

Leaning over the front seat so Miss Warring could see, I pulled out my upper lip.

"See. Here are the scars. I hope he doesn't hit me again."

"I hope not, too," said Miss Warring. "All right. Let's all get out. I'll carry Millie."

As we walked from the car and up the shoveled steps to the back porch, I looked at the big building around me.

"This is the biggest and prettiest house I ever saw," I exclaimed. "I think I might get lost inside."

"It's a very lovely home," said Miss Warring, "and I just know you'll be happy here." She knocked at the kitchen door. We waited a few minutes, and then a little lady with curly gray hair opened the door and looked out.

"Come in," she said, holding the door for us. "Take off your boots and put them right there." She pointed to a mat by the radiator just inside the door. "I'll put all the coats here on the chairs for now."

The four of us stood in the kitchen while Miss Warring introduced us to Mrs. Tanner. I looked at my new mother in her green dress with the small white collar and long sleeves. I looked at her brown shoes with a fan design on the front and box heels on the back and no laces. She was dressed up and wore pink lipstick and rouge and nail polish. She's very rich, I thought, to dress this way when she's not going anywhere.

We followed Mrs. Tanner through the kitchen and into the sitting room, which she said used to be her dining room.

"Muriel, sit in the chair by the window," said Mrs. Tanner, "and the girls can sit on these two footstools beside you."

"My, your fern is lovely, Fanny. How do you keep it so green and alive?" asked Miss Warring.

"Just a bit of..."

I didn't hear the answer because I was looking out the window at the front porch—so large with white pillars, and the wide front yard swept snowy clean by the wind.

"I think you'll enjoy these little girls, Fanny, and I know this will be a good home for them."

"Let's hope we get along fine, and I think they'll like being here with their brother," said Mrs. Tanner, smiling at us.

She's nice, I thought, and neat and clean and pretty, but she's very serious, not giggly and funny like Esther.

"Well, I have to get back to the office now," said Miss Warring, rising from her chair. "It's almost noon, and I have this report to finish. I'll see you girls in a few days when I bring your clothes."

Mrs. Tanner got up and walked with Miss Warring to the door while Millie and I stayed on our stools. I heard them say good-bye to each other, and then Mrs. Tanner came back to the sitting room. She took little steps and looked almost like she'd twirl into a dance.

"All right, Mary and Millie," she said gaily, reaching for our hands. "Come with me, and I'll show you your room."

We went up a long stairway that curved and had lots of wooden sticks under the railing. When we got to the top, we turned and walked down a hallway with a pretty fringy rug and into a bedroom. I put my school box on the big bed that had wood by the pillows and wood at the bottom where our feet would be. There was a fluffy white bedspread with blue flowers on it, and my eyes followed the many colored flowers splashed on the wallpaper from the bed to the window, where I could see my brother playing with his sled.

Mrs. Tanner was talking about a room of our own, and she walked to the closet where we would hang our dresses. She talked about "your room" and "making your bed every day and keeping your clothes hung up and dustmopping every morning."

I didn't care to hear about work, so I stayed by the window. I was up very high in the house and could see a long way. There were fields and fields of deep snow and tall green pine trees along the driveway to the cow barn. Billy was on top of the hill, where I watched him sit on his sled and go whizzing down. He walked back up and stood for a minute. Then he held the sled in his hands with his arms up by his waist. He ran with it and flopped his body onto it when the sled hit the ground. Away he went, down the hill and far out across the white, crusty field. I laughed down in my throat and wanted so much to be out there with him. You and I'll have lots of fun,

Billy, I thought, and I couldn't wait for him to come inside for supper so I could see him up close.

"And Mary?"

It was Mrs. Tanner speaking to me. "Yes?" I said, turning to her and seeing her push a dustmop across the floor.

"I want you every morning to use this dustmop like this and then take it over here, open the window and shake the mop. I'll show you how to open and close the window. Watch."

I moved out of her way and saw her turn the lock and raise the bottom half of the window. She pushed the dustmop out and shook, shook shook, pulled it back in, closed and locked the window.

"There, you see," she said, and placed the handle of the mop in my hand. "It goes in the closet."

When I had placed it in the closet and closed the door, she said we should go with her downstairs so we could talk for awhile before she had to start supper.

I followed her and Millie down the winding stairway, and pretended I was a princess and this was my castle and I was living with my fairy godmother.

When we were seated again, Millie and I listened.

"First of all," began Mrs. Tanner, "you will call me 'Mother' and you will call Mr. Tanner 'Dad'. Since our son has grown up and left home, we thought it would be nice to have children here with us so we wouldn't get lonely. I will have work for each of you to do because I can't take care of this big place alone. I'll show you the back room where you can play because I don't allow children to play here in the house. But you will have a nice place in the washroom. There's a toilet there for you to use and a sink where you wash up before you eat. You'll brush your teeth and comb your hair out there, too. The only time you are allowed in the bathroom upstairs is first thing in the morning when you get up and on Saturdays when I give you your baths.

"Now, I'll give you this *Sears Catalog* to look at while I go prepare supper."

She sat Millie in the big rocking chair and walked, in her little steps, to a basket near the fireplace where she picked up the catalog and placed it in my lap.

"There you are. Now be sure you look at it together," she said, leaving us alone in the room.

"Do you like her?" I whispered to Millie.

"I guess so," she answered. "She's bettuh than Muvver."

"She is," I agreed. "I like this house, and I can't wait to see Billy."

I opened the big catalog and turned to the children's section.

"Let's find dresses for Miss Warring to buy for us. How's that?"

"That good," said Millie, and we looked at each other and laughed, both so happy to be with a kind, new mother.

CHAPTER 9

Fuhrer Fanny

Supper was ready, and so were Millie and I. We wanted to see Billy, but Dad came in first. He was a jolly fat man in a plaid shirt and bib overalls. When he came in, Mrs. Tanner was mad at him.

"Franklin, you'd better not come to my table with those old smelly clothes on. You go right upstairs and wash and change. I'm trying to teach children manners, and look at you."

"Oh, Fan, don't get so excited," he said. "I'm on my way, back in a minute. What are your names?" he asked, messing up our hair. "Huh? Can you talk?"

"Never mind," she said. "I'll tell you later. Just get that smell out of this kitchen."

Billy came in the door. He had blond, curly hair and blue eyes and a big smile on his round red face.

"Hello, sisters," he said. "I remember when you were babies, and you still look the same."

"Oh, no we don't," I said. "We're not babies."

"We're not babies," said Millie. "You're a baby."

"Now, now," said Mrs. Tanner. "Stop arguing and be quiet at the table, too. Here comes Franklin, so we can sit down now. You sit in your place," she said, taking Mr. Tanner's arm and pushing him toward his chair. "Millie, you sit next to Dad. Billy, you're by the window across from Dad, and Mary, you're beside Billy and next to me. I always sit at the end of the table, so I can get up and get things."

We sat down. I didn't know how Millie felt, but I was afraid to be at the table with the grown-ups watching me. My stomach began to hurt, and I didn't feel like eating. I saw that Mr. Tanner had the plates in front of him, and I watched as he put helpings on each one and passed it, first to Mother, then to Millie, me, and Billy. He put the most on his own plate, and the least on Mrs. Tanner's. She reminded me of a bird because she was not very big, not even in her hands. I noticed that she stuck out her little finger when she held her fork and spoon, and I tried to do the same, but my fork turned sideways.

"How'd you do that?" I asked.

"Do what?"

"Hold out your little finger that way."

"Never mind. You just eat. When we have our meals, children are seen and not heard. No laughing, either. You eat like ladies. Billy knows what the rules are, don't you, Billy?"

"Yes," he said, "from you at my first meal here."

"Hmph. Won't hurt you any, either." She tapped my hand with her fork. "You're not holding that right, and neither is Millie. You don't grab it like it's a shovel. Haven't you been taught anything? Watch me, now."

She picked up her fork in her fingers, and we tried to do it just like Mrs. Tanner, instead of using our fists.

"There," she said. "Now hold it that same way all the time."

Later, in our room, I told Millie that Matthew died, and we both cried. Then, I told her that Matthew was God's helper and watched out for us.

"But now he's happy and safe in heaven," I said, and that made us both feel better.

Millie and I soon learned Mrs. Tanner's rules, and we learned how to do many chores inside and out. Mornings, we made our bed, and I dustmopped the room. I couldn't wait to get it finished so I could open the window and shake the mop. I liked to feel the cold air coming into the room, and I liked to see the little pieces of dust float down onto the white snow far below.

One morning, after several weeks of the same ritual, I decided that the floor didn't need to be done every day, and I didn't even touch the mop.

When I went downstairs, Mrs. Tanner was looking out the window over the sink as she washed dishes. Not turning, she asked why I hadn't dusted my room. She seemed quite angry, so I quickly responded.

"I did it." I lied because I didn't know what she'd do if I disobeyed.

"No, you didn't," she said.

I stood behind her and watched her washing dishes. How could she know? I wondered. She continued to look out the window.

I felt my face getting warm, but I said nothing. I looked past her out the window where I could see trees swaying. Oh, I thought, now I know! She didn't see the dust come down by the window. Maybe she won't say any....

"You didn't do it, did you?" she said.

"No."

She whirled around, dripping soapy water onto the braided rug under her feet.

"Well, let me tell you something, young lady. You do what I say, and don't you lie again. Now, get back upstairs and dust that room, and the next time you don't do what you're told and you lie about it, you'll get a whipping. Remember that."

I turned and walked slowly up the steps and into my room. I dusted and shook the mop hard out the window. But I didn't watch the dust fall onto the snow. It wasn't fun anymore, and I didn't feel good inside myself. I felt heavy and ugly and bad.

During the 1941 winter, after I'd turned seven in December, I think Mrs. Tanner wanted to keep me busy so I wouldn't get into trouble. She had Millie with her most of the time, showing her how things were done in the kitchen. She gave me more and more work, not only dustmopping my room, but sweeping the back rooms, too.

One cold Saturday in March, she said I had to learn how to dust the furniture. She had me follow her into every room where she demonstrated my new task.

"No excuse now for missing a thing," she said when we'd returned to the kitchen. "Next week it's your job. I'll put the cloth on a nail under the sink."

The sad day came, and I got the black gauze cloth, thinking that maybe if I did a terrible job she'd do it herself from then on. But, she had me follow her, and when we got to her bedroom, she pointed to the bed.

"There it is," she said. "Do that and everything else, dresser, chest, chair, radiator top, window sills, bedstand and washstand. Just don't pick up the pitcher and bowl because I don't want them broken. They were my mother's. I will inspect your work when you tell me you're through." She turned and left the room.

I felt trapped. She'd know if I missed anything; she was like a detective. She knew that I hadn't dusted my floor. Nothing to do but get started, I thought, and then I felt determined to do a perfect job. She won't find any dust when I get through, I promised myself, and I began to rub back and forth with the cloth on the wooden foot of the bed. There were fancy swirls that I liked going in and out of, and then I reached up as far as I could to do the headboard. I went from room to room, cleaning and looking at all the pretty things: pictures, jewelry, lamps, homemade quilts. Her bedroom and the guest room had fireplaces, and I wished that Millie's and my bedroom had one, too. I went to the back bedroom at the opposite end of the hall from ours, and it was the smallest room. She had said it was Dad's room. He just had a small iron bed, dresser, washstand and old rocking chair like the one Mr. Pitts sat in. The Pitts didn't have separate bedrooms. I wondered why Mr. and Mrs. Tanner did.

When I was finished, I went to the kitchen where Mrs. Tanner was making apple pies. "I'm all done," I said happily.

"All right," she said. "I'll check everything later. You go out to your washroom and sweep that and the back rooms. The broom and dustpan are behind the old cookstove. When you're through, you can play in the washroom until I call you for dinner."

"Can Millie come and play with me then, too?" I asked.

"After she helps me clean up the kitchen."

I finished the sweeping and went to the washroom to work on my favorite puzzle of moonlight on a snowy landscape. Millie came in when I was half finished and said she was ready to play out in the snow.

"Let's make a snowman," she said. "And where's Bilwee?"

I wanted to finish the puzzle, but Millie and I didn't get to play outside very often, so I put on my snowsuit and we went out to find Billy.

"I think he's sliding down that snowbank, Millie. Maybe we can all get on the sled and go together. How's that?"

"Funny," giggled Millie, and we ran to the highest snowdrift. Sure enough, our brother was there having a grand time. He was happy to see us, but when we were getting on the sled for the fifth trip down, we heard the familiar high-pitched call for dinner.

"Aw, she would hafta call us now," whined Billy, "just when we're getting started. But I'm hungry, so let's go."

He was at the back room door before Millie and I could get out of the field. "Slowpokes," he yelled and went inside to wash.

While we were at the table, Mrs. Tanner said she found some dust on two things, the floor lamp in the parlor and the rocking chair in Dad's bedroom. I remembered that I had rocked in the chair and thought about nice old Mr. Pitts, and had forgotten to dust it, but I didn't remember seeing any floor lamp in the parlor.

"So from now on," I heard Mrs. Tanner say, "I'm going to inspect your work, and if I find dust on anything that you were supposed to do, you'll get no dessert for Saturday dinner. You can have pie today because it was your first time dusting, and I'll excuse you. But I won't after today."

"I'm little, and I can't dust like you," I sputtered.

"I'll not have that sass," she said sternly. "I was dusting at your age, and doing everything else, too, so say no more."

I felt like running away from the table because I had tried hard to do a good job. Now I felt like I'd never do it perfectly, so that meant no more pie forever on Saturdays. Oh well, I thought, she makes the pieces too small, so I don't care.

"Get your elbow off the table," she said to Billy, "or you'll get a poke with the fork. You know the rules."

"Can I poke you and Dad if I see you put your elbows on the table?" asked Billy, sticking out his chin.

"No lip from you," said Dad, hitting his fist on the table.

We cleaned up our plates and waited for Mrs. Tanner to cut the pieces of pie for us. Even though my stomach hurt from what Mrs. Tanner had said earlier about no pie, I thought I'd better eat the small piece. It may be my last for a long time, I thought. It was cherry, not apple. I guess she made more than one pie. Cherry was my favorite, so I felt lucky, but I didn't think I could ever like Mrs. Tanner. She always looked like a grump, and she was too bossy and never said thank you for anything I did. She didn't have good manners, that was certain.

Later, when Billy and I were playing outside, and Millie was taking a nap, I asked him if he liked Mrs. Tanner.

"Are you being funny?" he asked. "I hate both of them. Dad's just like her when I help with the chores. He doesn't like the way I do anything, but he gives me more and more work, and I think he does it so he can yell at me more. I keep telling him I'm only eight years old, but he says I'm big for my age and strong as an ox. I like farm work, but I don't like being a hired man and getting no pay. I'm telling my father when I see him."

"Is he my father, too?" I asked.

"'Course he is. He's Millie's too. We'll all see him, maybe, if he has time. Sometimes he's in a hurry, but I think that's 'cause Mr. and Mrs. Tanner don't like him to be here."

"How come?"

"Aw, they say he's a bad influence for me, but I think he likes me better than they do 'cause he's my own dad."

When our father came on Sunday afternoon, I was resting on the sunporch couch, and Millie was upstairs in our bed. I heard the truck come up the driveway, so I ran through the parlor and into the kitchen to get my sweater.

"Where do you think you're going?" said Mrs. Tanner.

"To see my father," I said.

"Oh, no you're not. I will not allow him to corrupt you like he has Billy. As long as you live in my house, you will have nothing to do with your father. He's no good. Now, go back out on the porch and take your nap."

Billy came around the back of the house and knocked on the porch door. When I opened it, he asked me if I was coming out, and I told him what Mother had said.

"Well, I guess you'd better stay in," he said, "but I'll tell Dad what the old lady said. Don't worry, 'cause I know you'll get to see him someday."

I closed the door and went back to the leather couch where I put my face into the pillow and cried. I didn't remember what my father looked like, and I wanted to see him and hear him talk. When I stopped crying, I sat up and thought about Mrs. Tanner and how I disliked her and her house that I had to dust and sweep.

I'll get even with her, I said to myself. I'll think and think, and someday I'll get even, and she'll be sorry she was so mean to me.

Billy came to the sunporch after our dad left and told me about his visit.

"I wish I could stay with Mom and Dad instead of in this old hole," he said. "But Dad and Mom don't have any money. And what's worse, they've got two more kids. Dad said our brother, Mitch, who's three, will have to be sent to a home, but they're going to keep Ginny. She's one."

"Can Mitch live here with us?" I asked.

"Don't be so dumb. We don't even want to live here…"

"Oh, Billy," Mr. Tanner called.

"Get out, quick," I said.

He was gone in a flash, and I pretended to be asleep when Mr. Tanner came to the porch.

CHAPTER 10

The Incorrigibles

My brother was a rascal, and I admired his daring ways. We had such fun together through the winter, sledding, building snow forts, and playing fox and geese. He was 'it' most of the time because I could catch him so easily, even with his fancy dodging and dancing. I could run faster. We thought games would be even more fun with Millie, but Mrs. Tanner said that because Millie had her hands and feet frozen when she was a baby, she couldn't be out in the cold.

My times outside were so much fun that they made the times inside terrible. Mrs. Tanner said I had become too sloppy doing my work, and she wasn't going to put up with the same shenanigans that Dad did with Billy. So I got a whipping that she said would "straighten me up." I was taken to the washroom and told to lie over the commode, where a number of razor strap slaps were administered by Mrs. Tanner. She was a smaller Mrs. Pitts, and that made me afraid of her, but not the same kind of afraid. I was bigger now, and every time Mrs. Tanner did something to me that I thought was mean, I decided that one day I'd do something to her to get even.

Billy said I didn't have to be afraid of the old lady because he could beat her up if she hurt me too much.

"I'm not afraid of anybody or anything, not even when I get a licking from Mr. Tanner," he said. "What's a licking? I've had so many, they don't even hurt anymore."

One day, I was in the washroom putting a puzzle together, and I thought about the old problem that seemed to me would never go away. All three of us wet the bed! I'd wake up in the early morning and sense the dampness, and feel around quickly to learn whether Millie had wet the bed or whether I had. Sometimes, it was both of us, so that meant two things would happen. Mrs. Tanner would come into the room and say, "I can smell that stench. Are you babies? Should I get diapers for you?"

The second thing was, "Well, these sheets will be hung out on the line all day so everyone will know what you have done."

Billy had his sheet on the line many mornings, too. We'd make fun of him because he'd make fun of us, but Millie and I never made fun of each other. I felt sad for my sister when people were mean to her, and I guess she felt sad for me. I didn't know why Billy had to laugh at us, but I thought boys must like to pick on girls, even if they were brothers.

One morning in the spring, when Millie's and my sheets were on the line, Billy was calling us "diaper babies" and saying "shame, shame on you" when Mrs. Tanner came out on the porch.

"Don't you be acting like you're a goody-goody," she said to him. "I just went to your bed that you made this morning, and I could smell the stink a mile away. So, here's your sheet on the line, too."

Millie and I got back at Billy for teasing us. We called him everything he had called us, and we didn't stop all day long. Of course, he wasn't bothered with anything we said to him. When nobody was around but Millie and me, he said he was going to try to wet his bed every night.

Our father had been coming to see Billy all through the winter and spring, and now that it was summer, he'd probably come to visit more often. Billy told me that our father had told him that he shouldn't have to work so hard.

"Dad said I should just tell Old Man Tanner that I'm not going to do all his dirty work for him. The old man makes me shovel manure out of the cow barn. And now he wants me to work on the haybaler this summer. He said I could hook wires, whatever that means. My Dad said that was dangerous for an eight-year-old boy. Dad said I was a free hired man, and he said Tanner had enough money to hire ten men."

"But, Billy, Mr. Tanner will give you another licking with whatever that thing is," I said.

"It's a rein that they use when they hitch up the horses to the hay wagon," said Billy, "and it doesn't even hurt anymore."

"Listen, Mary, I got a good idea. Let's you and me run away. I got my piggy bank out of my room this morning and broke it open, and I got sixty-five cents. That's enough to take care of us for a long time."

"That is a lot of money," I said, "but I think I'm afraid."

"Afraid? What are you afraid of? I'd be right with you, and I'm not afraid. It's better to run away than stay here."

"How will we go so they won't see us?" I asked.

"I got it all figured out, Mary. We'll have to go over that big fence by the Veterans' hospital, run through the yard there and climb over the other fence to get back out again because we can't go around. After that, we'll be in old man Ferguson's alfalfa field."

"No, I'm scared of Mr. Ferguson. If he catches us, he might shoot us, because Mother says he walks around with a big gun all the time to keep people off his land."

"You just come with me and run fast when I tell you, and nobody will get us. I know the way really good. And we don't want to be here anymore. They don't like us, and we don't like them. Are you going with me or not?"

He started walking away from me, and I was afraid something would happen to him, so I followed. Billy climbed to the top of the high fence and I watched him, but when I tried, I couldn't make my foot stay in the wire fence holes. Billy told me to take off my shoes and stick my bare foot into the holes. That worked better, and I got over the fence and put my shoes back on. We got over the fence at the other end of the big yard and continued on our way.

"Where are we going?" I asked.

"To town," said Billy. "See, we're on Gilbert Street now, and when we come to the end, we'll be on Main Street, at the top of the hill."

When we were on Main Street by the railroad roundhouse, Billy told me to sit on the bench and wait for him to go get us some food. He told me not to talk to anyone.

"I'll come back here to get you."

I sat and watched him go down the road past Lou's Tobacco Store and over the railroad tracks.

"What are you doing here, girl?" a voice behind me said.

I jumped up and turned to see a very old man with a long white beard. He hobbled with his cane to the bench and sat down.

"Sit down, little girl," he said, with a squeaky laugh. "I don' bite. Jus' hot an' tired...cool here...tired. I been walkin' long way, an' my...cane's tired...hot from rough road an' hot sun." He cleared his throat. "Ahhahhem...what's yer name?"

"Mary."

"Mmmareee...whacha doin' here?" He looked up in the sky, reached to his back pocket, took out an old handkerchief and wiped his forehead.

"Waiting for my brother."

"Where's he?"

"At the store."

"Hmmm...ahhemmm. Mother know?"

"Uh huh."

"You're pretty. Go ta Sunday school?"

"Unh uh. Well, sometimes."

"Ever hear 'bout Adam and Eve?"

"Yes."

"You lissin. They lived in..." And then the old man coughed. He coughed and coughed, just like Mr. Pitts had done, and I thought he'd die on the bench. I felt very frightened until he talked again.

"Think of it ever' day, I do. Ol' Eve an' that apple—gave it ta Adam." He looked down at me. "Now, girl, we all gotta die...jus' everbody, an' my time's a comin'...yup. Time's a...comin'...soon...an' all 'cuz a Eve an' that apple. Ain't ita shame...coulda been heaven...on...earth fer us all."

"I better go," I said, very much afraid that he would die right that very minute.

"Naw, stay till yer brother gits back. I'll stay with ya."

I'd rather stay here alone, I thought. He's so old and shaky, I don't think he could help if someone wanted to steal me. And he talks too much about scary things when I want to be happy.

"People are evil with all their killin' an' cheatin' and lyin'...but everbody's gotta pay fer what they do...uh, huh...everbody..."

"You won't die yet, will you?"

"Probly...uh...ahhemm...tomorry."

I felt better knowing he wasn't going to do it on the bench.

"I wish you didn't have to die," I said softly, and then I saw Billy. "Oh, goody, here's Billy."

I jumped from the bench. "He's got candy for us. Bye, Mr. Man," and I ran to meet my brother.

We turned down the side street away from the sick, old man. I turned to wave good-bye, but he had dropped his cane and had his head way down like he was sound asleep, so he didn't see me.

Later, I told Billy the story the old man had told me.

"Aw, Mary, he's just a crazy old geezer trying to scare you. He doesn't know what he's talking about, 'cause I never heard that story. He just made it all up. Here's some gumdrops for you, and I got us a Milky Way—your favorite—huh?"

"Yes, that's my favorite. Thanks. But I think the story the old man told me is right. He said if we do anything wrong, we have to pay the price. And I learned in Sunday school a long time ago about Adam and Eve and the apple. So do you think we'll have to pay for running away, Billy?"

"No, because we aren't ever going back to the Tanners."

So Billy and I ate our candy until we felt sick and decided to save some for the next day. The sun was going down, and we had to find a place to sleep. We walked in the road after we came to Gilbert Street, and that was on the way to the Tanners.

"No, Billy," I squealed, pulling at his sleeve. "We can't go home. We'll get the worst whipping in the world if we go there."

"Nobody'll see us, Mary. Now, come on. I know where we can sleep. I don't feel so good, and I want to sleep."

We slept under the biggest and tallest tree I'd ever seen,

right in our own front yard. After we had been there awhile, I heard cars coming in the driveway, and I heard voices. One was Mr. Tanner. I heard Mrs. Tanner's voice a little later, so I peeked through my lowered eyelids to the front porch of our house, and there she was with three policemen who were shining a big flashlight on Billy and me.

"There they are," boomed a man's voice.

"Well, just leave them there," said Mr. Tanner. "We'll get them in the morning. They won't go anywhere tonight. Probably too scared."

Ha, ha, I thought. You don't know Billy. He's not afraid of anything and especially not you!

Billy whispered to me to lay still like I was sleeping, so I did. When the people were gone, Billy whispered again.

"First thing in the morning, we'll get up and run away again. I know where we can go—to our Dad's place, and he'll take care of us."

I was so excited thinking about that, I couldn't go to sleep.

When the sun was just beginning to come up, Billy shook me and said, "Let's get outta here. I gotta throw up."

We hurried to the small garden behind the house, and I waited for Billy to finish being sick. I heard one of our roosters crow from the fence post on the cow path, and I thought that Dad was probably already milking the cows.

When Billy felt better, he said we should go to the cornfield because nobody could see us there with the high corn.

We stood by the plants that were a little taller than we were, and I pulled off an ear of corn. I didn't like the taste, and I noticed that Billy didn't try to eat any.

"Let's play tag between the rows," said Billy.

"I can catch you easy," I threatened.

"No, you can't," he yelled excitedly and began running toward the woods at the back of the field.

"No, Billy," I screamed, "you can't go that way. There are wild boars in the woods. Come back, come back."

Then I heard a shout from the barn. I knew that Dad Tanner had heard me screaming, and he'd come after us. I watched him get into his truck and drive down the lane in our direction. Billy had run back to where I was standing.

"Come on, Mary," he said pulling on my arm, "we have to get out of here and go to our Dad."

But Mr. Tanner had gotten out of his truck and was running into the cornfield toward us.

"Don't you move, you damn little fools," he called. "You stand right where you are."

I stood still, but Billy ran away, back down the row toward the woods.

"No, no, no Billy," I screamed. "You'll get killed."

Mr. Tanner grabbed me by the back of my dress and told me to get in the truck, and then he ran after my brother. I knew he would catch Billy before the boars killed him, so I went to the truck.

I saw Dad grab Billy by his shirt and then put his arm around Billy's neck and half-drag him back to the truck.

"You're choking me," said Billy, "and I'm telling my dad."

"The hell you are," said Mr. Tanner. "You two are going back to the house and face the consequences. Just wait till Fanny gets hold of you. Bet you won't run away again."

I was too frightened and sick to even think of what Mrs. Tanner would do, so Billy and I rode to the house in silence, petrified when we thought of facing the fury of our foster mother.

CHAPTER 11

We Pay the Price

Mr. Tanner didn't say anything while he drove us to the back porch where Mrs. Tanner was waiting. I saw her green eyes staring at us and her fists pushed tight into her hips. We got slowly out of the truck and stood facing her.

"What do you two mean running away like that? We had to call the police and be humiliated in front of our friends and neighbors. What have you been eating while you've been gone, and where did you go?"

I looked at Billy for him to answer, but he just stared at the Tanners. I felt very frightened about what was going to happen to us, so I answered the questions.

"We went to town, and we ate candy, and we slept under the tree in the front yard, and..."

"Well, you'll both get a good dose of castor oil, and then you can sit in the sun right here on the concrete steps for the rest of the day," Mrs. Tanner said. "You'll get nothing but bread and water for three days, just like you're in jail, where you should be."

We took our castor oil, and a little later we paid the price for all the candy. I never had such a terrible stomach ache. I moaned and groaned all morning and went to the toilet at least ten times. So did Billy, but he didn't complain. The sun was so hot, I thought I'd burn up sitting on that concrete, and when I looked at Billy, his face was beet red, and sweat dripped on his shirt.

At dinner time we sat at the table, and there was a slice of bread on a plate and a glass of water. I didn't feel like my stomach wanted anything, but I ate the bread anyway and drank a little water, but Billy just sat with his hands on his legs and his head down.

"Eat that bread, Billy," said Mr. Tanner, but Billy didn't move.

"Starve then, you brat," said Mr. Tanner.

When the punishment was over, I was glad to get some good food, but it made my stomach hurt awful. Billy didn't say anything about his stomach, but he ate his food and I was glad because he hadn't eaten his jail food.

A few days later, Billy said we would pay back Mrs. Tanner for what she had done to us.

"What will we do?" I asked.

"We'll go to the cellar where she has all those jars of food, and we'll eat some," he said.

So I went with him, and we chose peaches and took the glass jar out back to the smokehouse.

"How do we get it open?" I asked.

"I'll break the top with a rock," said Billy. "We can eat with our fingers and then we'll bury the broken glass. It's easy. I've done this lots of times. Now you'll know how to do it, and you'll never have to be hungry."

And that's what we did for the next several days in the afternoon when Millie was napping. We didn't think Mrs. Tanner would ever notice that jars were missing.

On Labor Day, before I started third grade, Billy was taken away from the Tanners. He didn't know he was leaving until Sunday afternoon when Mrs. Tanner told us.

We were sitting at the dinner table and had just finished our pie when Mrs. Tanner said she had something to tell us. She said she was not happy to do what she had to do.

"Billy will be leaving tomorrow," she said.

"Why does Billy have to leave?" I asked, angry and scared about losing him and feeling my face getting red.

Mrs. Tanner ignored my question.

"Miss Warring will be here first thing in the morning, so,

Billy, you have your clothes packed in the box that I have put in your room," she continued.

Billy just stared, first at Mrs. Tanner and then at Mr. Tanner.

I felt like everyone was about to burst with anger.

Billy pushed his chair back, and, without saying excuse me or anything, he turned from the table and walked out the door.

I felt sorry for Billy, so I pushed my chair back.

"May I..."

"No, you may not," snapped Mrs. Tanner. "Sit right where you are until I tell you to leave."

Miss Warring came early on Labor Day and Billy got in her car with his box of clothes. He hadn't talked to me about going away because Mrs. Tanner made me stay in the house with her and Millie. I think the Tanners sent him away because they didn't like him, and they didn't want me with him. Maybe they thought he would make me bad. I know we did things that we shouldn't have, but I think Billy felt like nobody liked him, so he didn't care what he did. I cared about him, so I did what he wanted me to.

I didn't know where Miss Warring took Billy, but I hoped he was with our father. Whenever Miss Warring came to get Millie and me to go shopping for clothes, I'd ask her about Billy, and many times she said, "He's in a new home. He has trouble getting along with people."

I didn't see my big brother for a long time, but Miss Warring took Millie and me to meet our little brother, Mitch, who lived with a family not far from the Tanners. He was a cute little boy with blond hair and blue eyes, and when I saw him, I wanted him to live with us. But Miss Warring said the Tanners couldn't take care of more children. We visited Mitch several times, and it made me happy to have a little brother who was so sweet and good.

CHAPTER 12

Fanny and Foe

On Labor Day afternoon, I was in the washroom crying for Billy when Mrs. Tanner called me to come outside with her. She said that I should get busy and get my mind off what was bothering me, and the best thing she knew for me to do was to pull some weeds. She took me to the spirea bushes that grew along the driveway.

"You see under there," she said, pointing with her pink fingernail, "we need those weeds out of there before the cold weather. It'll keep your mind on something worthwhile for the rest of the afternoon."

She took my arm and pushed me toward the first bush. "Start here," she said and walked away. I watched the light green hem of her dress bump against the back of her legs when she took her little steps.

"Why don't you pull these old weeds?" my lips said, as I saw the sides of her bottom go up and down when she climbed the steps of the back porch. "Why do I have to do the things you don't want to?"

Squeezing my eyes closed, I stuck out my tongue in the direction I saw her go because I knew she wouldn't turn to look at me.

I turned to the weeds and cleared them from three bushes. I don't care about old weeds, I thought, and I picked up a stick and looked at the dirt packed down where I had stepped on it.

I drew a barn and a house. The flowers I made were small twigs stuck in the ground, and my trees were taller twigs. I drew Mrs. Tanner on the roof of the house and then I scratched her out. She's nowhere in my picture, I decided.

Just before supper, Mrs. Tanner came to see if I had finished. When she got to the fourth bush, she looked at me hiding there, and I watched her shoes as she went down the driveway looking under more bushes and making snorting sounds. Her shoes came back and stopped at my hiding place.

"Get out of there," she said. "Why isn't this work done?"

"I don't know," I said, as I crawled out and stood before her.

"You don't know? You don't know nothin'. You're lazy." She kicked the stones in the driveway and grabbed my arm. I jerked away thinking she'd hit me in the face.

"Come here to me," she shouted. "You don't get any dessert for a week, and you'll stay home tonight while we take Millie to see Uncle Henry and Aunt Zella."

I stood beside her, but I looked under the bushes that had no weeds. I don't want any of her old cake, anyway, I thought, and I don't want to ride in any old car with her. She took some steps toward the house and then turned.

"Go wash your face and hands for supper."

When supper was over, I dried the dishes. She didn't talk until I hung up the dish towel. Then she said I was to brush my teeth and go to my room where I should stay the rest of the night. I hurried out of the kitchen so she wouldn't see my tears. I wanted her to think that no matter what she said, she couldn't hurt me.

I stayed in the washroom until I heard doors slam. Through the window, I watched the car move slowly out of sight. Then, I went to the porch glider, sat down and swung it back and forth, bumping it into the windowsill because she had told us not to do that.

After a few minutes, I got up and walked to the bushes and crawled under them where I'd drawn my farm. I pulled a weed and then another and another, while I sang, "Pigweed, pigweed, go away, ragweed, ragweed you can't stay," and I didn't stop working until they were gone. She'll be surprised, I thought as I crawled from under the last bush. It was nearly dark, and I was afraid of boogiemen, so I ran to the back porch and swung happily while I waited for everyone to come home.

When I heard the tires grinding on the gravel, I was so excited, I could hardly wait for them. I hurried to Mrs. Tanner who helped Millie out of the back seat.

"What are you doing out of your room?" screeched Mrs. Tanner.

"I have a surprise for you to see before it's pitch black out here." I took her hand and pulled her so she'd come and see what I had done for her and be happy and like me.

She walked with me along the hedge to the end. "See," I squealed in delight. "The weeds are gone, 'cause I pulled every one."

"Humphf," she grunted. "Didn't you know that 'lazy man works best when the sun's in the west'?"

She turned from me and walked to the house, and I stayed in the driveway. I heard Mrs. Tanner's voice coming from the porch where she was talking to Mr. Tanner. "...never amount to nothin'...like her mother..."

I didn't want to hear anymore, so I ran farther down the driveway until her voice sounded like a drone with no words.

And then I remembered the boogiemen who were in the trees, and walked back to the porch steps. I stopped, thinking I'd wait for the Tanners to go to bed, but Mrs. Tanner called to me.

"Mary, get ready for bed. It's late."

I went through the darkness past her and into the back room. I like her in the dark, I thought. It's like she isn't there at all.

CHAPTER 13

Mrs. Shiner's Way

I walked to school Tuesday after Labor Day with the three Colley sisters and two Haskins brothers who lived up the road from us. We knew that Mrs. Shiner would be waiting in the school yard for us.

"There's Mrs. Shiner," said Betsy, the youngest Colley girl. "I knew she'd be right there by the old pump, just like last year."

"Yeah, but she's different this year," said Ronnie, giving a big stone a hard kick, "'cause she went and got married to some old man."

"He's not old, he's young and handsome," said Betsy.

"Good morning, everyone," called Mrs. Shiner. "Hurry, I have something to show you."

We ran to the pump and followed our teacher to the back of the school where we saw two new swings and a tall pole with ropes.

"What's that?" I asked, pointing to what looked like a huge maypole.

"Oh, that's what my husband, Philip, and I bought for you. It's called a maypole swing, and this is how it works."

She walked over to the pole and grabbed one of the handles with both hands and began running around. The pole turned faster and faster until her feet came off the ground and she was in the air.

"Hey, let me try," called Ronnie, and he ran to get one of the other handles. He ran until his feet were off the ground and he was flying through the air. But he looked like he would lose his pants. We were watching and laughing at how funny he looked flying round and round.

Finally, Mrs. Shiner called to us.

"Come, now, we must get inside and begin our new school year."

Inside, we saw balloons and crepe paper streamers everywhere. On the blackboard, Mrs. Shiner had written, "Welcome back, everyone. Let's have a great year together!" She had also placed name tags on our desks so we'd know where to sit, and I was happy to be the second person in the row by the windows. The glass came down as far as my desk, so I could sit and watch the wind move the trees and see the rain and snow fall and the birds fly.

I thought Mrs. Shiner was the best teacher in the whole world because she was always nice. She read us stories, and we read her stories. She played the piano and taught us songs. We liked to hear her sing, and she said she liked to hear us sing. I didn't think she liked one of us better than another.

I was proud to take home my report cards because they were very good, except for deportment, which was "satisfactory" or "needs improvement". Mrs. Shiner said she had to be honest and show that as a weakness because I talked too much when she was trying to teach the others. I knew I talked when I shouldn't, but I couldn't help it because I had things to say, and if I had to wait, I'd forget.

When we went out for recess, Mrs. Shiner came, too.

"I want to be sure nobody gets hurt," she said. "I know how some of you big boys can get a little rough sometimes."

Sometimes she'd sit on the top step by the door, or she'd sit in the grass around back. When we'd ask her to come and play tag or hide-and-seek or push us around the pole, she'd have as much fun as we would.

I felt happy in school. But then, in the afternoon when I'd think about going home to be with Mrs. Tanner, I'd feel sad. I liked playing with Millie, though, and Mrs. Tanner was letting us play together more now that Millie was older and didn't get sick a lot.

One afternoon in October, when we had finished our lessons with Mrs. Shiner, she stood at her desk and said she had to talk with us about the world conflict.

"We'll have a history class now for everyone," she began, "and you've probably heard your parents talking about the problems we're having with other countries."

We sat quietly while Mrs. Shiner told us about the war going on between Germany and other European countries. We had already learned that England and Germany had been fighting.

"I listen to Edward R. Murrow almost every night," Mrs. Shiner was saying, "and I'm afraid that one day before long, America will be forced to fight in this war. There will be many young men called to fight, and what we can do back home is pray for them and for peace in the world. As time goes on, I'll be talking with you more about this."

Mrs. Shiner stood at her desk for a moment looking down and moving the toe of her shoe back and forth on the floor.

She must be sad, I thought. Maybe she thinks her new husband will have to fight....

"Let's have a little singing time," said Mrs. Shiner, as she sat at the piano and began playing *Polly Wolly Doodle*.

"Come now, evvv-rybody sing...yes, sing right out," she shouted, laughing and playing loudly so we'd make lots of noise with our singing.

Sunday morning, Mrs. Tanner came to get Millie and me out of bed.

"Come on you two, get up. Mr. and Mrs. Shiner will be here to take you to Sunday school and church with them. I didn't tell you about it because you'd be too excited to sleep. They'll take you to their house for dinner and bring you home for supper."

Millie and I jumped out of bed faster than ever, except for maybe when it was wet.

"Huh, going to Mrs. Shiner's house?" I asked.

"I don't know her...don't wanna go," whined Millie.

"Yes, you do," I said. "Mrs. Shiner is the nicest lady in the whole world. You just wait and see."

"Well, I'd better not hear that either one of you misbehaved," said Mrs. Tanner as she looked in the closet for our clothes.

"We'll be good, won't we, Millie?"

"Uh, huh," nodded Millie.

Mrs. Tanner turned and held up two dresses I'd never seen.

"Where'd you get those?" I asked. "Miss Warring didn't buy them."

"Mrs. Shiner got these for you, along with hats and new shoes and socks," said Mrs. Tanner.

"They look like movie star dresses," I said. "I saw them in the Sears Catalog when we went to get clothes."

I took the hanger from Mrs. Tanner and looked at the prettiest dress I'd ever seen. It was red and white checked with pleats, and it had a white collar edged with red and white, and a short blue jacket and bow. I hugged the dress, loving it and the shiny black buckled shoes and red socks.

Millie's dress was red with little white flowers all over it, except for the collar that was white and trimmed with a red and white ruffle. Her puffy sleeves had little ties, and her shoes and socks were like mine. Her hat was red, mine was blue, and both had long ribbons.

When Millie and I were dressed, I thought we looked beautiful. Millie's curls framed her face, but I had short bangs and straight hair, so I knew I wasn't as pretty.

Before Mrs. Shiner came to the door to get us, Mrs. Tanner gave Millie and me each a handkerchief.

"Let Mrs. Shiner keep these in her bag for you, and if you need them, use them. And act like young ladies, not tomboys, especially you, Mary. I don't want to hear that you couldn't behave yourself."

She stood back and looked at us, first me and then Millie. She looked away and lifted her head. Looking out the window, she said, "I hear the car coming up the driveway."

I was so excited, I ran toward the door.

"No. Wait here until she knocks," said Mrs. Tanner.

When the door was opened, I saw Mrs. Shiner, and I couldn't believe my eyes. There she stood, smiling and looking like me in her red and white checked blouse, dark blue skirt and jacket, and blue hat with the brim turned up. I could see her light brown curly hair.

"Oh, you look like me, Mrs. Shiner," I said as my smile got bigger and bigger. "Except your hair is curly like Millie's and mine is straight."

She smiled at me and winked, "Doesn't matter about our hair—we're twins," she said and then turned to Mrs. Tanner.

"I'll have them back home about five this afternoon," said my best friend in the whole world, "and don't worry about them. We'll have a wonderful day."

"Thank you for taking them, Jean," said Mrs. Tanner, and turning to us, she said, "I'll see you girls later. Behave now."

We were getting in the back seat of the car when I heard the "behave now," and I wished Mrs. Tanner hadn't said that. My teacher will think I'm a baby, I thought.

"This is my husband, Philip," said Mrs. Shiner, after she got in the car and closed her door. "And Philip, I want you to meet two of the prettiest young ladies in town."

"They're just about as pretty as you," he said.

Millie and I brought our hands up to our faces and giggled. I knew it would be a fine day because I felt happy inside and pretty outside.

We were left at the door of our Sunday school room with a nice lady named Miss Marlowe.

"Come and have a seat," she said. "We have a big class today, and our lesson is about Adam and Eve."

I almost said I'd heard that one, but I was afraid to talk because I didn't know anybody.

"Let's begin our lesson with a prayer," she said, and I saw the girls and boys put their heads down, so I did and poked Millie's arm so she would.

"...and help us every day to be kind to one another. Amen."

I listened to the story Miss Marlowe told, and it was a lot like the old man's, but she wasn't angry with Eve for making us all die. After the story, we had to draw a picture of Adam and Eve in the garden with the serpent and the apples. I put flowers in my garden so I could have many colors in it. I drew the serpent with a smile on his face because I thought he must have been pleased to make Eve do something that God told her not to do. I thought maybe I was like Eve and Billy was the serpent who had made me run away with him and steal fruit.

After Mrs. Shiner came for us, we went to church with her and Philip. That wasn't as much fun as Sunday school because we had to sit still and listen to the minister. I didn't know what he was talking about because he used big words I didn't understand. I tried to be good and sit like Mrs. Shiner. I folded my hands in my lap like she did. She put her head down to pray and so did Millie and I. Some lady played the piano and everyone stood up to sing. I didn't know the song, but it had nice words about being in the garden early in the morning when the roses had dew on them. I wanted to learn that song because the music was pretty.

As we we left the church, Mrs. Shiner introduced us to the minister, and he shook our hands. "Come back again soon, ladies," he said.

That afternoon when Mrs. Tanner met us at the door, Mrs. Shiner told her what fine little girls we were and that she wanted to take us to church again.

"Anytime. It's good for them," said Mrs. Tanner.

And we did go many Sundays, and I learned a lot of things in Sunday school. My favorite lesson was about the Golden Rule: Do Unto Others As You Would Have Them Do Unto You. After I heard that, I sat in church and wondered if Mrs. Tanner knew that rule. I wondered if she'd like for Millie and me to yell at her or whip her with the razor strap. Sometimes I wished I could make her lean over the toilet seat and then I'd use the strap on her...right on *her* bare bottom. I wanted to laugh when I saw that picture in my mind. But then I thought I shouldn't want to hurt somebody if I didn't like being hurt. Why does Mrs. Tanner hurt us, I wondered, and quickly decided that it was because she went to church and not to Sunday school and she didn't know the Golden Rule.

The next night, when Mr. Tanner was listening to the news, I heard that the Japanese had bombed Pearl Harbor. I was helping Mrs. Tanner with the dishes, and I could hear everything the newsman said about bombs and Americans killed in Hawaii. I didn't know the Japanese were going to sneak up on people at Pearl Harbor, and I guess no other Americans knew, either. When Edward R. Murrow reported that terrible happening, I felt sick to my stomach, and I wanted to go hide under my bed. I felt nervous, and I wanted to talk about it.

"Why did they...?" I started to ask Mrs. Tanner.

"Shh, I'm listening," she said.

Well, I'm not listening anymore, I thought. I'll just ask Mrs. Shiner about this awful war and what's going to happen to all of us.

And that's just what I did the next day.

"We're going to talk about it the first thing this morning," Mrs. Shiner told me, "when everyone gets here and we get the room warmed up and we're all settled at our desks."

We talked all morning about President Franklin Delano Roosevelt and England's Prime Minister Winston Churchill. We learned about Joseph Stalin, Russia's communist leader, Hitler, the dictator of Germany, and Hirohito, the emperor of Japan. Mrs. Shiner said they were names we should remember.

"And each morning we'll have a short review of the war, and you may ask any questions you wish. I will try to answer them. But please do not be afraid, because even though the United States will have to be involved in this World War, we do not believe there will be fighting on our soil.

"As time goes on, we'll talk about things we can do to help. One of the most important things is to remember our prayers for all who are defending us, who are not only our men and women but those of our allies. Now it's time to begin our studies for today."

Mrs. Shiner turned toward the blackboard, and because I wanted to think of happy things and not about people dying, I took out *The Bobbsey Twins At The Seashore.* I opened it where I'd quit reading yesterday and instantly became Nan Bobbsey. I was a new person in a safe world.

*   *   *

Except for learning about World War II, third grade with Mrs. Shiner was good, even when she had to "administer disciplinary measures" as she called them. At times, I, along with several others, had to stand in the back corner of the classroom for talking out of turn. Boys who were mean on the playground had to miss recess. Sometimes students would have to stay after school and write things on the blackboard like, "I will try to think of others' feelings" or "I will not talk during lessons."

I think Mrs. Shiner liked to have us write on the board. She said it helped us remember things better. Quite often during study hour in the afternoon, before we left school, there'd be several of us writing line after line of the things we should remember.

In June, on the last day of school after our picnic, Mrs. Shiner asked us to sit around her in a rainbow so she could see all our faces.

"I have something to tell you," she said. "And you may think it is sad, but I want you to listen carefully to everything I have to say.

"Philip is a captain in the Army Air Corps—a fighter pilot—and he has been assigned duty in France. Since his parents are in Virginia, I have decided to live with them so we can all give each other support and strength while Philip is gone."

"You can't live with them," said Ronnie Haskins. "We won't have a teacher if you go."

"That's right," we shouted. "You can't go."

"I want you to think for a moment about how life changes," said Mrs. Shiner, holding her hand up for silence.

"Mary, you know about changes because you have had to move to new homes and get used to strangers both at home and at school. But, like Mary, the rest of you will have to adjust to many new things in your lives. And one of the most difficult lessons we learn is how to 'let go' of someone we love. That is what I have to do with all of you because you are so special to me. And just because we aren't together doesn't mean we can't still care about people who have meant so much to us. Do you understand what I'm saying?"

Oh, no, this can't be true, I thought as I sat staring at my favorite grown-up, the person I thought was so beautiful and nice, and the lady I wanted to be like more than anybody else on earth. I wondered how she could leave. What will we do when she's not here? How terrible this school will be without her. I could feel the tears fill my eyes, and before I could stop them, they rolled down my face. I heard voices....

"Yeah, I know what you mean, too," said Ronnie. "My uncle's in the Navy, and he's been gone almost a year now. He's my mother's brother, so she cried a lot at first, but I guess she's all right now."

"We know about it, too," said Connie, "because our dad had to leave a couple months ago. He's still in California, but he said he may be sent to Hawaii."

Bill Price said his older brother is gone and that his older sister, who is a nurse, wants to work for the Red Cross in Europe.

"So, you see, there are many people involved in trying to keep peace in the world, including the nurse who works for the Red Cross and the family members at home writing letters, saying prayers, buying savings bonds and giving each other strength to face their tomorrows," said Mrs. Shiner.

But I kept thinking about not having my teacher around anymore, and I began to cry. Then the Colley girls and Gracie Fisher cried, and then Helen Wesley and pretty soon all the girls were crying.

"Aw, be quiet, you dumb girls," said Ronnie, trying to act like he didn't care. "Who wants to hear all that bawling, anyway. She's not gonna jump off the world or anything. Make them quit, will ya, Mrs. Shiner, or I'm getting outta here."

"Mary, it's all right," said Mrs. Shiner, as she kneeled to put her arm around my shoulders. "You'll have another teacher in September, and you'll like her, too, so please don't cry."

I wiped my eyes and looked up at her. "I'll quit crying," I told her, "but I don't think I'll ever like another teacher."

Then I watched her go to each of her students and talk quietly as she had to me. And I knew I'd never be with any other teacher in my whole life that I liked as much as Mrs. Shiner.

Later that afternoon, I walked home alone so I wouldn't have to talk to anybody. I kicked stones when I felt angry at Mrs. Shiner for leaving, and I sat down in the grass and cried when I felt sad that I'd never see her again. And before I reached my driveway, I wiped my eyes so Mrs. Tanner wouldn't call me a big baby for crying. I wish she could be like Mrs. Shiner, I thought, and then I could be happy every day because she'd be more like a real mother.

I went into the kitchen where Mrs. Tanner was kneading bread dough, and I told her about Mrs. Shiner leaving.

"She's going to Virginia to live," I said, "and we'll never see her again. We sat around her in a rainbow arc and she told us about moving away. The girls cried, and the boys got mad at us, but Mrs. Shiner put her arm around each of us and said she'd always remember how special we are."

I couldn't say anymore because my voice was shaky and my eyes were going to cry again.

"Well, that's just Mrs. Shiner's way," said Mrs. Tanner, watching her fists punch the puffy dough. "Now, go change your clothes and help me with supper."

I went to my room and I thought: I know how love feels because of Mrs. Shiner, and I know how hate feels because of Mrs. Tanner.

CHAPTER 14

Wedding Blues

Millie and I were on the back porch glider one afternoon, and Mrs. Tanner was lying in her lounge chair when she said she'd take us to a wedding at the end of June.

"You can wear your Easter dresses that Miss Warring got you," she said, "and I expect you to be good girls between now and then. If you don't behave, I'll not let you go. It seems I have to tell...."

Oh, *you* behave, my mind said, but then when I thought about going to a wedding, I was excited. I'd never seen one. I did see a lady trying on a wedding dress, though, when we went with Miss Warring to get clothes. But I had never gone to a church to see how people got married. I imagined the bride would look like a princess, or let's see, like....

"Did you hear me, Mary?" said Mrs. Tanner in her snappy voice that made me jump.

"Yes," I said quickly, even though I hadn't heard.

"Why don't you go out to the flower garden behind the house and pull some of those weeds, and be very careful so's you don't get any new flowers," she said. "Put the weeds in the wooden barrel on the sidewalk, and see if you can fill the barrel before supper."

I got up to go, but she stopped me with a shaking finger.

"And by the way, Mary, I've seen you from the kitchen window playing in the dirt along the cow path under the pines.

I've asked you time and again not to play there because you'll get that nasty ringworm disease, so I'm telling you now to stay out of it."

She lifted her arm above her head and shook her hand in the direction of the flower bed. "Now go. I'll call you for supper."

I walked from the porch to the sidewalk that led to the weeds.

"Come along, Millie," I heard her say in her soft voice. "You and I will go in and have a nice nap."

"Go take your old nap," I whispered as I continued toward the garden. "You sleep and I'll work. You make me mad, you old lady."

When I got to the flower bed and stood looking at all the blossoms, I felt happy.

"They look so pretty," I said aloud, "and I guess they'd look nicer with no weeds, so I'll pull the easy ones like the chick-weed, pigweed, and ragweed, but not the thistles 'cause they hurt."

I worked for awhile and then looked where I'd been. I thought that Mrs. Tanner would be happy to see how neat the bed looked. Then I remembered her mean blah-blah-blah voice telling me about playing in the dirt, and her kind la-la-la voice when she talked to Millie.

"Mary do this and Mary don't do that...or that...or that," I said in a high squeaky voice. "Well, well nowah...I believe I weel do what I weeish," I said in my snooty grown-up voice. "I shall nowah go to thee cow path while you arah sleepinguh and ppllaay in thee dirt, and you will neverr, neverr know! I'll get even weeth you *now*, Ladeee Tahhnnerrah."

Throwing the last ragweed into the barrel, I began to prance on my bare feet, moving my behind from side to side and letting my head roll back and forth from shoulder to shoulder. I held my elbows at my sides and let my hands hang down at the wrists, and then I put my nose in the air and moved out of the garden, past the smokehouse and into the lane, where there seemed to be much more powdery sand than ever.

I looked at my hands, and they were greenish-black from all my hard work. I knew that if Mrs. Tanner saw them they'd look awful to her, anyway, so a little more grime wouldn't do any harm. I filled them with the soft, fine grains from the cow path, made a fist and then let a small stream sift out the hole by my little finger. The breeze blew some in my face, but I didn't care; it wouldn't make my face any dirtier than it was from sweat and weed dirt mixed.

"I'll show you, Fanny Tanner," I said. "This is how Miss Mary Easley gets even with you. But *you* will *never know* because I shall hurry to the garden before you get up."

I enjoyed my favorite pastime for awhile, and when I had placed little piles of the soft sand all around me, I stood up in my circle and said, "This is my world, and only Millie can come in." Then I heard Mr. Tanner cough, and I turned to look toward the sound. If he saw me, I knew I'd be in trouble. He walked into the milkhouse, so I swung my foot around to smooth out the circle I'd made and backed away from my spot, watching to be sure that he stayed inside the building. I kept walking backward until I was near the smokehouse, and from there I ran to the garden where I fell on my knees and began to pull furiously at a patch of dandelions, thinking that I'd better get the barrel full before supper. I hated that dandelion goo sticking on my hands, but I had to fill the barrel with something.

For the next few days, I was good as gold. I'd gotten even by playing in the off-limits dirt and was extremely proud of outwitting the napping Mrs. Tanner.

I did my work, and she couldn't find a spot I'd missed, so I got a big piece of pie for dinner on Saturday.

After that, I didn't play in the dirt. I remembered my pleases and thank-yous, and I kept my clothes hung up and my bedroom dustmopped. I was just plain good, perfect in every way, and going to the wedding was a sure-enough thing.

One morning, I came in from the washroom with Millie and sat down to breakfast.

Mrs. Tanner had bacon, eggs, and toast on our plates and a glass of milk for Millie and me and coffee for her and Mr. Tanner.

I picked up my fork and looked at Mrs. Tanner, who was watching me. Feeling quite smug about my goodness, I was sure she felt kind toward me and would grant permission to play with the kittens in the barn.

"May I go to the barn today to see the..."

Mrs. Tanner put her cup on the table and then her fists. She turned to me and looked into my eyes with her face close to mine.

"No, you may not go to the *barn* today or any day," she said slowly and sternly. "You and Millie *absolutely* are *not allowed in the barn*, and if you *ever* go there, you'll get a switching."

She kept her face close to mine and looked into my eyes and at my forehead.

"I knew it!" she shouted, jumping out of her chair.

She scared me so, I threw down my fork and moved my chair back.

"Franklin, look at her. Just look...there...on her forehead. Right there," and she pointed her finger at the spot.

"Uh, huh, I see it," he said, nodding. "Ringworm."

Oh, no, I thought. Now she'll holler and yell about playing in the dirt, and I'll have to sit and listen. But wait, she's not angry; she's not saying anything. I wondered why my behind twinged like it always did when I knew I was in bad trouble.

"You realize that you won't..." she began.

I pushed my chair from the table so I could leave because I knew she'd say I couldn't go to the wedding. I wanted to scream and cry and kick her and tell her that I hated her.

"You know what this means, Mary," she said quietly. "I'm sorry, because I wanted you and Millie to see that wedding, but I can't take you when you have this infection. Now, eat your breakfast."

She picked up her cup and sipped, looking out the window. I thought she was looking at the path where I had played, but she didn't say anything, so when I had finished eating, I asked to be excused.

"Yes, go make your bed, and I'll find some salve for your head," she said. "I'd better check you to see, too, if it has spread."

When I got in my room, I sat on my bed and thought about what I had done. I was bad to play in the dirt, and now I'd have to pay. But the price was too high for me. I felt the hurt beginning in my throat and going to my stomach. It wasn't like scraping my knee or stubbing my toe. It was a different kind of hurt, the kind that would make me cry, and even if I cried, it would still be there.

The day of the wedding, I stayed in the washroom so I wouldn't have to see everybody dressed up. Mrs. Tanner's brother, Uncle Henry, came to stay with me because he said he hated weddings.

"Don't you worry, little girl," he said when Aunt Zella brought him to our house the morning of the big day. "We'll have a good time."

And he was right. After everyone left, he came to the washroom to get me, and we played Chinese checkers and put puzzles together. Then he took me to the cow barn. The cows were in the field, so the huge room was empty. Uncle Henry showed me where the cows stood in the stanchions so they could be milked. I counted their standing places and there were forty.

"And they are Brown Swiss," said Uncle Henry. "They're about the prettiest cows you'll ever see, and they give good, rich milk."

We went to the back of the building, and Uncle Henry said the little stalls were for the calves that grew up and went to the pasture. He took me to the horse barn so I could pet the two draft horses, Sam and Nell, and we went to the hayloft and played with three yellow kittens until it was time to go back to the house.

When everyone came home from the wedding, Uncle Henry and I were sitting on the swing, so I had to see the fancy clothes after all. I was surprised that Mrs. Tanner could look so pretty. I liked her green and white organdy dress and big white hat with the green bow. I knew what Millie looked like because she had worn her dress on Easter, and Aunt Zella looked pink all over. Mr. Tanner's suit and tie were blue, and that's the first time I'd ever seen him dressed up. He looked like a stranger, but not for very long, because he went straight to his room to change his clothes and came back in his overalls.

"Got to get the cows and milk," he said. "Come on, Henry."

"Be right there," he said, as he pulled himself up from his chair, winked at me, and hurried to catch up with Mr. Tanner.

I thought I'd like to have Uncle Henry for my father, but I wouldn't want Aunt Zella to be my mother because she never talked to me, just looked at me and shook her head.

Mrs. Tanner took Millie's hand and asked Aunt Zella to go inside with her. "You stay out here, Mary, until Millie comes back. I'll call you when supper's ready."

I waited on the porch for Millie, and when she came out in her old play dress, I asked her if she had fun at the wedding.

"Yes, when I saw the bride. She was so beautiful, and her dress had a train that was way behind her on the floor," she responded. "The rest of the wedding I didn't like because I had to sit and not make a sound in church, and I had to be seen and not heard at the reception. Wish I could have come back home after I saw the bride."

"Good," I said, grabbing her hand and skipping across the porch with her. "Let's play with our paper dolls in the smokehouse, and I'll tell you about the fun Uncle Henry and I had."

Later, in bed, I thought about my troubles. I had wanted to see the Cinderella bride so badly, and I was sad about that. And I knew that the reason I missed it was because I'd played in the dirt. But, I had done that because Mrs. Tanner had made me pull weeds after I had been so good about doing everything right for a long time. To me, that meant that the ringworm and not getting to the wedding were Mrs. Tanner's fault. So, it was clear. I'd have to find a way to make her sad for making me miss what I'd worked so hard to see.

CHAPTER 15

The Bag Boys

When the Colleys and the Haskins and the Easleys walked to school the Tuesday after Labor Day in 1942, we didn't see a pretty teacher waiting for us by the water pump. When we went inside the little white school, we didn't see welcome signs and streamers everywhere. What we saw were the same desks and blackboards and windows, and a big person with short gray hair sitting in Mrs. Shiner's chair at a desk covered with textbooks and lined on two sides with yardsticks.

"Please be seated in your last year's desks," said the teacher. "When you're settled, I'll hand out your texts and supplies."

She pushed her chair away from the desk a lot farther than Mrs. Shiner ever did, and she stood up, but not very far. She wasn't as tall as Bob Preston, the handsome seventh-grader I had a crush on, and there was no smile from her. I didn't like her one bit.

"First-graders, call your names one at a time."

"Millie Easley, and this is my first day of school."

"All right," said the teacher. "Come get your books, Millie. Don't open them until I tell you what to do."

"Benny Hildebrand, and this is my first day, too."

"Just your names. Here are your books, Benny. Don't touch."

When she said, "Fourth-graders," I called out my name and then asked, "And what's your name?"

"Quiet," she said. "I'll do the talking. I'm Mrs. Hardison."

After books and supplies were handed out, she went back to her chair and sat looking at us one at a time and calling each name.

"I know all of you now," she said, "and we'll get along fine if you remember the rules."

Oh, no, not another *rules* lady, I thought.

Mrs. Hardison said that the yardstick was on her desk for a purpose; "And that purpose is to use it when I have to."

The next couple months of school were not much fun inside or on the playground. We played tag and kick the can and swung on the Shiner swing, but some of the seventh and eighth grade boys like Jimmy Darnell, Walter Haskins, Henry Smith and Billy Mason, caused us girls a lot of trouble. And Mrs. Hardison never came outside like Mrs. Shiner had, so the boys got away with everything. They chased us with worms, threw grasshoppers on us and tripped us when we were running. I was always on the end of the line when we played crack the whip. I felt like I was flying through the air before I tumbled down and rolled over and over in the grass. They wanted to put Millie on the end, but I took her place. She was too little to play a rough game.

Just before winter, Billy Mason found a burlap bag out by the shed beside the school. "Hey, Mary," he shouted, "c'mere and get in."

"No, I won't," I called back to him from the swings.

"Go get her, Jimmy," he said, "and you, too, Walter."

I saw the two of them coming after me, so I ran toward the front door of the school.

"Oh, no you don't," yelled Billy as he came running from another direction to block my path. I was surrounded by the three of them, and I screamed for Mrs. Hardison to help me, but I guess she didn't hear.

Walter and Jimmy took my arms and Billy and Henry grabbed my legs. They carried me to the bag and pushed my legs in. My sweater was off one arm, and my dress was up so far my underpants were showing. I was embarrassed for boys to see them, and I pushed my dress down when one arm was free. It didn't do any good. It was almost over my head by the time they got me in the bag.

"You fools," I screamed as they closed the top. "You'll kill me in this filthy thing.

"Help, I can't breathe," I shouted through the tiny holes of the burlap, while I tried to kick and dig my way out.

"Sure you can," Jimmy said, laughing. "See all those air spaces? We're gonna take you for a ride, so hang on."

"No, no, no," I screeched as I went bumping over the ground. "Let me out...let me out...."

It was the roughest ride of my life. I tried to sit as much as I could, because I felt like my behind wouldn't get hurt as much as my other body parts. I could hear the four boys laughing like fools, and I heard the girls screaming for them to stop. It seemed they ran forever, and I thought I'd surely die if they pulled me over rocks and bumped my head. They finally stopped and opened the bag.

"You can come out now," said Henry. "Wasn't that fun?"

I couldn't move for a few seconds.

"Are you dead?" asked Billy.

"No, I'm not dead," I shouted, "but you will be when Mrs. Hardison gets you with her yardstick." I crawled slowly out of the dark, dirty bag because every part of me hurt. But I knew I'd get everything working in a minute, and then I'd scratch their eyes out and kick their legs till they couldn't walk.

I ran toward Billy first because he started the whole thing, and all the time I tried to catch him, I shouted, "Don't you ever do that again, you bully. I hate you and all your dopey friends."

"Oh, we won't," said Billy, "only to your little sister."

Oh, no, not Millie, I thought. They just can't do this to her. She's little, and I know she'll die in there. She won't be able to breathe, and she won't know to keep her head up so it won't hit a rock. She'll get killed. I didn't know what to do, but I most certainly was not going to cry.

"You're not getting my sister, or I'm telling Mrs. Hardison," I shouted at Billy.

"Titsy, titsy, tattletale, poor little baby," he taunted.

"We got her," called Henry as he and Walter carried a kicking and crying Millie to the bag.

"Let her go," I yelled, and I kicked Billy in the legs.

"Get outta here, you cow pile," he said.

I saw that they had my sister inside and were running with her, so I ran as fast as my legs could take me to the swings and grabbed a seat. I clutched the board in its grooves where the rope had fit so I wouldn't drop it, and holding it over my head, I screamed for Mrs. Hardison to come and help as I ran toward Jimmy. He was coming at me bent over, ready to tackle, but I reached out with my weapon and whamed him on the head, and he fell down. Then I went straight for Billy, and because he was pulling the bag by himself, he couldn't run at all. His head was bent forward as he tugged the screaming and crying shape behind him. When I got close enough, I brought the board down on his back, and he fell to the ground and rolled around groaning. And when Walter saw that I had hit Billy, he headed for the school door, all the time looking back over his shoulder. Boom! He ran smack into Mrs. Hardison.

That was a great sight! My battle was finished, so I sat on the ground and helped Millie out of the bag. She was so scared, she was shaking, and her face was wet with tears.

"I w-w-wet my p-p-p-pants, Mary," she sobbed.

I wiped her face with my hanky and then helped her stand up. "Don't worry about that, Millie. They'll dry. I'm glad you're all right. Let's go tell Mrs. Hardison," I said, taking her hand.

But I didn't have to tell Mrs. Hardison, because I saw her talking to Billy, Henry, Walter and Jimmy, and she was leaning on the yardstick. I heard her tell them to get inside.

"The rest of you stay out here until I ring the bell," she said, looking over at Millie and me and the rest of her students.

The girls, along with Bob Preston, Benny Hildebrand, Ronnie Haskins and Joey Weston, Millie's and my best friend, had come to find out if we were all right. Betsy took a white handkerchief out of her coat pocket and began wiping Millie's face, and Connie had her arm around my shoulders. I wondered why all of them together hadn't tried to stop those four boys, but I didn't say anything. I didn't want them mad at me right then.

"Hey, Mary, I didn't know you could be so tough," said Connie.

"I can if somebody's hurting my sister," I said.

But inside, I felt like I'd cry any minute. I can't do it, though, I thought, because then I won't look like I'm tough at all.

We heard the bell ring and walked quietly to the school door. I wondered if Mrs. Hardison had whipped the four boys, but when we got inside we didn't see them at their desks. I think they were in the coatroom, because she sent people there when they talked during classes or if they were late for school.

I knew those trouble-making boys would continue to find ways to annoy Millie and me on the playground because they were just made that way. But the difference now would be that I'd take care of them in my own way, no matter what they tried to do.

CHAPTER 16

My Mother, My Father

Suppertime at the Tanners meant hearing them talk about the war. Most of the time I didn't listen because my teacher told me everything I needed to know. The trouble with the Tanners was their gruesome descriptions of dead soldiers and sunken ships, and hearing those details made me think we'd all be dead within a few days. Mrs. Tanner's favorite expression in 1942 was, "We're all going to Hell in a handbasket." She said the same thing over and over, and every time she said it, I imagined her sitting in a market basket while a man with horns and a pitchfork, and dressed in red, carried her to the door of a fiery furnace. I didn't want her to be thrown in, but I didn't want to be living with her, either.

I often thought about my parents and wondered what life would be with them. So, one night when I was tired of hearing the Tanners, I waited for them to be quiet, and quickly, before one of them could speak, I asked Mrs. Tanner if Millie and I could see our real mother and father.

"No," she said, and she made me jump when she banged her fork down beside her plate. She brought her face down to mine and said, "You don't *need* to see them. They're no good. Put their children out so other people would have to take care of them. Humph."

"Do you get paid for taking care of us?" I asked.

"Don't be so sassy," she snapped. "That's none of your business."

Aha, I thought. She does get paid. I wonder how much.

"I want to see what my parents look like, don't you, Millie?"

"Yes," answered Millie. "I want to see my real mommy and daddy and talk to them."

"I don't want to hear anymore about it."

"I'm going into town in the morning. You want to go?" Mr. Tanner asked his wife.

"You know, I have to...."

I didn't hear them. I was pretending I was living with my parents.

My mother and I are doing dishes together, and she's talking about school and telling me to study hard, and I'll do it because I like her so much. We're pulling weeds with Millie in the flowers, and we're talking and laughing together, the three of us. She looks at my report card and says, "My goodness! How smart you are—just like your daddy." I have a beautiful doll that I'm taking for a ride in her carriage. Millie's doll is in her carriage, and we're walking beside each other and talking like grown-up ladies and...

Oops, I jumped when Mrs. Tanner spoke. She spoiled my daydream.

"Mary, get up and let's get these dishes done." I excused myself from the table and took the towel from the rack beside the sink.

"I'll see my mother someday," I said to Mrs. Tanner.

"Maybe you will, and maybe you won't," she said.

I thought of a wonderful idea as I was drying a white dinner plate and saw my reflection, and wondered if I looked like my mother. I decided to ask Miss Warring if Millie and I could see our parents. She might take us to their house, or maybe she'd tell them to come to the Tanners to see us.

I knew Miss Warring would be coming to get us in a few days to buy me a new winter coat and leggings. Millie would wear my old winter clothes, but she needed long stockings and new shoes. My shoes were too big for her, and I didn't wear stockings anymore, I wore knee socks.

I couldn't wait to get in the car when Miss Warring came on a Saturday morning to take us shopping. As soon as she had turned the key in the ignition, I asked her about our mother and father.

"Millie and I want to see our parents, don't we, Millie?" I said. She nodded.

"What makes you think you want to see them?" asked Miss Warring.

"We want to know what they look like," said Millie, "and we want to know if they like us."

"And I want to know why they left us outdoors in the winter, and can we go live with them?" I asked.

"One question at a time, please," said Miss Warring. "Your mother left you because they had no money, and she thought if she left you on the street in town, somebody would find you. They are a nice-looking couple, and you do look like your mother—and a little like your father. But, you will never live with them because the courts have taken you away from them, purposely, so there'll be no danger of neglect again."

"What's neglect?"

"That just means that you weren't cared for as you should have been, not enough food or clothes."

"That's sad," I said, "but I still want to see them. Can we?"

"I'll see what I can do," promised Miss Warring. "Here we are at Buster Brown, so we'd better think of clothes now."

"I want saddle shoes," said Millie.

"Me, too. Can we get some?" I asked.

"I'll have to see the prices first, and we'll have to see whether you need shoes yet."

"I'll put my feet in that machine that can look through my shoe and see how much room I have left," I said, "and I bet I'll need new ones."

"Nuh, uh," said Millie. "No fair, 'cause I have to wear your old coat and you get a new one, so you can't have new shoes, too."

"Well, you wouldn't want me to get curled toes from wearing small shoes, would you?" I argued.

"I will look in that machine when you put your feet there, and I will see if you have curls," said Millie.

Inside the store, Miss Warring was talking to Mr. Webster,

the owner, so Millie and I ran to see how much longer I could wear my old shoes. I tried to push my foot up to the toe, but I still had plenty of room for growing, and we both knew what that meant.

"See," squealed Millie, looking down through the glass at my toes. "You can't have new ones, just a new coat and leggings. Let's go see what shoes I will buy."

"Go look at the shoes yourself," I said. "I'm looking for my new coat when we go to Carlson's General Store."

"Look at your ugly coat," said Millie, giving me a push.

"All right, girls, that's enough," said Miss Warring. "You will behave like ladies beginning right now." She took Millie's hand and they sat in chairs in front of the stacks of boxes that went from floor to ceiling.

"Saddle shoes, please," said Millie in a loud voice.

Mr. Webster said that the two-tone brown leather saddles were just one dollar and ninety-eight cents.

I turned away from them and went to the back of the store where I looked at the men's boots. I saw a pair of arctics that I liked and thought I'd ask Miss Warring if I could have them. I knew my old boots wouldn't fit my spring shoes.

The arctics idea was all right with Miss Warring, so I got those, and Millie left the store in her shiny and beautiful two-tone saddles.

At Carlson's, I got a navy wool plaid-lined snowsuit with embroidered red and yellow wool flowers down each side of the front of the jacket. It cost ten dollars and ninety-eight cents. When I tried it on and looked in the mirror at the store, I felt very rich.

"And I want to buy a kerchief to wear on my head instead of a dumb old hat," I said to Miss Warring.

"You'll have to wait for that," she said. "There's a red stocking hat that matches the suit, and it will keep you warmer than a kerchief."

I didn't like the hat because it mashed down my hair, but I had to take it. I decided I'd wear it only to keep my ears warm.

When we got home, I didn't tell Mrs. Tanner anything

about our parents coming to see us, but I just knew it would happen.

One summer afternoon, we had just finished the dinner dishes and Mrs. Tanner said Millie and I should take a nap, when Mr. Tanner said he heard a car in the driveway. He went out the kitchen door with Mrs. Tanner, Millie, and me behind him.

"It's them," said Mr. Tanner. "The Easleys," and he looked at me and then turned his face away.

I grabbed Millie's hand and swung it back and forth. "Our mother and father," I shouted to her.

Millie, jumping up and down, squealed with delight, and I was so excited, I couldn't hold back my happy squeal.

We ran down the steps to the front of their old car.

Our mother got out holding our little sister, Ginny, and our father pushed two crutches out the driver's door and pulled himself up so he could walk. But he couldn't. I was shocked to see his feet dragging on the ground as he moved to lean on the front of the car.

Why did Miss Warring say they were a good-looking couple, I wondered. My father was crippled, and my mother was very big around. They laughed, and I saw perfect white teeth. They're like mine, I thought. My mother had brown hair and blue eyes, like Millie. My father had dark hair and deep blue eyes. He was handsome in his face and shoulders and down to his stomach, but then he wasn't.

"What happened to your legs?" I asked.

"I was in an accident," he said. "I won't ever walk, but I get around all right. Come here, you two, and give me a hug."

Millie and I ran to him, and our mother watched.

"What beautiful girls you are," she said. "And you look so healthy and happy. Are you happy here?"

I looked up at Mr. and Mrs. Tanner who were standing on the porch, and I was afraid to say no. At this minute, I was very happy, and Millie was smiling up at her real daddy, so she was happy, too.

"Yes," I answered. "but can we go home with you?"

"Not today," said our father, "but someday maybe we can be together, if only for a long visit."

He handed the crutches to my mother and reached for Millie and me and held us tight against him. Leaning forward, he said, "Hug me around my neck." I looked into his face and saw tears coming down, so I hugged him as tightly as I could.

We hugged our mother the same way, and she laughed.

"Oh, that felt so good. I wish I could have hugs like that every day. Now let's talk about school and about your home here."

I looked toward the porch and didn't see the Tanners, but I thought they must be listening from the kitchen. I'd be afraid to say anything bad about them to my parents.

We talked a long time about not liking Mrs. Hardison and missing Mrs. Shiner, but we didn't say anything about living with the Tanners. My father asked us if we were happy, and I said, "I guess so," hoping that he would somehow know that we weren't.

Finally, our mother said it was time to go and let Ginny sleep.

"Come here, girls, and give me another hug," she said.

We moved slowly away from our father and put our arms around our mother's waist. I tried to hug Ginny, but she cried and pulled away from me.

"She's just tired," said my mother. "You two be good, and maybe we'll see you again."

I took Millie's hand and backed away. Our father sat in the car, pulled his legs in, and put his crutches in the back seat. My mother got in her side, and they closed their doors at the same time. I heard the engine sputter and stop, then start and sputter some more as the car moved backward down the driveway. Our parents smiled and waved good-bye, but Millie and I just stood holding hands and watching them go. I looked at Millie's trembling lips.

"Don't cry," I whispered, "Mother will say we're babies."

"Come on, you girls. You have to take a nap this afternoon because company's coming tonight. Mary, you go out to the sunporch, and Millie, you come with me into the house. You can sleep in your room."

I wanted to talk with Millie about seeing our real mother and daddy, but Mrs. Tanner moved Millie's hand out of mine and took her in the house. I heard steps behind me and turned to see Mr. Tanner going down the driveway to the barns.

I didn't want to move until I had put the picture of my very own mother and father in my head and had remembered everything they said. It had been a special time, but I could never live with them, I knew. So, after this, whenever I thought about them, I'd be happy, but I'd also be sad.

CHAPTER 17

The Singer and the Rock

Hitting the big boys at school with the swing board didn't stop them from bullying the girls and younger boys.

Millie and I were called "welfare kids" and were told we weren't any good because of our parents. They were no good because they didn't take care of their own kids, and the taxpayers had to do it.

"We gotta pay for all your food and clothes," Billy Mason told us, "and we even gotta pay somebody for taking care of you."

All I could say was, "Well, I can't help what my parents do."

When they were tired of teasing Millie and me, they pestered Joey with the nickname they gave him.

"You know why you're 'Crazy'?" they asked. "'Cause you have fits, that's why."

And then Joey cried, which was the worst thing he could have done, because he was mimicked and picked on even more. I tried to tell him never to cry, but he said he couldn't help it.

"It hurts to be hated," he said. "You think I like having fits? I'm always afraid of dying."

I knew how he felt by being "different" because Millie and I were, and we knew that was why no one could like us.

Connie tried to make the big boys leave us alone, but they chased her and twisted her arms behind her back until she hollered "Uncle". She told Joey, Millie, and me one day that we'd just have to ignore the bullies and try to have fun by ourselves.

"Walter, Billy, and Henry will be gone next year to the high school," she said, "and I'll bet you they'll get beat up by the big guys there."

That was a comforting thought for me, and since it was now the winter of 1943, I knew we didn't have much longer with them.

One day, when there wasn't much snow on the ground, Billy, Henry, and Jimmy took Joey to the gravel pit next to the school yard. Everyone knew it was off limits. They said they were going to bury him and put him out of his misery.

"Just think," they laughed, "no more fits."

I screamed for them to leave Joey alone, but they told me to shut up and mind my own business as they dragged him down the snowy side of the pit. Joey wasn't making a sound, and I was proud of him for not crying, but I was worried he might have an attack.

About the time they got him buried, Mrs. Hardison rang the bell to come inside, and the three came running back.

"You're not leaving him buried under stones, are you?" I asked.

"He'll dig out," they yelled as they ran inside the school.

I didn't go inside. I went to the pit to save my friend, and he was so thankful, he made me a promise.

"I'm gonna marry you," he said, huffing and puffing after pushing stones with me. "You've saved my life."

"Oh, Joey, you would have gotten out by yourself."

"I didn't want to get out," he said. "I don't care if I die. I think it would be good because I'd never have another seizure or be laughed at."

"I don't laugh at you, Joey. I know how you feel, just like I feel. We aren't as good as the others. You have these seizures, and I'm a welfare kid."

"Yeah, that's it."

"But, just maybe all these kids are wrong," I said, "because I learned in Sunday school that God loves us, and I think He does. And I also learned that if you ask God to help, He will."

"Aw, I never heard that stuff."

"Well, I did, and you can believe me. I think when we're in trouble or someone is hurting us, we should say, 'help me, God,' and maybe He will."

"You do that, Mary, but I think you're a little goofy, and I think we'll be in awful trouble for not getting to our desks when we should."

"I'll just stand up and tell Mrs. Hardison what happened."

"Oh, sure, and get us both killed next time at recess. You better just keep quiet," warned Joey.

I helped him up the hill, and we went into the school where Mrs. Hardison stared at us from her desk.

"The next time you hear the bell, you come in," she said. "Both of you will stay after school and write on the blackboard one hundred times, 'I will come in when I hear the bell.'"

I raised my hand.

"Put your hand down, Mary, and study your arithmetic."

I stood up and felt my legs go shaky, so I put my hand on my desk to steady myself. I was so mad that I knew I wouldn't sit down until I'd told her what had happened.

"You have to listen to me, Mrs. Hardison. Joey was buried in the gravel pit, and I went to help him get out," I explained angrily.

"Why were you in the gravel pit, Joey? You know that's a dangerous place, and you're never to go there."

"Because some people took me there," he answered.

"Who took you there?"

"I'm not telling, because if I do, I'll get beaten up. I didn't do anything wrong, and neither did Mary, and we shouldn't have to stay after school," Joey said, his voice getting louder and louder. "I'll just tell my parents that you never know what's going on out there, and..."

"That's enough," shouted Mrs. Hardison. "Sit down, both of you, and I shall have a talk with all sixth-, seventh-, and eighth-graders at the end of school today."

You had better have a talk, I thought. You don't even care how Joey feels or how I feel. I'd like to punch you in that fat stomach. I looked right where I thought her belly button would be and imagined I was punching her right on target. But then I felt bad to think such a thing, because she had said she'd talk to the older students. Maybe she is going to make things better, I thought.

I opened my arithmetic book and began to work the multiplication problems.

For the next several days, Mrs. Hardison came out during recess, and we had good times on the playground. She had made things better, and I wondered how she did it.

On Friday of that week, as on every Friday, Mrs. Hardison said we would have our "down time". That was when she played the piano, and we sang our favorite songs.

"...and so today I'm going to have a little different program," said Mrs. Hardison from her piano stool. "I want Mary and Millie to come to the front of the room first and sing 'Playmates,' that we learned last week."

I was so surprised, I couldn't move, and I looked over at my sister. She was looking my way and must have felt as I did.

"Come on up," she coaxed, holding her hands out toward us.

We went to the front of the room, and she began to play the song, the chorus for the introduction and then the downbeat for the first verse.

"Playmate, come out and play with me, and bring your dollies three...." We sang both verses and the chorus twice, and when we'd finished, everyone clapped as we returned to our seats.

"Very good," said Mrs. Hardison. "Now, I want Joey Weston to come up here by the piano. Come along, Joey, right here," she said, pointing to a spot at the corner of the upright.

Joey, my friend, got up from his desk and shuffled reluctantly to the front of the room. I heard a couple boys make snorting sounds as Joey moved to the spot where he was to stand. I supposed that if he sang, the big boys would call him a sissy, and I wondered if Mrs. Hardison was doing the right thing for Joey.

I was afraid he'd get sick since he seemed so scared, but he put his hands in his pockets, and without piano music, Joey began to sing.

"When I was a lad and O' Shep was a pup..." he sang.

And we listened. Not a sound was heard except for Joey's clear, fine voice as he pealed the words about Jim and his dog, Shep.

My eyes filled with tears when I heard about Shep being sick, and I could tell that Joey could feel the hurt, too, just like Jim, but he did not stop singing until the song's end, even though tears streamed steadily down his face. I was proud as could be of Joey Weston. He could do what nobody else could— sing with the best voice I ever heard.

When he finished, there was a lot of sniffing going on at the desks behind me. Joey wiped his eyes with his shirt sleeves as he walked quickly to his desk. The clapping did not stop until after he was seated. I turned to look at him, and I saw the biggest smile on his face I'd ever seen. When I looked around the room, I didn't see looks of dislike for the boy who was different. I saw looks of surprise and wonder.

The next Friday, around song time, Mrs. Hardison told us to put away our work. "We have some serious business to discuss," she said.

The not-too-tall, somewhat plump teacher told us more about the war—about tanks and guns and warplanes, about dying, bombs, and air raids, and about self-preservation.

We listened to every word, and I was frightened. I wondered if everyone felt as I did.

"We don't know," she explained, "when we might be bombed in our country. You have to know how to protect yourselves, and I'm going to show you something we can do if we have an air raid warning. We'll have a drill now, which means get up quickly when you hear me ring this bell three times, like this."

She picked up the long-handled bell and gave it three quick rings. We jumped up, obeying her but also startled by the loudness of the clangs.

"Put on your coats and boots, everything you have to keep warm, and follow me to the field."

We hurried to the coatroom and put on our winter clothes and walked to the alfalfa field beside the school. Henry and Walter darted toward the woods. They didn't take life and death seriously like the rest of us. But Mrs. Hardison's shrill voice carried far into the stillness.

"You two get back here, or you'll stay after school."

The two ran back in line.

"Now," she said, as we stood before her, "scatter around, not too far away. Get down on your hands and knees and circle your arms in front of you. Then tuck your head into the circle."

We scurried to various spots, I being sure my sister was near me so she wouldn't be afraid.

"Watch me now," shouted our leader. And using one of the boys as an example, Mrs. Hardison showed us exactly how to attain the position. We knew when we were in correct form, according to "Sergeant" Hardison, because she called out to us.

"The enemy pilots will think you're just rocks in the field."

I remained stationary and didn't hear a sound from anyone until the next order echoed across the field.

"Get up and come inside."

As I scrambled to my feet and reached for Millie's arm to help her up, I felt secure in the knowledge that I could fool the enemy in the air anytime just by being a "rock" in the field.

Back inside, after we hung up our snow clothes and got settled at our desks, Mrs. Hardison walked to the piano.

"Song time," she shouted. "What shall we sing?"

"How about George M. Cohan's 'Over There,'" said Bob Preston.

And so we sang the 1917 World War I song with new awareness: "...send the word, send the word, to prepare...and we won't be back till it's over, over there!"

CHAPTER 18

Wonderful Winter

The rest of January and all of February and March brought the best of snows and cold, crisp, clean air. On a February day, I sat in school looking out the tall windows at the white, inviting mounds that lay waiting for the feel of mittened hands making snowballs and black-booted feet tracking out designs for fox and geese. I watched the snow falling quietly on trees and fields, and I felt excited about the sight that, to me, was so pretty and peaceful. And then the wind began to blow, slowly at first and then faster, until the white powder was swirling so thick I couldn't see the swings. I wanted to be out there, out there away from mean boys, away from books and papers, pencils and pens and black inkwells. And I wanted to be away from this teacher, this loud-talking, mean-looking teacher, a person I tried to like, but couldn't.

I looked away from the windows and thought about school. Being here with Mrs. Hardison was the opposite of being with Mrs. Shiner. In second and third grades I was happy, knowing I was with a teacher who liked me and the work I did. But now, in fourth grade, I'd grown tired of hearing Mrs. Hardison's crackling voice teaching me about compound sentences and rivers in Russia and multiplying nines. I didn't want to give her another book report or turn in another arithmetic lesson because of what happened a couple days earlier.

"Your writing is atrocious," she had said. "I can barely

read it. Why don't you take your time and not be so sloppy?"

And when she saw my arithmetic problems, she said, "Look at this mess. You don't have them in line so that you can add them right, and that's why they're all wrong. And stop drawing pictures on your papers. I don't want to see scribbling. I want to see your work. What's the matter with you? Don't you care about anything? Go to your desk and do page thirty-six again."

I watched her crumple my papers and throw them away, and then I walked to my seat and carefully rewrote my book report. I was writing straight columns of arithmetic when she called to me.

"Mary, bring your papers."

"I'm not finished."

"Don't sass me. If they aren't finished, you'll get a zero."

And because that's how it was with Mrs. Hardison, every day when I walked to school with Millie and the others, I wanted to go down another road that would take me away from this teacher. She and Mrs. Tanner are alike, I thought. Both mean.

But since I didn't know how to find another home, I walked on with Millie beside me. Millie, the little sister I had to help every morning. She couldn't put on her boots, so I did it. She couldn't comb her hair, so I did, and sometimes when I got tired of it, I pulled too hard and made her cry. Sometimes I was sad when I made her cry, and sometimes I didn't care.

The best days of winter were when I played in the snow alone. Millie couldn't go out because her hands and feet got so cold from being frozen when she was a baby.

After school, I'd say, "I'm staying out," to Mrs. Tanner.

"All right, and don't get wet, or you'll catch cold," she'd say, quickly closing the door.

I looked to the west to see the sun. It'll be dark by six, I thought, and I'll have to go in, but now I'm going to the summer garden and build myself an igloo.

With shovel in hand, I began digging at the foot of the highest drift. When I got tired of shoveling, I dug with my hands and worked until I could crawl inside the hole and nobody could see me. "My igloo is done," I said, and I went outside to look. "It's perfect, the most beautiful igloo I ever saw, and I did it by myself."

"Ma-reeeeeee. Ma-reeeeeee."

That was Mrs. Tanner's high-pitched call for supper. I was sure half the world could hear. They'd run for cover, I thought, because it would hurt their ears.

"See you tomorrow after school, Mr. Ig," I said, jumping out of my hideaway. "I'll bring a book called *The Bobbsey Twins at Snow Lodge* and read to you." I patted the top of the drift and then turned away. "Hope it's not too sunny tomorrow," I called as I hurried to the house. But if it does get sunny and Mr. Ig melts, I'll just go sledding, I thought, as I washed my rosy cheeks and cold hands in the warm water. And when it snows again, I'll build another igloo. There's so much to do in the snow, and I can do it just for me without having anyone tell me what's wrong with it.

I dried my hands and face on the towel and went outside, where I stopped, before going in to supper, and looked at the bright, full moon glowing in the gray sky. And then, looking far away, I saw millions of tiny sparkles, diamonds in the snow, I thought.

I shivered in the cold air, and glanced toward the kitchen where I'd have to go. "Winter is wonderful," I whispered, wrapping my blue sweatered arms around myself, "and it belongs to me."

CHAPTER 19

Final Report

When I should have been working on lessons at my desk, I was looking out the school windows.

My beloved snows were whipped about and then crusted over by fierce March winds, and the persistent April showers broke up the smooth whiteness with tiny rough gullies that twisted and turned down hillsides and across fields. I watched the ballet of the swings in the wildest winds and their day-long resting when ropes and wood were saturated by repeated rain and drizzle.

May Day came and we danced around Mrs. Shiner's maypole swing with bright colored streamers in our hands. I didn't think it was much fun, but Mrs. Hardison said it was what people did the first day of May to celebrate spring.

The little schoolhouse was too warm, so we opened the windows, and I felt like I was outside. A robin flew into our room, but it didn't stay long when we squealed and jumped around trying to direct it to freedom. I wished I could have gone with the bird.

Thinking of summer made me sad because even though I'd be away from school troubles, I'd be with Mrs. Tanner every day for three months. That meant pulling weeds when I'd rather run down the lane with Millie to the wheat field or play house under the big walnut tree. Or it meant dusting and sweeping and helping wash clothes and dishes instead of playing paper dolls with Millie in the smokehouse.

I struggled through to the end of fourth grade, and when I got my report card, I saw that Mrs. Hardison had written a note to Mrs. Tanner.

"Fanny," it said in printed letters, "I hope Mary will work in fifth grade. She won't pass unless she does."

"I don't care whether I pass or not," I said to her note.

The end of school brought cheers and giggles and good-byes inside, and shouting and screaming outside. The older kids chanted their favorite verse as we hurried down the sidewalk to the gravel road: "No more pencils, no more books, no more teacher's dirty looks."

When Millie and I said good-bye to the Colley girls and turned to walk up our driveway in the warm June sunshine, I asked my sister if I could see her report card. She handed it to me, and I looked at what she had done in her first year. My eyes widened and my mouth fell open.

"Look at all these excellents!" I exclaimed. I felt as though she had betrayed me. "How could you do this?"

"I like school," she said, "but I didn't get excellent in reading."

I felt better. "Why not?"

"I don't know what the sounds are, like t-h and g-h."

"Well, I like reading, so I'll help you with it. I wish you could help me with multiplication and geography and New York history."

"I will," said Millie. "I'll help you with everything."

"How do you think a first-grader can help a fifth-grader?"

"I'm a second grader now, Mary, so I will listen, and you tell me everything you know, that's how, and..."

"It would take me ten years to tell you, because I already know four years' worth of everything."

"A-a-a-n-d," continued Millie, "if you tell me everything you know, then I'll know it, too, and I can help you."

"Millie, that doesn't make sense. You have to tell me what *I don't know*, and..."

Just then, we turned the corner, and there sat Mrs. Tanner in her favorite redwood lounge, and I was not happy.

"Let me look at your reports," she said, rising from her chair and reaching for the cards.

Millie placed hers on Mrs. Tanner's outstretched hand.

I watched Mrs. Tanner open the report and read it. "Very good," she said, "but you'll have to work harder in reading."

"I'll help her," I said, placing my card in the upturned palm.

Even though I felt like running, I stood quietly as she looked over the Mary E. Easley, June 1943, fourth grade report card. I watched her face as she read the message on the back and shook her head.

Keeping her head down, she looked over her glasses at me. "Did you read her note?"

"Yes," I said, backing away to dodge the expected slap.

"Then you know what's expected of you." She reached for my arm, but I didn't let her touch me. Instead, I took the card from her and was walking to the washroom when I heard her call.

"Supper's in an hour."

And then, "Now, Millie, come here and tell me...."

I hurried into the little room and closed the door, so I wouldn't have to hear the happy "Now, Millie" voice. Why did she like Millie so much and not me? I wanted to cry, and I felt the sting in my eyes, so I looked in the mirror and watched the tears run down my face. I jumped when I heard a knock.

"Can I come in, Mary?" asked Millie, as she opened the door.

I wiped my eyes quickly with the back of my hand. "Yes, you *may,*" I corrected, not really wanting her right now.

"We have all summer to play together," she said softly.

I looked at her pretty blue eyes and brown curls. My little sister, and I loved her so very much; no matter what had happened or might happen, I'd always feel the same about her.

"Yes, we do," I said, "and I think we should go to the smokehouse and see if all our paper dolls and books and puzzles are where we left them on Saturday. And let's see if the little mice come out and look at us like they did then."

In agreement, she took my hand and led the way out into the sunshine, through the petunia-lined path of the flower garden and down the grassy hill to our small brick playhouse.

CHAPTER 20

Summer Senses - Part I - Bad Dads

Part of my trouble in life had nothing to do with mischief making, but much to do with bladder control. No matter how determined I was not to wet the bed, it happened anyway. And, of course, it wasn't something that could be hidden from Mrs. Tanner or that could go unpunished. All she had to do was come to our door in the mornings to get us up, and a mere whiff could tell her. Sometimes Millie and I both had lost control, and sometimes just one of us, but it may as well have always been both because we didn't like to see the other get a whipping. It seemed, too, that when the sheets were hung across the driveway, we both felt guilty.

"You do it just to cause trouble," Mrs. Tanner said. "I know you could hold it if you tried. Everybody else does."

After awhile I got used to the whippings she gave with the razor strap, even though the sting was so bad that Millie and I didn't even try to sit down until we had to at meal time.

One night, though, I outwitted the world's greatest morning whiffer. At some hour during the dark night, I felt the urge to relieve myself, so in my dream, I got out of my bed and stumbled to the cane-bottom chair in the corner of the room. I was in the bathroom, I thought, on the commode.

In the morning, at the first rooster crow, I opened my eyes and stretched, looking over to see Millie sleeping. And then, oh, no, I suddenly remembered the dream and frantically felt the sheets, above me, below me—dry! Ah, it was just a dream. But, oh, oh, the chair. I threw off the blanket and sheet and jumped out of bed.

When I reached the chair, I felt the seat. Dry. "Ohhhhh," I said softly in relief. I glanced under the chair and there, truth be told, was a puddle, plain as day. Oh, no, I thought. What can I do? If she sees this, she'll beat me until I can't walk and tell everybody what I did. My stomach churned at the thought of pain and embarrassment.

I looked around the room. The blanket. No, not that because it would smell bad for a long time. I know what I'll do, I thought, as I hurried to the closet. I grabbed the dustmop, went back to the terrible pool and moved the chair out of the way. *plop!* I set the mop in the middle of the circle on the floor and swished it around so that every trickle disappeared. I lifted the dustmop, heavier now, and carefully carried it back to its closet corner and closed the door.

I got in bed where Millie was still sleeping and making little snorts through her nose. My head sank back onto the soft feather pillow, and I smiled to myself. Nobody will ever, ever, not in a million years, know about this!

I didn't like to hear Millie's snorts anymore, so I shook her.

"Don't wet the bed, Millie," I said softly.

"Ummm...I...wooonnn," she mumbled.

When Mrs. Tanner opened our door a few minutes later, I saw her nose wiggle. Our window was open, so I hoped the smell went out.

"Millie, let's go to the bathroom before we have an accident."

We hurried past Mrs. Tanner, who hadn't said a word, and I felt pleased with myself that I had outsmarted her.

My side of the bed stayed dry for awhile, but that didn't mean my life was trouble free.

One July afternoon when I was weeding, I looked at the smokehouse just beyond the flower garden and decided I'd play there for awhile because the sun was too hot to work. I didn't like being hot and sweaty. When I turned to leave the flowers,

I saw Mr. Tanner come out of the barn and walk down the lane toward the cow pasture, making the barn a safe place for me to go.

I wondered how big the kittens were as I wandered away from my work. I decided to go see for just a minute. Mrs. Tanner and Millie were taking naps, and I felt I shouldn't have to work while they slept. Mrs. Tanner had told me over and over, *"Stay away from the barn."* But I didn't know what could be so bad about a girl going to the barn to see the animals.

And, with that bit of positive thinking, I ran, stopping now and then to look back at the house. I finally slapped my bare feet on the cool concrete of the barn floor, and there was Mr. Tanner. I hadn't seen him come from the field, but there he was cleaning gutters.

"I came to see the kittens and calves," I shouted above the scrape of the shovel.

"Where is Mother?" he asked, standing the wide, dirty shovel against the whitewashed door.

"Sleeping. You won't tell on me, will you?"

"Nope," he said as he walked up to me and put his hand on my shoulder. He smelled just like the manure, and I was afraid he'd get dirt on my dress, so I moved away from him.

"Whatsamatter, I won't bite," he laughed. "Come on, I'll show you the kittens. Follow me."

"I know where they are."

"How do you know?"

"I just know that your kittens would be in the hay like they were at the Pitts', and calves would be out here near the cows."

"Umhm, I hear your tall tale, girlie."

I ignored his remark. "Are there any calves here?" I asked, pointing to the little stalls at the back of the barn.

"Nope. They're too big, so they're out grazing today."

I followed him to the hayloft, and he knelt in front of me while I picked up and hugged each of the four kittens.

"Like 'em, don't you?" he said.

"Yeah, especially this white one, and I'll call her Snow-ball."

"It's not a her," he said.

"Well, him then."

"The little hers will grow up and have kittens," he said in a low voice as he swung around to sit beside me. "And so will you."

I looked at him and giggled. "Not kittens, babies."

"How old are you?"

I moved away so he wouldn't be touching me. "I'll be ten in December, but Mother doesn't know what day."

"Don't know when your birthday is...doesn't matter...."

I looked at him sitting there beside me, and he was staring at me, my face, my dress, my legs. I felt strange, even a little frightened.

"Like Milky Way candy bars?" he asked in a whisper, putting his arm around my waist and pulling me close to him.

I looked at his bib overalls and at his bare back and belly under them. "I can't eat them," I said. "Mother said candy would make my teeth rot and..."

"Maarreee. Maarreee."

"Mother's calling," I said, putting down the kitten and moving away from him. I stood up and brushed off the pieces of hay from my dress.

"No, down," he said, reaching for my arm.

I didn't know why, but I was afraid of Mr. Tanner right then. He had never hit me or hollered at me or anything, but he didn't seem like the right Mr. Tanner.

"Mother'll whip me if she finds me in here," I explained, and I ran out of the loft and through the cow barn. When I went out the door, there she stood, with a switch in her hand! She hit the side of my left leg. Snap, snap, snap. And I screamed. I pushed past her so I could run away, but she grabbed my arm and pulled me to her.

"Oh, no you don't," she shouted, and took hold of my earlobe and pinched with her sharp fingernails. I thought the blood would run down her arm from my ear.

"Ow, ow, let go," I cried.

"You'll walk in front of me all the way to the house," she said, letting my ear go. "I've told you time after time not to go to the barn. You'll mind me or suffer. You have no sense!"

I stepped away from her and she switched my legs hard and fast.

All the way to the house she'll hit me, I thought, and I cried loud and tears dripped off my face.

After several more steps, I stopped and turned to look at her.

"Stop hitting me!" I screamed, wanting the world to hear.

But her lips were tight and she didn't say anything; she just kept swinging that switch. I turned and walked fast, then faster and faster, until I was out of her reach and could run. I turned the corner at the pine trees and ran, and I knew she couldn't catch me.

"Come back here...come back here...you'll get worse...."

I didn't care what worse she'd do. That would be later and my legs hurt now, and I didn't want them to be hit anymore.

When I got to the pasture, I ducked under the electric fence and went to my favorite walnut tree where I sat in the cool grass.

I looked at the red stripes that went from my ankles to the hem of my dress, and I felt sorry for myself. Why does she get so mad about going to the barn, I wondered. I love to see the animals and hold Snowball, but I don't think I'll go back. I don't like the way Mr. Tanner looked at me.

After awhile, I left the shady spot and went to the flower garden where I pulled weeds around the daisies and phlox. And when I began to feel quite hungry, I heard Mrs. Tanner call me for supper, so I went into the washroom and scrubbed my dirty hands and face.

Mr. and Mrs. Tanner didn't say anything to me about what I had done, so I enjoyed my meal of mashed potatoes, sliced ham, green peas, applesauce, bread and butter, rhubarb pie and milk.

When Millie and I were in the smokehouse later, she saw my striped legs and asked me what had happened.

"I got switched bad when Mother caught me in the barn."

"Why did you go there?" asked Millie. "You knew she'd hit you."

"I went to play with the kittens. Why does she hate us to be there?"

"Because she wants us to be ladies like her."

"Well, I don't ever want to be like her," I said. Then I whispered in my grown-up lady voice, "Look, Millie, there's Millicent Mouse coming to visit this evening."

We watched the small brown creature crawl along the concrete ledge below the bricks and above the dirt floor.

"Where's your husband, Millicent?" I asked.

She stopped to look at me, and I sat very still so she wouldn't run away. I thought she had the cutest little face with such big brown eyes, and her fur was like brown velvet.

"I wish I could pet her," I whispered to Millie.

Just then we saw another mouse come up out of the hole in the corner of our little house.

"There's Bartholomew," I said to the lady mouse. "He's coming after you. Better run."

But the two mice stayed on the ledge, and before long, two more appeared with them.

When Bartholomew got close to Millicent, she ran from him and went back in the hole. When the two little ones saw him, they ran back with their mother.

"Bartholomew must be mean," I said.

"He's leaving," said Millie. "He doesn't like them."

"I think they don't like *him*," I said, and picked up a paper doll. I wanted to tell Millie what Mr. Tanner had done, but I was afraid she'd tell Mrs. Tanner, and I'd be in trouble.

"Here, Millie, you dress Cinderella in her tattered clothes, and I'll tell you the story. How's that?"

"Why do you always tell me that story, Mary? Why don't you tell me about Snow White or Hansel and Gretel? You always tell the same one."

"I like this story the best because, just like Cinderella, I have to do all the work and stay home while all of you go away."

"Girrrrls. Girrrrls. Time for bed," screeched Mrs. Tanner, so that was the end of our play and our talk.

Later when Millie was asleep, I was on my knees looking

out the window and thinking about what had happened to me in the afternoon. Even though the scratches on my legs still hurt, I thought more about how strange Mr. Tanner's face had been when he was sitting beside me, and I wondered why he had looked like that. And why was Mrs. Tanner so angry when she found me in the barn? And why didn't Mr. Tanner try to help me?

I heard voices. They were talking.

"....so I'll see you in the morning," I heard Mr. Tanner say, and I think he was at the other end of the hallway.

"Be quiet when you get up, Franklin. You wake me every morning, and you know I don't want to get up at five o'clock."

I could hear her plainly, so she was standing at her door beside ours. "Oh, hell," said Mr. Tanner.

His door slammed, and a few minutes later when I was back in my bed, I heard him yelling, "Ow, oowww. Damn. Damn it all, oohh."

I waited to hear Mrs. Tanner's footsteps in the hall going to help him, but she didn't leave her room.

Maybe he just stubbed his toe, I thought, as I crawled into bed and turned on my side to look out the window.

Summer Senses - Part II - Cat and Mouse

The next day, Mrs. Tanner was rolling out pie crust, and she had flour on her apron and hands when I came through the kitchen with my dusty cloth on the way outside to shake it. I almost laughed when I saw her so messy.

I looked at Millie sitting in Dad's chair at the table and holding her face in her hands.

"Take your elbows off the table," I said to Millie.

"Don't have to," said Millie, "Do I, Mother, 'cause I'm not eating." Mrs. Tanner glanced at me, and her glasses slid down her nose.

"Don't be gawking and causing trouble," she said. "Leave Millie alone. Get out if you've finished your work. You make me nervous."

She's still mad about the barn, I thought, but I am too. I

felt flutters in my stomach because she was trying to get rid of me. I couldn't hold back my feelings.

"Millie's in here with you," I shouted, "and she's watching you. What's the difference if I watch you, too?"

Mrs. Tanner whirled away from the table, dusting the flour down the front of her apron and onto her black shoes and the green linoleum.

"Now look what you've made me do," she sputtered as she shook the rolling pin at me. "And don't you be sassing me. Who do you think you are?" She slammed the rolling pin on the table and said in jerky, loud words, "You juss git outta here! Now!" And she pointed to the door, never taking her eyes off me.

I stood and stared at her.

"Don't yeeww dare defy me," she drawled in a low voice between clenched teeth.

I kept looking into her eyes and at her face, which was just above mine. I don't want to be near this old witch, I thought. So I turned and left the room. The door slammed hard behind me.

I walked down the gravel driveway toward the barns. What could I do to *hurt her?* I thought. I could go right into the cow barn and sneak out the back when she came after me. I knew she'd be watching me from the kitchen window. But I turned away from the buildings and walked, instead, down the lane to the cornfield, where I thought about the cats and wondered how many kittens were playing in the hay today. Dad had said several nights ago that Cinnamon had a new litter.

"We need those mousers," he had said, "and Cinnamon's the best we have. Maybe her kittens will take after her. I'll take them all to the wheat bins, can't keep the damn mice outta there."

The poor little tiny mice, I thought. How awful that cats eat them. Oh, it makes me sick to think about it. How would it look to see a cat eat a mouse? Hmm...I wonder. Phewy, I can't think about it.

I walked back to the house and wondered if I'd get pie for dinner.

When I reached the porch, Mrs. Tanner was there. "Where have you been? I've been looking all over for you. Don't be going away when I need your help. And look at your feet. Been on the cow path, haven't you? I hope you get every disease coming and going, and where are your shoes? Why aren't they on your feet?"

"'Cause I hate shoes in the summer."

She drew up her shoulders, opened her mouth and then closed it. I saw her chest rise up as she sucked in air through her nose, held it a minute, and let it out slowly.

"Go wash your hands and face—*and feet*—for dinner and put on your shoes before you come in my house!" She turned suddenly and went into the kitchen.

I didn't want to go there with her, but I was hungry, so I hurried to the washroom.

At the table, Dad told Millie he had a surprise for her.

"What is it?" she asked all smiley and excited.

"You'll see," he answered, laughing and winking at her.

"Can I have a surprise, too?" I asked.

"Who knows?" he mumbled as he stared at me through squinted eyes.

His look made me uncomfortable, so I turned to Mrs. Tanner.

"No," she said, "you don't deserve any surprise."

I watched her dig her fork into her scalloped potatoes, and then my eyes fell on my plate where I'd mixed my potatoes, carrots, string beans, and applesauce to make them taste better. I ate the mixture quickly before she'd see it.

Saturday went by with no surprise for Millie, which pleased me, but Sunday was different. Mrs. Tanner sent me to sweep the back room and garage because I hadn't done a good job on Saturday.

I had a pile of dirt ready for the dustpan when Dad rushed in.

"Where's Millie? I got something for her," he laughed, pushing an old cigar box at me.

I could hear rustling through the closed lid.

"What is it?"

"Never mind. Just tell me where's Millie?"

"She's in the kitchen with Mother," I said, but I already knew what he had in the box. I'd witnessed mice in the smokehouse enough times to know their scratching when I heard it!

He walked through the back room, across the porch and into the kitchen, and all the while he was laughing. I followed him and waited on the porch to hear Mrs. Tanner, as I knew I would.

"*Eeeeeeeek*, Franklin," she screamed. "Get those filthy things out of my house."

The next instant, Dad was on the porch with Millie. They came to the garage and walked through my dirt.

"You got me my white mice?" squealed Millie, jumping up and down. "Where'd you find them?"

"Out in the wheat bins. You want them?" he said, handing the box to her.

"Wow, six and sure I want them." She opened the lid. "Ooooo, they're so cute; what pretty babies you are," she said, putting her face almost into the box. "I'll take good care of them, too. Thanks, Dad."

"Can I have one?" I asked Dad.

"Nope. They're Millie's," he said and left the room.

I watched him go out of sight and wondered why he'd give me Milky Ways but not white mice.

"And your name is Victoria, after the old queen," I heard Millie say. "And you'll be Franklin, after Dad, and you're Henry, because Uncle Henry is a nice man. And this littlest one is Joe, and then we will have…"

"Why not one named Fanny?" I asked sarcastically. "You love her so much. And don't you dare name one after me. I hate the squirmy ugly things. Besides, Millie, mice aren't supposed to have people names. They need mouse names."

"They do?"

"Yeah, names like Nibbles, Squeaky, and Creepy," I said.

"Oh, all right. That's what they'll be," she said. "But I need two more names, so I'll think of these myself. Let's see…ah…"

"Why not Ugly and Pukey?"

"Because nobody's ugly. I'll say, Scratchy and Scrippy."

I thought she picked good names, and I felt left out, so I said, "Hey, Millie, can I have one of them?"

"No," she grinned, hugging the box close, "you can't. Dad gave them to me. They're mine. You can find your own and leave mine alone. I'm going out in the yard and play with them."

"Wait a minute, Millie," I argued, "if I had six white mice, I'd give you two or three."

"I don't care. I'm not giving you any." She left and disappeared around the corner of the house.

Later in the afternoon, I was sitting on the top cellar step in the back room when Millie walked by me and put the cigar box on a tool shelf. I saw that she had poked small holes in the lid.

Several days later, I was taking newspapers to the attic when I heard the familiar squeaking and scratching inside the mouse house. I took the attic steps two at a time, dropped my armload at the top banister post, and hurried down. I went straight to the squeaks, took down the box and forced the strings off at the corners. When I opened the lid, I saw the tiny white mice that were mostly pink. They ran into the corners and tried to hide under the straw, but I uncovered them.

They are so tiny, I thought, and so wrinkled. They don't look a thing like our smokehouse mice. How could Millie think they're cute.

They had long, naked tails and little teensy eyes, not big brown ones like Millicent Mouse and her family. I didn't want to touch these creatures. In fact, I decided I didn't even like mice anymore. I didn't blame cats for eating them. Mrs. Tanner said they carried disease. And I didn't like them because Mr. Tanner gave them to Millie and not to me.

Just then, I heard a meow and looked up to see Snowball coming into the garage. He ran over to me, and I put the box on the floor so I could hug and pet him, but he didn't want a hug. He pounced on the mouse house, so I picked it up and held it away from him as he stood on his hind legs trying to reach the good meal.

"Mee-oww, mmrrooww," he whined, twitching his long, white tail.

"Snowball," I said. "You're my best friend in the whole world, but you cannot have Millie's mice." He rubbed against my legs and purred, and I reached down with one hand to pet him.

"Mmrroww, mmrroww."

"Poor thing. I'll bet you're hungry, aren't you?"

I looked at Snowball wanting the mice, and I thought about Dad telling me that they were for Millie and for me to leave them alone. And I thought about Millie telling me to get my own, and then I thought about Mother and how she was good to Millie and mean to me.

"Snowball, you're the only one who likes me all the time," I said. "Here, kitty, have one," and I held one small, wiggly mouse by the tail.

The cat jumped on his hind feet, batted his meal with his front paw and then caught it in his mouth.

I set the box on the floor and turned away and left the garage, knowing that Snowball would have a feast. I didn't think any part of his meal would get away.

When I saw the cat leave the garage and trot down the driveway, I went back and put the pieces of scattered straw in the box. I covered it with the lid, placed it on the shelf and went to the smokehouse to play with paper dolls.

What will Millie do? I wondered. She'll hate me forever, but I don't care. Dad won't like me anymore, and Mother can whip me if she wants to. I'm glad I did it. I got even with every one of them for being mean to me.

After we'd had supper, I hid on the attic stairs, because I knew Millie would come then and get the box off the shelf.

"My mice are all gone," she whimpered, and then she screamed and cried both at the same time. "*My mice are gone.*"

The box hit the floor, and I heard her feet go plat, plat, plat, plat on the concrete as she ran. When the kitchen door slammed, I came out of my hiding place and picked up the box, put the straw in it, and placed it on the shelf.

I went out of the back room to the field behind the house where I sat under an arbor of twisted vines.

White mice are hard to find on the farm, I thought. She'll never have them again, and I'm glad.

CHAPTER 21

The Fort

Millie and I played in the summer every day after her nap, and it was better than always being by myself. We had happy times playing house with our paper dolls, pretending we had nice husbands and sweet babies and happy homes.

After Labor Day, we were back in school with Mrs. Hardison, and I was struggling with my fifth grade lessons. Sometimes, I did very well and surprised even myself, but most of the time, I wasn't interested.

The weeks passed. In December 1943, I was ten years old, either on the 7th or the 9th. Nothing was different on my birthday, except that I felt myself getting old, too old to stay around the house and play with a little sister, and too old to be in the house and bossed around by Mrs. Tanner.

New snow lay on the ground on the morning of the 9th, the day I chose to celebrate, and the small flakes continued to fall. Snow made me smile, and just watching it come down was a perfect present.

After breakfast, I turned to Mrs. Tanner who was washing dishes at the sink. "I'm going out to play," I said. I didn't ask her if it would be all right; after all, I was ten and too old to ask permission. And since I got no response from her, I went into the washroom and climbed on the box so I could look in the mirror. I studied each feature of my reflection: blue eyes, round nose, mouth with the two peaks in the middle of my top lip, and the smooth skin on my square-shaped face. I look like June Allyson, I thought. My blond hair is short and straight and turns under. I smiled at myself, and made my eyes crinkle like hers did in the magazine picture.

"I think I'll be a movie star," I said to the Mary in the mirror "I'll live in a mansion with Millie and Snowball."

From the corner of my eye, I saw my snow clothes hanging on the back of the door, so I stepped down from the box, pulled the clothes to the floor and dressed for the winter day, snapping my arctic boots last and feeling the snugness that would keep out the wet snow.

When I stepped outside into the gray and white day, I stood watching the flakes lose their shapes in white air. The gray light of the morning and the snow falling around made me feel free, separated from everyone who could tell me what to do or how to act.

First, I'll build a fort, I thought, as I walked toward the back of the house. Maybe I'll build two, one for Millie and one for me. Then, we can have a war and try to break them down.

In an area far from the house, I looked across the space at the crooked limbs of three apple trees that held snow in their curves, and at the black branches of the walnut tree that reached up through the grayness and disappeared.

I walked to the walnut tree and began to clear the snow from the foot of it. This is where I'll have my fort, I thought. This tree is my friend, because I come here when I'm sad, when I read, and when the summer is too hot. Now, in winter, it will be a part of my fort.

When I had cleared my space, I began rolling balls of snow just big enough for me to lift. I stacked the fort three rows high. When I had finished my fort, I cleared another place by an apple tree and made Millie's fort. My hands were cold, so I went inside to warm them at the radiator, and Millie came in while I was there.

"Want to play war?" I asked.

"No, I want to make a snowman," she said.

"But I built some forts for us, and I have some snowballs for you to throw. How about if we play war first, and then we'll make a snowman right here on the porch so Mother can see it from the kitchen window?"

"We'll play war." She started for the back of the house and ran to the walnut tree. "I want this one."

That was my spot, but if I didn't let her have it, she wouldn't play. "All right, Millie, you can have that fort. What you do is throw snowballs to make my fort fall, and I'll make yours fall."

Millie was two years younger than I, and she stayed inside so much that she wasn't very strong. She couldn't throw snowballs very well. I helped her throw at my fort for awhile, and then we both threw at her fort, and neither of us did much damage.

"Time to build a snowman," shouted Millie, clapping her hands to get them warm.

"How about if we make it right here on the battlefield?" I asked.

"Nope. I want to make it so Mother can see it, on the porch in front of the kitchen window, just like you said."

I remembered what I had promised, so we went to the porch and worked on the snowman, rolling the balls as large as we could and still be able to lift them on top of each other. As I was poking the holes where the eyes should be, I looked over at the kitchen window and saw Mrs. Tanner watching us. She had a little smile on her face.

This makes her happy, I thought. Now she'll like me better.

"Look Millie," I said. "Mother's watching. She likes it. Go ask her if she has something we can use for his eyes and nose."

"Don't want to," said Millie. "Hands are cold, and I'm going in."

I didn't say anything as I watched her disappear behind the closed door. I was mad at her for leaving me. When I turned around to leave the house, I saw Mr. Tanner coming from the barn, so I ran to meet him.

"Hey, Dad. Come and see my forts out back."

"Why would I want to see them?" he teased.

"Because I made them," I said.

He walked beside me to the back of the house. "How'd you know how to build them?"

"At school, but the boys play against the girls, so we get beat."

When we got to the field, he stood and looked at the forts. "Which one's yours?" he asked.

"Mine's by the walnut tree. Want to play war?"

"Yeah," he laughed. And he went to the other fort and threw snowballs at me before I could get to my tree.

"Don't hit me," I called. "Hit my fort, and I'll throw at yours."

"Here goes," he yelled, and he threw many big snowballs until my fort was nearly gone. Then he said he had won the war.

"Remember, Mary. To the victor go the spoils," he shouted.

When he was gone, I jumped up and down on the round shapes I had put in his fort until there was nothing left, and then at the walnut tree, I built my fort up again. As I walked slowly from the field, I looked at his big tracks coming and going in the snow.

"He doesn't have spoils now," I said, "because my fort is perfect."

CHAPTER 22

A Story of Easter

The winter months were cold, snowy, and windy, and Mrs. Hardison's loud slow voice talked about General Patton's invasions in Europe and about precipitation and condensation. And while I heard her drone, I pretended to study. But day after day, I sat at my desk, kicked my heels against the old wooden floor and drew pictures of snowmen and fluffy blue clouds and red tulips.

Just before Easter vacation, when report cards were due, Mrs. Hardison called each student to her desk, delivered a report, smiled and wished each one a happy Easter. Except me. When the others had left, I was still at my desk, feeling my face get hotter and hotter.

"Mary Elizabeth Easley," she called, rising from her chair, and dropping her voice on my last name.

I walked slowly and stood before my teacher. In her hand, I saw the tan, folded card with my name neatly printed. I could not make myself take it, so Mrs. Hardison grabbed my right hand, placed the card on it and bent my fingers over the edge.

"Take it," she said sternly, and then, just above a raspy whisper, "and face the consequences."

I turned and walked out of the school into the road. I didn't want to be with anyone. I knew I was dumb, but I didn't want to hear it from them. I wondered what Mrs. Tanner would do to me, and I wished I had somewhere else to go.

Maybe I'll go right by the house, I thought, and keep walking until I find my father's place. I'll just quit school and get a job. When the police find me and want to take me back to the Tanners and make me go to school, I'll scream and holler and tell them I'd rather go to jail.

I know I can't do that, I reasoned. Where would Millie be? She'd have to live at the Tanners without me. I guess I'll have to do like Mrs. Hardison said and "face the consequences". I just hope they aren't too terrible. It'll be a thrashing with the razor strap, no dessert forever, and no going visiting forever.

I kicked a stone as I neared the driveway and wished with all my heart that I had someplace else to go.

Millie was waiting for me by the bushes and said we'd go together the rest of the way.

"I won't let Mother be mad at you," she promised.

"Millie, there's nothing you can do. Mother will be mad, and she'll do something awful to me, I know; my bottom tells me."

We were at the steps, and Mrs. Tanner was on the porch waiting. Millie quickly handed her a good report card, and I tried not to hear the nice words from Mrs. Tanner. They made me feel sad because they were never said to me. She took my report card, read it, and stared at me. I watched her face become angry: mouth turned down, eyes opened wide and cheeks turned pink. She pushed her glasses down her nose and then dropped her hand to her side.

"What's the matter with you?" she asked. She lifted the card and her eyes went to the grades. "Unsatisfactory in deportment and failing arithmetic and social studies, English, reading and penmanship. You are failing fifth grade."

She pursed her lips and held out the card to me. I took it and could feel the warm spots from her fingers. She put her hands on her hips, squinted her eyes together and moved a step closer to me.

"I won't even sign it," she hissed.

I looked down and saw the black toe of her shoe move closer to me.

"Look up here," she ordered.

I lifted my head and I was so scared, I felt sick to my stomach. But I heard every word.

"I will never sign that thing. I will have nothing to do with your indifference and obstinance. You're lazy and good-for-nothin', just like your mother and father. She's in jail today and all because she's plain no good, and he's got the police looking for him every other week. *You are like them! You'll never amount to anything.* I don't know why I try with you. You're nothin' but trouble for me."

She turned and walked away. Then she grabbed the handle of the screen door and stood there. I wanted to scream and tell her not to say terrible things about my mother and father, and make me feel like I was just a piece of dirt in the world. I wanted to say that she and Mrs. Hardison made me bad because I knew they didn't like me. I wanted to tell her how very sad I felt all the time because I didn't live with my real mother and father, and I wanted to know why nobody liked me.

Suddenly, Mrs. Tanner whirled around and swung her arm at me. I ducked.

"Go stand behind the door in the corner. Just go," she shouted, grabbing my elbow and pushing me into the kitchen. "Get out of my sight! *out—out—out!*"

I ran through the kitchen and into the corner, where I'd already spent many hours in seclusion. The door swung open so far that it made a triangular space. I sat on the floor between the dustmop and carpet sweeper, but my legs felt cramped, so I stood with my head resting on my folded arms against the wall. I noticed my report card still in my hand, so I slid it under the corner of the rug where I'd never have to see it again.

How long was I going to be here this time? I wondered. What could I do for fun? I had already memorized the pattern in the wallpaper. I thought first about capitals. Concord, New Hampshire; Augusta, Maine; Montpelier, Vermont; Dover, Delaware. I liked that one, I thought. It reminded me of a song, "There'll be bluebirds over the white cliffs of Dover, tomorrow just you wait and see. There'll be love and laughter and peace ever after—tomorrow when the world is free." I imagined the bluebirds, with their orange and white breasts, flying over the

sharp white corners of a glacier, and I saw happy people hugging each other and laughing together after the war. I didn't
want to think anymore. It made me sad. I knew I would never
be happy like those people. I wanted something to do, just
anything that would take the sad feeling away.

I moved my finger up the thin, red line on the wall as far
as I could reach and then down the wider stripe to the right.
"It's torn," I said softly. Taking a small loose patch, I pulled it
very slowly up, up until it ripped off just above my head. Then
I pulled the paper that had loosened beside the bare spot. I
pulled little strips until half the wall, from the door molding to
the corner, was nothing but blotchy dry paste. I had my fingers
on one small paper I had missed just below my knees when
Mrs. Tanner called from the kitchen and made me jump.

"Mary, wash your hands for supper."

The scraps, I thought. What'll I do to hide them?

"Maaarree," she called again.

I snatched up the small papers and stuffed them in my
dress pockets. When I walked into the kitchen, Mrs. Tanner's
back was turned, so I hurried out the door and emptied my
pockets in the trash barrel.

Saturday was cleaning day, and Mrs. Tanner hadn't seen
my handiwork on her wall, so I thought by the time she did
discover it, I'd be too old to be whipped. But I had worried so
much about it that I wished I'd never done it. I was setting the
table for the noon meal when she said she'd forgotten to dust
the hall floor. As she went toward the swinging door, I could
see in my mind her hand reaching...her eyes not seeing....

"Mary, come here," she shouted, and her voice trembled.
"What have you done? Get in here this minute!"

The white plate almost fell out of my hands, but I put it
safely on the table and walked to her. I twinged everywhere,
and I knew why. I had done something horrible this time.
When I got near Mrs. Tanner, she slapped my face so hard that
I fell back against the wall and onto the floor. Before I could
move, she grabbed a handful of my hair and pulled me up. "Get
to the back room," she ordered. "I'll be there." I was shaking
and crying, and through my tears I could see her angry face. I

backed away from her and ran out of the kitchen. In the wash-room, I expected to get the worst whipping I'd ever had. And I did.

Later, at the table, I didn't feel much like eating. For one reason, my sitter hurt from the sharp stings, and for another, swallowing was difficult after a long crying time. She told Mr. Tanner what I'd done, and what she'd done to me, and he said he ought to give me another one. That comment made me shiver.

After dinner, while I was washing dishes, Mrs. Tanner told me to turn and look at her.

"I want to talk to you," she said.

I shook the suds off my hands and faced her.

"We will not talk to you—not I, not Dad, and not Millie. As far as we're concerned, we can't even see you," she said, and she looked just above my head. "Come to meals on time. Go to bed on time. Do not talk to us."

When she'd left the room, I decided she could do her own dishes, and I wiped my hands on my dress and left the kitchen. I sat in the washroom at my makeshift table, a board over the sink, put my head down on my arms and cried.

"I'm so bad," I sobbed, "and I c-c-c-can't h-h-help i-i-t."

After awhile, when the hurt inside was gone, I took the box that held the thick pieces of my favorite puzzle, emptied them onto the board and began turning them right side up, three pieces for the large moon and many pieces for the snow and the frozen pond.

"Bad, bad, bad," I said, but another feeling inside kept telling me I wasn't bad.

"No, I'm not," I agreed. "I'm good. I can be good if I want to."

I put my knees onto the stool to make me taller so I could look at myself.

"No, I am not bad. Mrs. Tanner is," I told the mirror girl. "She doesn't talk nice to me. She hits me before I can explain, and she puts me in the corner where she won't have to see me. That's why I took the paper off the wall, because she's mean."

I looked at my red eyes and watched the tears fall and

licked them off when they got near my mouth. When they stopped falling, I went back to my puzzle.

The next Saturday, I dusted as usual, and I tried not to miss anything. In the dining room, I wiped the backboard light of the buffet and then the candlesticks on the left side. I moved my cloth over the surface of the crystal bowl that matched the candlesticks. But the bowl was not empty as usual. I saw first some cellophane papers and then inside them, I saw yellow sugary chickens. I picked up a package with a chick in it, looked closely at it and saw the tiny black, candy eyes. I wish I could eat you, I thought, but I'd better not.

I ate dinner and Mrs. Tanner gave me apple pie for dessert, so I knew she hadn't found dust on anything. I had done a perfect job!

Later, because Millie was staying close to Mrs. Tanner these days, I went to play alone at my table where I thought about the puffy, yellow chicks and how good they would have tasted. When I was tired of staying in the small room, I put on my coat and went outside where I walked to my walnut tree and sat on the cold ground. Spring had not yet come to Gallaway, so I didn't see soft, green grass or tiny purple violets that bloomed very early and made me feel happy. I sighed and looked around the field where nothing grew in winter. The grape arbor held twisted vines with dead leaves, and tomato stakes were lying on the ground with parts of the brown, rough stems clinging to them.

I'm alone, I thought, and I've been good a whole week. Still, nobody talks to me. Why should I try? I'll do just what I feel like doing. They can't hurt me.

When I saw Dad go up the lane from milking the cows, I walked away from the tree and back to the house, where I washed and went to the table for supper. I tried to eat everything on my plate, and even though the succotash tasted spoiled, I ate it anyway, so I could have white cake with chocolate frosting.

Mrs. Tanner talked about Veronica's wedding in May. "I hope she'll be happy," she said and wrinkled her forehead. "What do you think of Arthur?" she asked, looking at Mr. Tanner.

"He's all right, I guess. Pass me the gravy." He took the

yellow bowl from her and spooned the liquid on his potatoes and beef. "What time we s'posed to be...."

"Oh, Mary," Mrs. Tanner interrupted. "We're going to see the Pomeroys this evening."

I put my fork down and smiled up at Mrs. Tanner. I get to go this time, I thought, because I've been so good.

"And I want you to go to your room and stay there," I heard her say. "Take a book to read, but you are to stay in your room and go to bed when it's dark. We'll be home late."

I looked down at my plate and then pushed myself away from the chocolate frosting. I didn't want it. I stood up, pushed my chair under the table and hurried away. I took my coat from the hook, put it on, wiped the tears as they fell and went outside.

"Mrs. Tanner will never like me," I mumbled. "She likes her niece, Veronica, and she likes Millie. What can I do to make her like me?"

At seven o'clock, I stood on the back porch as the three of them got in the car. Mrs. Tanner held the front seat forward so Millie could get in the back.

"Hurry up," she said. "Veronica wants us there before dark."

As the car moved, I watched the dust curling up from the wheels, and when it had settled, I threw my head back and looked at the sky.

"I hate you Mrs. Tanner!" I shouted. "You are a...a fool. You are cow piles...and you are ugly...ugly as a...a...wild boar."

I sat on the step where she had made Billy and me sit after we had run away, and I looked down the path to the tall red barn where she had switched me.

"Huh," I said, "I'll go there the first chance I get." I turned to the other side of me and looked at Mrs. Tanner's kitchen. "And I'll never wash another dish."

I had declared war on Mrs. Tanner.

I watched the stars coming out all over the sky, and I found the Big Dipper before I decided I'd better get to my room. I was hungry, though. I could get a piece of cake, but she'd see the crumbs. I looked at the cake dish still sitting on the stove, but walked by it and started up the stairs in the hall. On the

third step, I turned to look toward the dining room. The yellow
chicks, I thought, and I went back down the steps and over to
the French doors. Turning the glass knob, I walked into the
dining room and around the long table until I stood facing the
cabinet and the sparkling, round dish.

"Hmm, let's see," I whispered, as I counted the clear, paper
packages...two, four, eight. My stomach was empty, so I picked
up three rustling papers and put them down the front of my
dress. I took two more and hid them with the others. I heard a
noise. I listened for voices or a car door. Nothing. I took one
more chick, two left.

Maybe six are enough for me, I thought. But two don't
want to be left alone. I'll take them. I quietly left, clicked the
door behind me and tiptoed to my room.

Closing my bedroom door, I pressed my hand against the
top of my dress just to hear the noisy papers. Those little yellow
sugar chicks were all mine. I took them out of the hiding place,
one by one, and lined them up on my bed. The first package was
half open and the sugar drifted out onto my bedspread. I held
the chick by the head and sunk my teeth into the soft, puffy
marshmallow. In two bites, it was gone. The next square package was closed tight, and when I pulled it open, the candy fell
to the floor. I scooped it up and ate the chicken whole.

"Mmm, yum, yum, you are so good and sweet," I said.
"How about another?" Gulp, chew, chew, swallow. "And will
you have another, Mary? Yes, thank you, I believe I shall."

Let's see now...one, two, three, four of the Tanner lady's
chicks left, I thought. I opened all four packages, took out the
candies and set them in a row, one behind the other.

"Hee, hee, hee. I'm the wicked witch, and I'm going to eat
you!"

I put two in my mouth at once and then the last two, and
my cheeks were puffed out so much, I could hardly chew. But I
swallowed the soft little critters in no time and hid the wrap-
pers under the mattress.

"That's what mean old Mother Tanner gets for making me
stay home," I said, "and I bet I had more fun than anybody at
the Pomeroys."

The next day was Easter, and while we were finishing breakfast, Mrs. Tanner asked Millie to come and help her set the table for the dinner guests.

"Hiram, Alice, Veronica and Arthur are coming to dinner. You, Millie, may eat with us if you can remember your manners. Don't talk with your mouth full, and don't talk unless you're spoken to, and don't..."

"Don't do this, and don't do that," I whispered as the two of them swished out of the room. I stood in the hallway and listened.

"Now, where are those yellow chicks I was planning to use with the place cards?" I heard Mrs. Tanner say.

"I dunno," said Millie.

"Well, they aren't here in the bowl. Oh, maybe I put them in the kitchen cupboard. Wait here, Millie. I'll be right back and show you how to set the table."

I heard the thick heels of Mrs. Tanner's black shoes clunking their way to the kitchen. I wanted to run, but she'd know I was guilty. When she saw me, she stopped dead in her tracks. Her eyes got big, and her mouth fell open. "You, y-y-you," she stammered, and I ran.

In the washroom, I grabbed my coat and was outside in a flash. Sly and spry, I thought. Through the garden I went, past my walnut tree, up the hill, and into the cornfield where the scarecrow hung without his straw. I was getting out of breath, but I ran on, and if she was calling my name, I could not hear. I'll go to town and I won't come home until Easter dinner is over and all the company is gone, I thought. And nobody today can have a better feast than I had last night on all those sweet, yellow chicks.

I walked down the long street in town, past the Buster Brown store where I had gotten saddle shoes and black arctics, and past Harvey's Drug Store where Miss Warring had taken Millie and me to get sundaes. I looked at the rings in the jewelry window before I stood in the middle of the street and looked to the end both ways.

"I don't know the way to my father's house," I said, "because I've never been there. What is the name of his road?"

I sat on the bench in front of the roundhouse where the

old man had told me about Adam and Eve, and I remembered Sunday school and what I heard there about Jesus on the cross and about Him coming out of the grave. Our teacher said that when He died on the cross it was a sad thing, but it was a good thing, because it meant we could go to heaven when we died. I liked to think of heaven. I knew it was a place where nobody hated anybody and where nobody could get hurt. I'll be glad when I get there, I thought.

I'd missed dinner and felt hungry. I knew it was almost suppertime, and I'd have to go back. There was nowhere else for me to go, and being alone in the night frightened me. So I got up and ran up Main Street and onto Gilbert Street.

When I was once again under my walnut tree, I felt safe, but I was very tired.

I'm afraid to go back to the house yet, so I'll just take a nap right here, I thought. How can I ever go back and face...a noise from behind startled me.

"Mary, where've you been?" said Mr. Tanner's voice, and I jumped up."You've missed your dinner. Sit down where you were, and I'll come and sit with you."

I sat again and watched him walk toward me and sit on the ground next to me. He wore his bib overalls and red wool shirt, so I knew he'd been milking, and I could smell the whitewash of the cow barn on his clothes. He put his hand on my leg just above my knee and under my dress. When I tried to push his arm away, he dug his fingers in.

"You look pretty, Mary," he said. "You've got roses in your cheeks, and that makes your eyes look even bluer. You're going to be a pretty girl someday. You'll fill out." He put his hand on my chest.

I felt very nervous. "Are there more kittens?" I asked, pushing his hand away. "And how is Snowball? Why doesn't he come to the house to see me? Is it time for..."

He didn't answer any questions, but scooted around until he faced me, and then he inched closer so his legs were on each side of mine. I could smell manure on his big workshoes. He pushed my dress up above my knees, and I tried to back away from him.

"Don't move," he whispered. "Sit very still. Don't talk."

He lifted my dress and looked at my legs all the way up and then reached over, unbuttoned my coat, and opened the front of it. He put his hand on my chest again, and I wanted to push it away and get up and run, but I was afraid of him, so I didn't move.

He put his face close to mine and his mouth on mine, and I moved my head back quick. "Don't," I said. "I want to get up."

He took hold of my shoulders with his big hands and pulled me up close to him. He shouldn't do this to me, I thought.

"No, I don't like it," I stammered, struggling to get away. "Let me go," I said in a loud voice.

"Be quiet," he ordered, as he took his hands away and let me move from him. "Mary, don't be afraid. I ain't gonna hurtcha."

He got up off the ground and reached for my hand, but I got up by myself. I saw him put his hand into his front overall pocket, and he brought out a Milky Way.

"Here, eat it," he said. "You must be hungry. Haven't eaten since breakfast, have you, and it's almost four o'clock."

We walked slowly away from the tree to the lane.

"Thank you," I said, taking the wrapper off the candy. I didn't want to eat it, but I was hungry since I'd missed dinner.

I felt all prickly and afraid, and I wanted to talk about something so I could forget what he did. "What's Easter?" I asked.

"I dunno," he said. "I'm not religious like Fanny. She said it's about the Resurrection."

"What's that?" I asked.

"Dunno. But I'll tell you what I think Easter's all about. It's the one Sunday in the year when the women spend their husband's money buying fancy duds and big hats and going to church so's they can impress each other."

"I learned in Sunday school that it's about people killing Jesus, and He was the best man who ever lived. He died, and He was buried, and then He came back to life and went to heaven."

I had been looking for violets while I walked, so I didn't notice that he was way ahead of me and hadn't heard me talking.

"Oh, here's a little bitty violet and you smashed it," I called out to him. I stopped and bent down. "Poor, little thing."

I pinched the tiny, limp stem from the ground and ran to catch up with him. One by one, I took each tiny petal between my fingers and smoothed the crinkles made from his foot.

"There, now it's all fixed, and if I put it in water, it'll stay pretty."

"It's no good now," he said laughing. "Once it's picked, it won't bloom again."

I looked at the small flower lying in my opened palm as Mr. Tanner and I walked in silence up the lane. When I saw the kitchen door, my legs got shaky, and my mouth felt dry. I didn't want to go on, so I stopped.

"I'm afraid to go where Mrs. Tanner is," I said.

"Aw, don't be afraid. She won't hurt you."

"She'll probably whip me," I argued.

"Don't worry," he said softly. "I won't let her hit you. I'll tell her I took care of it."

"What will you tell her you did?"

"Never mind. Go in the back room and clean up for supper, but don't wash those roses off your cheeks." He laughed and laughed as he walked on ahead of me. But after a few steps, he stopped and turned around. "And don't tell anyone, not even Millie, about our secrets."

I watched Mr. Tanner go inside, and the door slammed behind him.

I like Milky Ways, I thought, but I don't like to have Mr. Tanner put his hands on me. He likes me, though, because he said I was pretty. And he's not going to let Mrs. Tanner whip me. Maybe he's my friend, but I don't like what he did today.

In the washroom, I filled a glass, dropped the violet in and watched it float on the water. Then I hung up my coat, turned on the water again, and took the Ivory bar from the side of the sink. The soap smelled clean, and I rubbed it in my hands until they were all sudsy. I washed my mouth where Mr. Tanner's mouth had been.

"I don't like those secret things," I said, tasting the soap with my tongue as I talked and then spitting into the sink.

I put lots of suds on my cheeks and rubbed them hard with the white bubbles, and then I made a thick paste with the soap and patted it on my face so it would stay there. I placed the box under the mirror, climbed on it and looked at my face. "I like those cheeks," I said to Mary in the looking glass. "The roses that Mr. Tanner liked are gone. Now maybe he won't do bad things to me anymore."

I dried my face and hands and walked out of the small room to the porch and into the kitchen where my leftover Easter dinner was waiting.

CHAPTER 23

The Secret

After the two-week Easter vacation, it was back to school. My war with Mrs. Tanner became more complicated when she got messages from Mrs. Hardison. Every Friday, I carried home a sealed envelope, but Mrs. Tanner ripped open the letters and quickly read them to me: "Mary has improved in reading, but is not working on her history lessons; Mary's conduct on the playground is deplorable; Mary did not do her arithmetic homework all week." And then with a "hmmph," she pushed the letters into my hand, turned and walked away.

And as if my lessons didn't cause me enough trouble, I wet the bed just about every night. When I awoke in the morning, I'd feel my side of the sheets, but it didn't matter whether I was wet or Millie. I felt the same fear of a whipping for both of us. Some mornings there wasn't a dry spot anywhere.

On Memorial Day, the sheets had hung since early morning and I had been teased by Sam, the hired man, his family, the Tanners, and their son, Ted, who came for dinner.

In the afternoon, Mrs. Tanner said she didn't feel well and was going to sleep while Millie napped. She told me to stay in the washroom until she and Millie got up. I told her I would, but I knew exactly where I'd go and what I'd do there.

I walked past the cows' stanchions to the back stalls and climbed a three-rung ladder to a small haymow, where I found my favorite mother cat, Butter, and her five kittens. I sat down where I could rest my back against a beam and where I could see the open barn door. If Mother comes, I'll know, I thought. Butter walked over to me, and I patted her yellow head.

"You have a fine family," I said. "There's a white baby like Snowball, two yellow and white, and a yellow that I like best. I'll name her Butterscotch. How's that, Mommy?" Butter purred as I scratched her ears.

How soft each one felt as I held it close to my neck. They were quite wiggly, so after I cuddled each one, I put it back in the hay, except for Butterscotch. I placed her on my legs and tickled her belly, and she grabbed my hand with all four paws and tried to bite my fingers. Then she turned over and stumbled to her mother for milk. As I sat in the quiet peacefulness of my little corner, watching the happy kittens frolic in the security of their mother's care, I longed for such a safe and happy feeling. Finally, Butterscotch wobbled in the uneven layer of hay back to me and I picked her up, held her in my arms, and gently rubbed her head until she went to sleep.

This is one of the best afternoons I've ever had, I thought. I wish I could come to this place every day and play with these little darlings. I love them, and they love me. My eyes wanted to close, and I thought it would be nice to take a little nap while my baby was asleep in my arms. I put my head back against the beam and saw the sunlight from the open door spread a wide path on the dirt floor to the top of the ladder that leaned toward me at the edge of the loft. I closed my eyes. I heard Butter purring as she lay curled beside me, and I smiled in my special moment.

I'll doze...for...a...little...whi...No, a shadow!

I opened my eyes and saw the dried dirt on Mr. Tanner's shoes that were pointed at my bare feet.

"Mary," he said in a growly voice, "come with me."

"Why?" I asked, keeping my head down.

"Just come with me," he repeated.

I lifted my eyes to his face and my stomach began to hurt. "Butterscotch is sleeping," I whispered.

"Put the cat down," he said. "Come with me to the other haymow."

I glanced to the top of the high ladder and hugged Butter-scotch closer to me. She awoke and jumped from my arms.

"It's a long way up there, and I don't want to be that high," I said, patting Butter, who stood beside me purring.

Mr. Tanner took my arm and led me to the short ladder. I climbed down, hoping I could run when my feet hit the floor. But he held my wrist as he walked to the door and used his free hand to roll it down to the floor, closing out the sun. He couldn't fasten the latch; he would have needed two hands to do that. I was glad I wouldn't be in a locked barn with him. If he would let go of me for just a second, I knew I could run through the cow barn and get away. But he held my wrist until we were standing at the bottom rung of the tall ladder.

"You climb," he said. "I'll be right behind you."

I looked up at his red, wet face that wasn't smiling. Sweat dripped off his nose, and he brushed it away. I was afraid, and I wished that Mrs. Tanner would call so I could go.

Mr. Tanner put my right hand on the third rung of the ladder and my left foot on the first one, and then he slapped my bottom and told me to get going. I was trapped. My stomach hurt worse every minute, and I was afraid I might fall off the ladder. If that didn't happen, I was afraid of what Mr. Tanner was going to do. I felt his hot breath on my legs and my stomach churned.

"Let me down," I said. "I'm scared...it's too high...let me..."

"Come on," he said, "you can do it. You're bigger than you think." I moved up four more rungs, and his body was against my back. I remembered the other times when he'd been alone with me and wondered what he would do this time.

He leaned against me, and he smelled hot and oily like his tractor. The wooden rungs of the ladder pressed against the tops of my legs and my chest. A shiver moved under my cotton dress, but I didn't know why because the barn was very warm. I climbed two more steps and then his hands were under my arms, and he lifted me into the pile of hay. He stepped around the side of the ladder and stood beside me. His eyes were on my face, on my neck, down the front of my dress.

"Lay down," he ordered.

"It's too scratchy, and I don't like it," I complained.

"Don't talk. Lay back," he said hoarsely.

I leaned back carefully on my elbows and felt the jabs of dried stems on my back and arms. His hands were on my legs pushing up my dress and reaching for my underpants.

"No, no," I shouted, and he covered my mouth with his hand.

"Don't say a word or make a sound, or I'll hit you," he hissed as he pushed my dress up all the way.

I closed my eyes because I didn't want to see him looking at me. He took his hand from my mouth, but I kept my eyes closed and felt him pushing me where I was ashamed for him to look.

"D-d-d-on't," I whimpered.

He slapped the side of my leg. "Be quiet," he puffed as he pushed against me and made me sink deeper and deeper into the hay.

I was scared, so scared that I started shaking. He's doing something awful, just awful, I thought, and if Mrs. Tanner comes in here, I'll get a terrible whipping. I could feel the tears roll down the sides of my face and into my hair.

"Stop it," I cried. "It hurts. I don't like it. Let me go."

I looked at his face and the sweat dripped off onto my bare stomach. His eyes were half-closed, and his mouth was open. He looked like some strange person.

Suddenly, I heard a loud rumble down below on the barn floor, and I knew someone was opening the door. Mr. Tanner stopped moving, and I could hear the hired man's tractor engine. I thought he would drive in, but he didn't. He turned off the tractor and called.

"Hey, Franklin, you in here? Franklin? Franklin? Where are you?"

Mr. Tanner moved away from me. He raised himself from his knees, walked to the ladder and looked down.

"Hey, Sam...I'm...uh, up here working. Whaddya want?"

"The cows are in the road. Hurry before they get hit! I'll get the truck and be right back."

"Yeah, do that," called Mr. Tanner, and then he turned to

me and caught my chin with his hand. He gave my head a shake. "Don't ever, ever say a word," he whispered, "not to anybody. It's our secret. Stay here until I'm gone, and then you get back to the house as fast as you can. Remember—not a word!" He jerked his hand away, reached into his pocket and threw a Milky Way at my feet. Then he turned his back, went to the ladder, and was gone.

I let the tears fall as I got up and brushed off and smoothed my dress. I buried the Milky Way deep into the loft. He's bad for what he did to me, and I'm bad for being here where he could catch me, I thought, as I stumbled through the hay to the ladder. I didn't want to look at him ever, ever again.

I hurried down the ladder and out into the sunshine. I felt so sick in my stomach that I tried to vomit, but I just gagged, and even though the sun was hot, I felt cold. I'll never go back, not even to play with Butterscotch, I thought. I never want to see a barn again.

CHAPTER 24

D-Days

Mrs. Hardison handed out report cards on the last day of school.

"You're excused for the summer and may leave now, except for Mary and Millie Easley," she said. After good-byes were joyfully shouted, and the other students had left the room, our teacher asked the two of us to come and stand at her desk.

She handed my sister her report and told her how proud she was of Millie's progress in second grade. "I look forward to seeing you in the fall," she said with a smile.

"Now, Mary," She paused. "I know you could have done the work, but you didn't. I could understand your insolence and laziness if you were living with your parents, but you're not. You're with fine, highly respected people, and you should be thankful that people like them take in children like you.

"Mrs. Tanner is a lady, always a lady, and a wonderful example for any child. Mr. Tanner, why, he's a rock in our community. He's on the school board, and in the Kiwanis and Masons. Plus, he's one of the best farmers in the county! If you'd only apply yourself and..."

I was tired of her speech, and I wanted to tell her what he had done on Memorial Day. Then she wouldn't think Mr. Tanner was such a great man. But she'd never have believed me. I didn't want to think about him and that awful, awful day. I listened again to Mrs. Hardison.

"So, I'm sure you'll work hard for me next year, won't you?"

I didn't say yes or no.

She breathed a long, deep sigh. "Well, it's up to you," she said, placing the report in my hand. "You failed!"

I wasn't surprised. I hadn't studied, and I knew I wouldn't pass, but now that it was final, I felt sad.

When we were outside, Millie took my hand and swung our arms. "It's all right, Mary. I know you could have passed if you wanted to."

"No, Millie, I'm just dumb"

"No, you aren't," argued Millie, giving my arm a jerk.

"I'll probably be no good, just like Mrs. Tanner says, but I don't care. I don't care about anything...or anybody...but you."

We walked far behind the others, and I worried about having to see them in September. I couldn't bear to think about it, so I decided I'd hide somewhere every day and not go to school. And if the truant officer happened to find me, and if he asked me who were my parents, I'd say I didn't have any. It was true, I didn't have *my* parents, so I didn't have any.

There was nothing to do now, though, but go where I didn't want to go, to the Tanners. I stopped walking, and Millie looked at me.

"What's the matter?"

"It's other kids, Millie. When I see them with their parents, they look happy. When I read the Bobbsey Twin books, the mother and father are nice people who love their children. Why can't we live like that? I feel like I'm different. Do you feel that way, too?"

"No, 'cause we look like everybody else. But maybe if we lived with our own mother and father, we could be happy."

"I don't know. Do you suppose they'd whip us and send me to the back room when company came? Or, would they hug us and kiss us goodnight when they put us to bed?"

"I don't know, Mary, but let's be as good as we can, and maybe Mother will be nice to us. Will you, Mary? Will you be good?"

We turned into our driveway, and not wanting to make

that promise, I let Millie's hand go so I could kick a little stone.

"I guess so," I grumbled. "But I wish, more than anything, that we could stop wetting the bed and getting whipped."

We had reached the corner of the house, and I felt afraid about the consequences facing me.

"Wait, Millie. Uh,...oh, just stay with me till Mother reads my report card, will you?"

"Yes, and if she wants to use the razor strap on you, I'll tell her it's too late."

"You're the best sister in the world, Millie. I hope you'll always be with me."

"Sure I will," she giggled.

"I don't know. Billy was sent away. I guess I could be, too, if they don't like me. Oh, no, we're here," I groaned as we stopped under the kitchen window, "and I'll bet Mother'll be on the porch waiting."

Millie presented her report card first. While Mrs. Tanner read it carefully, I turned my card over and over in my hands, and when I glanced up at Mrs. Tanner, she was smiling at Millie.

"You've done so well. Keep it up next year."

Still holding my sister's card, Mrs. Tanner turned to me, and her smile faded. "Mary, give me yours!"

I knew she expected nothing. I didn't disappoint her.

"You've made your bed, now lie in it."

Millie smiled. She was happy that there would be no whipping.

I was relieved about that myself, but I didn't understand what Mrs. Tanner meant. What did my bed have to do with school?

June 6th had been D-Day, so almost every day there was talk about the war. The Tanners talked to each other and sometimes to their son, Ted, when he came by for supper.

"The American people can breathe a little easier now," said Mrs. Tanner one Friday night.

"Yeah, we're gonna win this war," said Ted, banging his fist on the table. "I just wish I could have helped!"

"Hold on a minute there, son," said Mr. Tanner, "we've got

the Japanese to worry about, too, ya know. Don't forget them. They're real fighters, and they don't give up easy. They have those suicide..."

I didn't listen anymore because I didn't care. I thought D-Day must have been about some battle we'd won, and I wondered if I'd ever win my battle against Mrs. Tanner. I didn't care about Mr. Tanner, didn't even look at him, but Mrs. Tanner...huh! I just knew that someday I'd get even with her!

"Millie, sit up straight!" ordered Mrs. Tanner, and I sat up, too.

"And Mary, I want you..."

"C'mon, Ted, let's you and me go in the other room and talk," said Mr. Tanner. They stood up and I watched as Ted kissed his mother's forehead before he followed his father into the sitting room.

He must like her a lot better than I do, I thought. No wonder, I'll bet he never had to clean her house or pull her weeds!

"...to dust my guest bedroom tomorrow," continued Mrs. Tanner, "...my Victorian room at the end of the hall across from Dad's room. We'll be having some company next week. The newlyweds, Veronica and Arthur, are coming for a couple days while their house is being finished. Don't miss a thing in that room, either. You hear?"

"Yes," I said, but I thought about their wedding that I didn't get to see because I brought home a bad report card and then pulled paper off the wall. I was still angry that I hadn't been allowed to go.

Saturday morning, I went to the guest room, pushed the door open and looked inside at the bed with four tall posts. I walked into the room and looked at the royal blue canopy with the scalloped edge and the bedspread that matched. I saw the same kind of material at three tall windows as my eyes followed the color around the room. I walked to the long dresser with a high mirror and then to the dry sink, where I touched painted blue roses on the bowl and pitcher. I looked to the right, at the fireplace that filled one corner of the room, and there on the mantle was a surprising thing—a shiny memento—

two layers of the cake that Mrs. Tanner had brought home
from Veronica's wedding. I looked at the bride and groom on
the top layer, safe inside a sealed glass. Mrs. Tanner had said
it would last forever in its container.

"Forever, huh?" I whispered, looking at the pink and white
sugar roses placed around the bottom layer. My mouth watered
when I saw the sugar bells on the top layer around the happy
couple.

I certainly would like a piece of that cake, I thought. I
looked down at the black cloth in my hand and remembered my
promise to Millie.

The wood on the dresser and dry sink matched the mantle.
When they were clean, I looked at myself in the mirror.

"This room is very lovely," I said, looking over my shoulder, "and I'm the princess who lives in it." I touched my hair
daintily with my palm and smiled at myself.

"Mary! Dust!" shouted Mrs. Tanner. I whirled around, and
she was in the doorway.

"I am dusting," I said. "And this is the most beautiful room
I've seen. It must be like a room in a palace."

"I want it done right. You hear me?"

"Yes. I will do it right." I watched her turn and leave, and
I stuck out my tongue. "You'll be sorry for being mean to me,
Old Lady," I whispered, watching her disappear down the wind-
ing staircase.

I got busy with the dresser, dry sink, bed, rocker and
window sills. I saved the mantle for last. I dusted and dusted
and stared at the delicious looking cake. There's got to be a
way, I thought.

I walked to the doorway, stepped outside and listened.
Hmm...she was running water down in the kitchen. Good. I
walked back to the mantle. Just a taste, that's all I wanted, a
tiny taste.

I thought of the yellow chicks and how good they had been
with their sweet, sparkling sugar. I turned the round container
until I could see the backs of the bells, and there I saw where
the top and bottom were sealed. I carefully pulled the top up
and the bottom down until I had made a small opening, and at

that place, I stuck in my little finger and dug at the icing. I put my finger in my mouth and savored the sweetness. Mmm, it was delicious! When I had finished a bit more tasting, I turned the container so that it looked perfect, just like it did when I first saw it. I walked from the room and, taking one last look at the cake, I closed the door behind me.

Veronica and Arthur did not come to visit that week, so the next Saturday morning, Mrs. Tanner said I'd have to dust the Victorian room again.

"I feel certain that they'll be here tomorrow," she said.

"I'll do a good job," I said cheerfully.

"Well, be sure you don't break anything, and do everything like you did last week."

"I will," I answered. It's her fault, I thought, as I entered the room. She said to do everything like I did last week, so I'll have to dust *and* taste the cake! This is my battle against her that I will win.

When I left the room, the back half of the souvenir was gone, but the newlyweds wouldn't notice, because the front looked the same.

I won't get into it again, though, I thought, because Mrs. Tanner will see if I take anymore. But, wait a minute. I won't care if she does know. In fact, it'll be my victory if she finds out, because she can't make it whole again! No siree. Whipping me won't even help her.

Wednesday afternoon, the newlyweds arrived in their new black Ford. I watched from the back room as Arthur opened Veronica's door. They're the prince and princess, I thought, and they will sleep in the royal bedroom with the half-gone cake that I have prepared for them.

They stayed two nights, and the next Saturday, Mrs. Tanner said she'd clean up the guest room for the next visitors and close it up again. Later, I was doing dishes when Mrs. Tanner called my name.

"M-M-Mary," she said just above a whisper. "How c-c-c-ould you?"

I turned to look at her, and she stood just inside the kitchen, holding the damaged memento. She had tears in her eyes when she looked at me. I felt prickles all over and wished she'd go away.

"You didn't let me go to the wedding," I blurted out.

I saw her hands shaking and thought she might drop the cake. And then, watching her lips tremble as she tried to speak, I was sorry for what I'd done.

"This can never be replaced," she whimpered, and then she turned and left the room. I heard her sobs as she went up the stairs.

I turned to the dishes and looked out the window at the trees moving back and forth in the summer breeze. Yes, I was glad I had hurt Mrs. Tanner by destroying her treasured memento, because she had hurt me so many times by things she had said. I could not forget many of her angry, bitter words.

I have won this battle, I thought. This is my D-Day. But I don't feel good about being mean and making a person cry, not even if that person is Mrs. Tanner.

CHAPTER 25

Attic Attack

After the wedding cake incident, Mrs. Tanner said I should dust only the downstairs and she'd do upstairs. That was fine with me, the less dusting the better.

But one Saturday morning in July, she apparently thought I didn't have enough to do, so she told me to sweep the attic over the garage. We were having breakfast, and every time I looked across the table at Millie, I could see Mr. Tanner out of the corner of my eye, and I knew he was looking at me. He made me feel uneasy when he stared like that, so I didn't look at him.

Why was he watching me? I was afraid of him.

"Franklin," said Mrs. Tanner, setting her coffee cup in its saucer. "I need sugar for my pies, so go to the store right away."

Good, I thought, he'll be gone a long time this morning, so I w....oh, oh, Mrs. Tanner is giving instructions.

"....have to take the broom with you, and empty the dustpan into the old box that's up there. Do you hear me, Mary?"

"Yes," I answered. As I left the table, I thought it would be a good idea to do the attic when Mr. Tanner was at the store, so I told Mrs. Tanner that I'd sweep right away.

"No," she said. "Do the dusting in the house this morning, and after the noon meal, you can go to the attic."

"It will be too hot in the afternoon," I complained, knowing that Mr. Tanner was hearing all this and afraid of what he was thinking.

"You heard me," she said, and with a wave of her hand motioned for me to get on with my dusting.

After dinner and drying dishes, I dragged the broom behind me up the rickety steps to the attic. I stepped around the wooden banister at the top step and looked at the mess, and then walked to the papers sprawled before me on the floor. I looked at the rest of the hot, smothering place. Newspapers lined the wall just beneath the broken window above the back porch. Mice scratched in the far corner where the *Life* magazines were stacked, and fallen *Farm Journals* lay in a line from the wall to the center of the room. Above me, cobwebs with dead flies stretched from rafters to roof. I looked back at the stairway, and near the railing lay two rust-stained gray and white striped mattresses, half against the banister and half on the floor. How nasty they are, I thought, as I dragged the broom to the far corner of the room and began sweeping.

As I swung the broom back and forth, I counted the boards I had cleaned—one—two—three, and then I looked toward the steps where I thought I heard a creak. There, on the top stair, stood Mr. Tanner.

"C'mere," he whispered.

Oh, help me, God, I said in my mind. Don't let it happen again. I grasped the broom tighter in both hands and looked in his eyes.

"No!" I said.

"Shhh. Not so loud," he cautioned. He squinted and then grabbed a corner of a mattress. He pulled it over to his feet and let it drop.

"Right here," he said, pointing and looking at the center of the mat and then at me. He lifted his hand and made a "come here" gesture.

I stood motionless, staring at him and wanting to scream because I was afraid, so afraid.

"Do as you're told," he hissed, kicking the mattress. Sweat dripped from his forehead. "Get over here and lay down—now!" He reached into his overall pocket and held up a Milky Way.

I remembered the day in the loft when it was hot, and he was heavy, and he hurt me.

"Leave me alone," I said, "or I'll tell Miss Warring what you did to me in the barn."

"She won't believe you," he laughed. "Nobody would ever believe anything an Easley kid said 'cause you're all liars." His voice was getting louder because he was angry, and I wished Mrs. Tanner would hear him. "Now, get the hell over here if you know what's good for you, or I'll give you a licking you'll never forget."

He was walking toward me, and I thought I'd hit him in the mouth with the handle of my broom if he got too close. "You'll be so damn sore, you won't sit down for a week after you get a strappin' from me."

He whispered through clenched teeth, "Who the hell do you think you are? You ain't nothin'." He was in front of me and reached for my arm. I'll show you who's boss, you..."

"Fra-a-ankli-in—Fra-a-ankli-i-i-in," screeched Mrs. Tanner in her highest pitch. "Frankli-i-in, come here."

"Old woman," he said, and pointed his finger at me. "Don't you move, damn you. I'll be back, and you be here!"

I had not moved, not even a twitch, since I had seen him, except to tighten my grip on the broom, but as soon as he was out of sight, I ran to look out the jagged hole of the broken window and watched for him to reach the kitchen door where I saw Mrs. Tanner waiting. When I saw him there, I hurried with my broom down the steps and out the back door. I ran, dragging the broom and thanking God, down the lane to the cornfield. I may have to hit him with this, I thought, so I'll keep it with me. But he didn't come to the field where I stayed until I heard Mrs. Tanner's call for supper. At the table, I pretended there was no such person on earth as Mr. Franklin Tanner.

The next morning, I awoke very wet. I reached to the edge of the bed. "Millie," I said, "feel your side of the bed. Is it wet?"

"Uh, huh," she answered with a whimper.

"Oh, no. We're in trouble again."

"Maybe she won't do anything," said Millie.

"Guess we'd better go tell her. I'll take the top sheet, and you take the bottom," I said.

We dressed and carried our soiled bedclothes into the kitchen.

Mrs. Tanner looked up from the stove where she was stirring oatmeal.

"Take them to the washtubs," she said, "and I'll do them later."

We passed Mr. Tanner coming to breakfast, but he just looked at us and grunted. Then he closed one eye, and screwed up the corner of his mouth. "Both of you, huh? Well, well, now we'll see about this."

I thought he sounded angry, but he had a strange grin when he had said, "Well, we'll see about this."

"Millie, his voice was loud," I said.

"Will he do something to us?" she asked. "He never has."

"Yes, he will do something, at least to me, and I think it will be very bad," I said, remembering his threats from the day before.

When Millie and I walked into the kitchen for breakfast, I heard Mrs. Tanner say, "Are you sure, Franklin?"

"Humph. Just wait and see right after breakfast."

We ate our oatmeal and drank our milk. He had eggs, ham, toast and coffee and was still eating when Millie and I asked to be excused.

"No," he shouted. "You damn little fools, sit right there until I'm through."

This doesn't make sense, I thought. I know he's mad at me about yesterday, but Millie didn't do anything. Why is he mad at her? I had never been so scared. I wished we could run away.

When he had finished his coffee, he told us to follow him, and he led us out to the concrete porch and turned us around to face the door. "Stay there," he shouted and went into the back room. I heard him go in the washroom, and when he came out, he had the razor strap in his hand. "I'm damn tired of you two wetting the damn bed every night. You're gonna get a licking you'll never forget. So bend over and touch your toes, and if you straighten up at any time, you'll get two hard shots instead of one. *Over, over!*" he shouted.

As I was putting my head down, I saw Mrs. Tanner standing in the kitchen doorway watching. She won't let him do this, I thought.

When I was bent over, I knew my cotton underpants showed because my dress was so short, and I didn't want him to see them.

Whack! He hit me so hard I nearly fell. He hit Millie, and she screamed.

"Shut up," he yelled, and I started to cry because I knew he had to be furious to hit Millie so hard.

Whack, whack, whack. I got three hits so hard I thought my skin would fall off, and I screamed, long and loud, so I wouldn't hurt so much. But he didn't care. He kept hitting and hitting, so hard, so terribly hard, and when I raised up because of the pain, he hit me over and over again, one strike after another with as much force as he could. I thought he wanted to kill me, and I truly believed that he would hit me until I fell dead.

Then I heard Mrs. Tanner's voice calling for him to stop. I saw her black shoes as she ran over to him, and as I tried to straighten up, she was pushing him.

"Damn women," he shouted, throwing the strap and walking down the steps and into the driveway.

Go to the barns, I thought. Go far away, and I hope I never have to see you again.

Through the blur of a thousand tears, I saw Mrs. Tanner help Millie into the house. I turned and, barely able to walk, I made my way, one short step after another, to the flower garden. I could not think of sitting down anywhere, so I stood near the garden fence and cried. I had never hurt so badly on my behind and back and legs, and I thought they had to be bleeding. I wondered if Millie was hurting, too, but Mrs. Tanner would take care of my sister and make her feel better. I wondered why she didn't help me.

I was afraid Mr. Tanner would come to find me, so I left the garden. I went into the washroom, closed the door and pushed the lock into place so he couldn't get in. With trembling hands, I washed my face with cold water and suddenly felt very tired, so I carefully lowered my throbbing body to my hands and knees, and then down flat on the cool linoleum floor, and fell asleep.

CHAPTER 26

Bleeding Hearts

Several days passed, and I spent most of my time in the flowers. When I had learned to pull weeds, Mrs. Tanner told me the names of her favorite flowers: petunias, always pink because she liked the color pink; small yellow marigolds because she liked them better than the large ones; and Shasta daisies. My favorite was the bleeding heart. I had picked many of the blossoms and looked for the blood inside during my summers of weeding. Of course, I never saw any, but I knew the little hearts were sad; the name alone told me that, and I understood because I knew what sadness felt like.

On this Friday afternoon, I sat near the spot where the bleeding hearts had sprung up, budded, blossomed, faded, withered and disappeared. But I knew that next spring, the tiny leaves would appear and the plants would grow larger and higher. Long pinkish stems would sprout buds which would swell until a pink heart would hang there with the tiny red droplet beneath it.

A week had gone by since Mr. Tanner whipped Millie and me, and it had been a very strange time. Nobody talked, except Millie and me when we were alone in our bed. During the days, Mrs. Tanner kept Millie in the house with her. I asked my sister why she didn't come out and play with me, and she said Mother wouldn't let her be with me because I'd done too many bad things.

"But, Millie, I've done a lot of good things, too. Do they count?"

"No, I guess not. Maybe all the wrong things were too bad to make the good things good."

The next morning, when Mrs. Tanner came to get us up, she carried a box with her and went to the closet. I saw her take my dresses off the hangers and put them in the box, and I felt a lump in my throat. I was going to cry. I threw off the sheet and blanket, sat on my side of the bed, and lowered my feet to the floor. Then I walked around to the foot of the bed and stopped.

"What are...you...doing?" I asked just above a whisper as the tears rolled down my face.

She sat the box in the closet and walked over to the bed where Millie was sitting up.

"A lot of things have happened while you two have been living here, and I can't take the strain anymore from all the trouble we've had. We think it would be better if we separated you two, and so Franklin and I've decided that you, Mary, should be taken to a new home. We'll keep Millie because she's younger, and we can teach her to behave. I haven't been able to do anything with you. We'll all be happier this way, so both of you get dressed, bring the sheets downstairs, and go wash for breakfast. I'll finish this later, and I'll get a box for you so you can pack your other things."

She left the room, and I was still by the bed crying. I turned to look at Millie who was looking at me. I saw the lines her tears had made on her cheeks.

"Don't cry, Millie. Just be very mad, and you won't cry. That's what I'm going to do. And someday maybe they'll bring you to live with me."

"I won't cry anymore," said Millie, and she jumped out of bed and began dressing.

After the noon meal, I came out of the washroom with my box of books, puzzles, and paper dolls. When I walked into the back room, I heard Mr. and Mrs. Tanner talking.

"It's too bad," said Mrs. Tanner, "that they have to be separated, but if she stays, she'll ruin Millie."

"It's better," said Mr. Tanner. "That Mary is nothing but trouble, and she'll just get worse. Imagine what she'll be when she's older. I feel sorry for the Shays who think they want her. So far, Millie's been a good kid. What is she now, eight? She'll be easy to handle with her big sister out of the way. We won't have to put up with that lying and stealing anymore. I could see she was just wearing you down, Fanny. Some of these kids are just bad, and they'll never be anything else. You mark my words, Mary will be a menace to society, hasn't got a good quality in her as far as I can see. Ah, yes, life'll be lots easier for all of us."

"Millie is a sweet little girl by herself," said Mrs. Tanner, "and I'll enjoy having just one. I'll make her into a real little lady."

I turned and went to the washroom where I thought I'd cry, but I didn't.

"I'm so mad at these people I don't even care," I said, as I slammed the box on the floor. "I suppose that horrible man thinks he's a perfect somebody. I'd like to go out there and sock him in the mouth and then tell his wife what a cow pile he is."

But I knew if I did all that, there'd be no telling what would happen to me, and he would keep on hurting me. I tried to convince myself that I was going to a better place anyway, but when I thought of Millie, the tears started. I was afraid I'd never see Millie again.

Now I know what a bleeding heart feels like, I thought. It hurts all over just like I do. Everything is so mixed up. I don't think I'm half as bad as Mr. Tanner, but I'm the one he says is bad. He can tell everyone what he thinks of me, but I know how bad he is, and nobody can ever know because I'd be called a liar, and he'd be called a good man.

After a minute, I wiped my face on the towel. I'll just be good and mad about this whole thing, I thought, and I won't cry another tear. I'll just think about the wonderful new home where I'll be living and where I'll be very happy.

I went out to the porch where Mr. and Mrs. Tanner were sitting in their chairs, and I walked over and sat on the glider.

"Where's my sister?" I asked.

"She's putting away the dinner dishes," said Mrs. Tanner. But she didn't look at me; she looked at Mr. Tanner.

I don't care, I thought, I don't want to see her old face anyway.

"What's the temperature today, Franklin?" she asked.

"I'd say it's over 90 and humid as hell, and we need..."

A few minutes later, Millie came out of the kitchen and sat with me on the glider. She was putting a dress on a paper doll when I heard Miss Warring's tires grinding on the gravel. I watched as she drove the car slowly around the curve and stopped at the porch steps. Miss Warring got out of her new black car and walked up on the porch.

"Good morning, Miss Warring," said Mr. Tanner, standing and stretching out his hand to her. "Good to see you."

"Good morning," she said. "It's good to see you, but this isn't something I'm happy to do." She looked at Millie and me sitting on the glider. "Are you sure?" she asked, looking down at Mrs. Tanner, who was still sitting in her chair.

"It's best," said Mrs. Tanner rising. "They understand."

I stood up, turned to my sister and said, "Bye, Millie."

"Bye, Mary." She held her doll in her arms close to her, but she didn't look at me. Her lips were pursed and tightly closed, so I knew she was trying not to cry.

I walked to stand beside Miss Warring with my packed toys.

"Oh, here," said Mrs. Tanner, holding up her box for Miss Warring. "These are her clothes."

"Come along, Mary," said Miss Warring, turning and walking toward her car. "We'll get there early so you can get acquainted with everyone before supper."

She put the boxes in the trunk, opened the car door for me to sit in the front seat, closed it, and went around to get in on her side.

I did not look at anyone, or say good-bye to the Tanners, and if they said good-bye, I didn't hear it. When I got in the car, I looked straight ahead out the windshield, and I was glad when Miss Warring drove the car away from the back porch. Inside I hurt more than I ever had, the kind of hurt that just hung there like the sheets on the line. But I knew I couldn't take it down and put it away, not ever, until I'd see my sister again.

CHAPTER 27

Mary's Here!

Miss Warring turned left out of the Tanner's driveway onto the familiar school road that I had walked for more than three years. We drove along the pasture land and past the house where the Great Dane lived. When we were opposite the gravel road going left to school, she turned right and drove over the railroad tracks.

I'll remember every turn, I thought, so I'll know the way back to Millie. If it's not too far, I'll just sneak away from my new home and visit her. She'll be so surprised to see me.

We rode up a hill, and tall thin poplars lined the road. I remembered seeing them another time, when the wind was blowing the trees over so far that I thought they might break. They didn't, though, they stood straight again when the wind let go. I decided to be like the poplars, strong, and that meant not crying, even if I wanted to. I heard Miss Warring talking to me.

"...and they have a little boy of their own and a welfare girl your age," she explained.

"And what are the parents' names?" I asked.

"Gloria and Nathan, and you will like them."

"You said I would like the Pitts and the Tanners, too, but I didn't, and I know they didn't like me. I don't think I'll like these people, either, and I especially won't like them because Millie is not with me."

"Just wait and see, Mary. And maybe, if you had a better attitude, you'd be happier. I think it's a good idea to separate you and Millie for awhile. I think…"

"How can it be a good idea when it makes me so sad?"

"Just wait and see. This is a younger couple, the ages of your own parents, so maybe you'll get along better with them. Will you try to be a good girl for me?"

I wanted to tell Miss Warring that she shouldn't ask me to be good. She should ask the new parents to be good. If they were, I would be.

"There's the house ahead on the left."

"Boy, that didn't take long," I exclaimed. "I won't be too far away from Millie."

I looked at my new home, and it was old. The outside was wood with no paint like the Pitts' house. When we turned into the driveway and drove around to the back of the house, I saw three chicken houses and two large barns, all without paint.

This is not neat looking like the Tanner's house and barns, so maybe I'll like it, I thought. Mrs. Tanner was so fussy, she wanted me to clean, clean, clean.

"Oh, they have a car here that's from far away, and it's a big, fancy car, too, Miss Warring. Maybe we should come back later when they don't have company."

"No, that's all right, Mary. Gloria said her brother, Ralph Blair, and his family would be here from Long Island."

"Oh," I said. I was disappointed, because I knew they'd send me to the back room like Mrs. Tanner did when she had guests. "I guess I'll have to stay in the back room until they leave, won't I?"

"I just don't think so, Mary. Now, stop worrying about everything, and just enjoy yourself. These are very nice people, and I think you'll find them much different than the Tanners."

I knew Miss Warring was trying to make me be nice, but I was so afraid to be in another home with so many people I didn't know. What if nobody liked me? I absolutely did not want to walk up those back porch steps to the kitchen door.

"Come along, Mary," said Miss Warring as she opened my car door. "Everything will be fine. You'll see."

I moved slowly across the seat and put my feet on the ground. Miss Warring took my hand and pulled me up. Then she let my hand go and said to follow her. I heard people talking and laughing in the kitchen. They sounded happy.

"Hi there, Miss Warring," said a cheery voice. "Where's that Mary? Is she hiding? I see her feet," and I heard the lady laugh. I peeked around Miss Warring and looked at my new mother.

Gloria Shay had short, dark curly hair and wore glasses. She wasn't much taller than I was, and she was plump and laughing. I liked her blue-flowered cotton dress with the white buttons down the front and her brown sandals. I looked at her while she and Miss Warring talked there on the porch. Mrs. Shay winked at me.

I guess she's all right, I told myself, but I'll just wait and see.

"So, Mary, are you ready to meet everyone?" asked Miss Warring.

"I guess so," I answered, looking down at my saddle shoes and wishing they were sandals like Mrs. Shay's.

We walked into the room, and Mrs. Shay took my hand and patted it. I looked up at her, and she was smiling and seemed to be twinkling everywhere. I had to smile back at her.

"Mary's here," she said, looking at everyone, and then at me. "And we are delighted to have you with us. Nathan's in the barn and will be back very soon." She swung her arm toward the table. "The man over there is my brother, Ralph, Uncle to you, and beside him is his son, Ralphie."

They grinned and waved at me, and Uncle Ralph said, "Welcome aboard."

"Jane will be here in a minute," said Mrs. Shay. "She went upstairs to put on a dress. She's about your age, so you'll enjoy each other, and Nathan Junior, we call him Gordy, is still taking a nap, and..." Turning, she called out, "Ralph, where's Nila?"

"Oh, I'll get her," he said, pushing his chair back and standing.

Oh, my, I thought. He's the handsomest man I ever saw,

and I looked again at his blue eyes, wavy blond hair, round face, broad shoulders and big smile. I watched him walk around the table and go into the dining room. "Hey, Nila," he called, "come on down. Mary's here." When he walked back into the kitchen and sat again at the table, I stared at him. He looked like a movie star.

Just then, Nila and Jane came into the kitchen together. Jane was a little taller than I and much thinner, but she was laughing when she met me, and I liked her. Nila was short and small, sort of like Mrs. Tanner, but her face and smile were pretty. She had on a seersucker culotte dress and white sandals, and I wished I had an outfit like hers. I was wearing a thin, cotton dress with just underpants and my saddle shoes and socks. That's what I always wore. Sometimes I was afraid people could see through my dress. I wished I could have worn a slip to hide what I didn't want to show.

"So, that's everyone, Mary, except, oh, here comes Nathan now."

The door opened and there stood my new father, Nathan Shay. Tall and thin, with dark curly hair and brown eyes, he was much, much younger than Mr. Tanner. He held out his hand and said at the same time, "Oh, Mary's here." We shook hands. "Glad to meet you, little girl." He winked, first one eye and then the other, and laughed.

"Come over here, Mary," called Ralph, "and sit with me. Right here," he said, patting his legs.

I went quickly to Uncle Ralph and sat right on his lap and had a wonderful, happy time with this new family.

After the supper dishes were finished, I asked Mrs. Shay where my boxes of clothes and books should go.

"If you'd like, Mary, we can go upstairs now, and I'll show you your room," she said.

"I'd like to see it," I said.

She led me through the hallway to the stairs, and turned left at the top. There was my room. We walked in, and I saw a window straight ahead with a green shade and thin, white curtains flipping in the August breeze.

"This is a pretty place," I said as my eyes followed the

yellow striped and flowered wallpaper around the room and back to the white iron twin bed which was covered by a yellow and white seersucker spread. As I looked along the hem of the bed cover, I spotted a chamber pot. Oh, now I won't wet the bed, I thought. I can sit on my pot anytime I want to, because it's my very own. And I already know how to dump it and clean it because I learned that at Mrs. Pitts' house.

Suddenly, I felt so happy, I wanted to talk and laugh and have a good time with everyone in the Shay house.

"Think you can take care of your own room?" asked Mrs. Shay. "Can you keep it pretty like it is now?"

"Oh, yes," I exclaimed, "and may I get my clothes and hang them in the closet over there? And I have books and puzzles. May I bring them up here, too, and put them on the table by the window?"

"Of course, you may. Let's go downstairs and get them. Think you can find your way back to the kitchen?"

"Yes, I can. I'm used to a big house, and I like this one."

"Oh my, I almost forgot," said Mrs. Shay. "I have to show you where the toilet is. Forgot all about that most important detail."

I followed Mrs. Shay through a door at the back of the kitchen.

"Out here's the woodshed," she said. "Could be a garage, but we use it for other things. Got a dirt floor, so it's a storage place," she continued, as we walked to the tiny house. "Here 'tis. Our lovely bathroom!" She pushed the door open, and I saw two familiar looking boards over the seating places.

I thought an outhouse in the house was funny, but I liked the idea because it meant I didn't have to walk down a dark path. I knew I could pull the string like Mrs. Shay had done, and a light would shine.

When we were in the kitchen again, Uncle Ralph told me to come and sit with him. He put his arm around me and said, "We like you, Mary, and you'll like us, too, I bet." I thought about the little kittens I had hugged and wondered if they had felt like I did now, all warm and happy. I thought that if I had been a kitten, I'd be purring.

The only thing that would have made everything perfect in my new home would have been to have my little sister with me. But I knew that Mr. and Mrs. Tanner liked Millie very much, and they didn't like me. But these people made me feel very special. It was a brand new feeling. Yes, Mary's here, I thought, and she's glad to be here!

CHAPTER 28

The Shay's Mary

The first night in my own bedroom I found to be a little bit scary, a little bit nice, and a lot lonely. I'd always been in a room with my sister. The first night without her, I missed her so much. I thought about her in that big bed at the Tanners, and I felt like crying, but I didn't want to cry. Crying made me hurt too much inside, and it wouldn't bring Millie to me. No, I decided I wasn't going to cry. Instead I would think about this new home and how nice the people seemed, especially Uncle Ralph. I closed my eyes and saw the image of his face, and then I felt a cool breeze and opened my eyes to see the sheer curtains moving slowly like a lacy cloud. I had put the shade all the way up so there'd be more moonlight in my room, and I wouldn't be afraid of the dark.

And then, in the stillness of the room, I could almost hear Millie talking to me, telling me good night. Oh, how I wished she were right beside me, and how I wished Miss Warring would bring her to this house to live with me. I couldn't help it, the hurt came inside me, and the tears rolled down the sides of my face as I cried quietly. I didn't want these people I'd just met to hear me and think I was a baby. After awhile, I got out of bed and went to the window where I knelt on my knees and looked out through the screen. Everything was different: my room, the house, the barns, the trees, the people. I could see up the road to the neighbor's house, and I heard a dog bark.

Otherwise, the night was quiet. Even the breeze was silent as it pushed the curtains across my face, as if to wipe my tears. But I was all right and ready to crawl into bed. I felt tired and I wanted to sleep in my own special room that Mrs. Shay had decorated just for me.

I lay on the cool white sheets and ran my fingers over the crinkles of the seersucker spread.

"Oh, my gosh!" I said, and sat up in bed. "What if I wet this bed! Oh, no, I just can't do that. There'd be my sheets hanging outside somewhere for Uncle Ralph to see, and Ralphie, and Mr. Shay. I'll have to stay awake all night, so I won't mess up this bed!"

I propped my pillow and sat up.

"The pot, yes, the pot, it's right here," I said as I hung over the side and pulled the white vessel out onto the small braided rug. "I'll keep my hand right here on the rim, and that will remind me in the night to get out of bed when I have to go."

I looked at the window and out at the dark sky with the bright moon. I remembered Miss Curtis in Sunday school had told us that God would never leave us. I thought it must be true, but I hoped He'd never leave Millie, either. I whispered, "Dear God, take care of Millie and thank you for my new home. Amen." I watched the curtain go this way and that way, back and forth and back and forth....

I awoke suddenly when a rooster crowed right outside my window. I had never heard such a noise. My hands moved quickly over my sheets.

"Hooray, they're dry," I whispered, and I leaned over to look into the pot. It was empty. "And I didn't even have to go after all! Thank you, rooster, for waking me early."

I jumped out of bed, put on my clothes, pushed the pot back under my bed, and tiptoed downstairs so I could get to the toilet before anyone else got up. Then, I went into the backyard where some of the young chickens were pecking at the ground. I heard strange noises above me, and when I looked up, I saw some of the bigger chickens in the trees. That was a sight, and a funny one that made me laugh.

"Birds are supposed to be up there," I said to one fat white hen, "not you."

"Hey there, Mary, what are you doing up?"

It was Mr. Shay, standing in the door of the milk house with a shiny silver pail.

"I just woke up," I said, "and I like being outdoors early in the morning. What are you doing?"

"Milking these cows. Why don't you come down here and talk to me?" he asked.

"No, I better not," I said. "Mrs. Tanner said girls shouldn't go to the barn."

"Okay, suit yourself," he said, and walked back to his cows.

"Why, Mary, it's so early. What are you doing out of bed?"

I turned around and saw Mrs. Shay inside the screen door.

"I like to be outside early," I said. "It's a happy time."

"Want to help me with breakfast?"

"Sure." I turned away from the chickens and went in the house where I set the table for eight. "What a lot of people eating here! There were just four at the Tanners."

"Yep. The more the merrier, I always say," said Mrs. Shay.

"What should I call you and Mr. Shay?" I asked, putting the last spoon at my place.

"I like to be called 'Mama', and he can be 'Daddy'", she said.

"I guess Jane calls you Mama and Daddy, huh?"

"Yes, we were Mama and Daddy when she was young, and we are now, too." She chuckled and continued, "And, you know, we're used to it, and if you changed our names, we wouldn't know us."

I laughed, too, when she said that, and to me, her laughter was a very happy sound, like she wanted me around.

"Well, Mama," I said, trying out the name, "what may I do now to help?"

"There's not much else until everyone comes to eat. Then, you can help put the food on the table. Why don't you go to the barn with Daddy and see the cows?"

"You mean, I can go to the barn, and you don't care?"

"Of course you can. You can go anywhere you want in the

house or outdoors, as long as you stay close to home. We have over a hundred acres, so that should be enough space for you, shouldn't it?" And her special laugh rolled out of her mouth and around the room.

"Oh, boy, I can't believe I can go to the barn any old time I want to," I said, hurrying out the door and straight to my new freedom.

"Well, you did come to see me, huh?" said Mr. Shay. "Have you ever seen the cows milked? Here's a stool for you, move it along as we go down the line."

"I bet I could milk," I said. "It doesn't look like it's hard."

"Nope, not hard if you know how," laughed Mr. Shay. "You just keep watching, you'll learn a lot of things."

Mr. Tanner had said those words to me, and I didn't like to hear them from Mr. Shay. But I looked at his face, and I thought he was a good man who would not do the bad things to me that Mr. Tanner had done.

My new daddy went on milking his cows and saying, "Damn you, get off my foot," or "Damn you, move over, you stubborn old mule." I just listened and watched and felt sure that I could milk, too. I liked the smells of fresh milk and hay, and I didn't even mind the smell of the gutter. It was part of a barn. I heard a "meow, meeoow" by the outside door and there stood a snow white cat. I couldn't believe it, another Snowball!

"Hey, Daddy, what's that cat's name?" I asked.

"Oh, I call it Fluff," he said. "Won't hurt you."

"C'mere, Fluff," I coaxed. "Come and see me." I talked in my itsy bitsy voice and knelt so I wouldn't frighten it. I stroked the soft fur. "I can't believe you're here," I whispered. "You are my Snowball, aren't you?"

I turned to Mr. Shay. "I'm calling him Snowball," I said. "Is that all right?"

"Yep, but it ain't a him, it's a her."

"Doesn't matter," I said. "Snowball fits either boy or girl."

When the milking was finished, we walked to the house and went in for breakfast. Mr. Shay and I had to wash our hands at the pump in the high sink. I didn't like that because it looked just like the one in Mrs. Pitts' kitchen, and that made me think of what she did to Millie. I felt sad, but Uncle Ralph walked in the room as I turned from the sink, and he winked at me, so I didn't feel sad anymore.

Then it was breakfast time with all of us around the table. Ralphie sat on one side of me and Jane on the other, but I hardly knew they were there because Uncle Ralph sat across from me, and I gazed at him all through the meal of juice, bacon, eggs, toast and milk.

The next few days were wonderful. We took the Blairs to town shopping, and we went to the amusement park where I rode on the merry-go-round, the ferris wheel, and the bumping cars, all with Uncle Ralph. We went to the lake where everyone but me went swimming. Even though Daddy and Uncle Ralph tried to teach me, I was afraid of the water and didn't think it was that important to swim. During the evenings, we played card games, and I had never heard so much laughing and teasing. This was a new kind of life for me, and I was beginning to like it!

At the end of the week everyone was sad to see the Blairs leave. Even though Ralphie said he'd write me letters and I said I'd write back, I wasn't thrilled at all. I was in love with Uncle Ralph, and I was brokenhearted thinking I'd never see him again. On the Sunday morning when they were saying the good-byes, he asked me for a hug. He shouldn't have. I put my arms around his neck and told him I'd never let him go because I wanted him to stay forever. Mama finally, and very sternly, said for me to let Ralph go.

"But I'll never see him again," I whined, taking my arms away and letting them drop at my sides.

"You don't know that," she said. "He'll probably be back up here in a couple years. Long Island isn't that far away."

"Don't worry, little girl," said Uncle Ralph as he got into his shiny white convertible, "we'll see you again."

He started the engine, called good-bye and waved as he backed the car out of the driveway.

"I hate good-byes," I snapped, and walked down the yard, scaring the chickens and making them run every which way. I went into the barn to find Snowball, and I stayed with her until it was time for dinner, the noon meal. I thought I'd better go help Mama. It sure seemed strange to call her what a baby doll says, "Mmma-ma". But "Mother" didn't fit her. She was too happy and jolly.

"Mama, could I help get dinner?" I asked, bounding up the steps and through the kitchen door.

"Yes, as soon as you wash your hands. Can you peel potatoes?"

"Sure I can if you show me," I said.

So I learned to peel potatoes, and she left them just as I'd done them, even though they had spots of skin here and there that I'd missed. I was afraid she'd yell at me for not getting every spot clean, but she just cut them into quarters, put water in the pan and placed it on the large wood stove which made the kitchen very warm on the hot August day.

After Jane and I dried the dinner dishes, I asked her if she liked to read, or play Old Maid, put puzzles together, or be outside.

"I don't like outside much," she said. "It's too hot in summer and too cold in winter. I don't care about reading, and I'm not very good in school, either. I like puzzles and Old Maid, though."

"Well, I like to read," I said. "I've read all of the Bobbsey Twin books, and Old Mother West Wind Stories, and I'd read more if I had the books."

"What grade you in?" Jane asked.

"Why did you have to ask me that?" I asked angrily.

"What's the matter. I didn't do anything to you?" she whined.

Mama turned to look at us, her hands dripping water and suds.

"Jane, don't say anymore. Why don't you go see what Gordy is doing. He's in the side yard at the swing. He should take a nap, so see if you can get him. You're good with him. Read him a story."

"All right. I'm glad to get away from that grouchy Mary, anyway."

Jane threw her dish cloth on the table and pounded her sneakers on the linoleum floor as she left the room.

Mama dried her hands, leaving dishes in the sink and asked me to follow her to the dining room where we'd have a "nice little talk".

"You want to tell me about school?" she asked after we sat down.

I looked into her face and saw a faint smile, and even though I was embarrassed to tell her that I'd failed fifth grade, I wasn't afraid to tell her. I just didn't feel like talking about it, and I guess she got tired of waiting for me to speak.

"Mary, your teacher here in Shadwell is Mrs. Keller. I have talked with her about you and so has Miss Warring. Mrs. Keller said she will give you a couple of tests a few days before school starts, and she'll decide what grade is right for you. You don't have to worry about a thing, because I don't believe you'll have to repeat fifth grade. But I'll tell Jane not to mention it again to you, and she'll understand. Here she comes with Gordy. Look how good she is with him."

The two walked through the dining room into Gordy's room. I could see that he liked Jane very much.

I decided that, in many ways, this was a very happy home.

Mrs. Keller gave me the tests on the Friday before school started. The reading, spelling, arithmetic and handwriting tests were easy for me. She asked questions about the history of New York and the Erie Canal, and the mountain ranges and rivers of Europe and South America. I knew most of the answers, and she said I'd learned a few things, and then she laughed.

"You'll do very well in sixth grade, Mary."

I wanted to hug her and tell her I'd do just fine in her school, but I didn't know her, so I just said, "Thank you."

She reminded me of Mrs. Shiner: young, pretty, and nice. I knew school would be fun with Mrs. Keller, and I was thrilled to be in sixth grade. I'd be one of the "older kids" and it felt good to think about being a big kid instead of a little one.

I couldn't wait to get home and tell Mama she was right. I wouldn't have to repeat fifth grade! I hurried out of the small white building and onto the gravel road. Down I ran to the four corners of Shadwell Center, turned right, and ran from the Grange Hall to my big wooden home. I skipped up the steps of the back porch and into the kitchen, where I saw Mama at the stove, stirring with a wooden spoon.

"I smell butterscotch pudding!" I shouted. "And guess what! I don't have to repeat. Imagine that! I don't have to repeat fifth grade. I'm going right into sixth. Isn't that wonderful news? I'm so happy, and I like Mrs. Keller a lot, and I like the schoolhouse and the playground and the tall flag pole by the front door. Isn't everything wonderful? I laughed and twirled around in my cotton dress and saddle shoes. Isn't everything wonderful?"

"Yes, it is, Mary," said Mama, still stirring the pudding, "and so are you."

CHAPTER 29

Mrs. Keller's School

Shadwell Center's School No. 5 in Gallaway, New York, was the greatest in the county, I thought, and Mrs. Keller was the perfect teacher. I quickly learned that she didn't have "favorites" and cared very much for each of her students. We were given jobs to do around the small, white schoolhouse. The boys were to bring in the wood for the round black stove at the back of the room during cold weather. They were to rake the school yard in fall, mow the grass in warm weather, keep the weeds out of the playground and trim the low branches of the trees so we wouldn't get hurt running into them while playing. The girls kept the coatrooms neat, swept the floor, washed windows and dusted the desks and tables. On the first day of school each year, Mrs. Keller assigned the very special and honorary duty of flag bearer to a student of her choice. She emphasized the importance of respect to our flag and loyalty to the duty assigned. I heard her call the name of Ellen Thompson, the seventh grader, as flag bearer for the year 1944–1945. I hoped that the next year, or the next, she would call my name.

This country school, the same as the last, had eight grades, and Mrs. Keller taught all twelve of the students.

Mrs. Keller told us that everybody helps in her school.

"When you finish all your lessons, you look around and see if you can help the younger students. You may help in any subject in which you've earned an eighty-five or better," she said. "But help only if you're needed. We must allow students to try to solve their own problems. If you aren't sure how to help with a certain problem, ask me. We will have plenty to do in this little school, both in work and in play."

I was there for almost two months before I had a disagreement with my teacher. On that particular day, she helped me realize that if I took time to think, and was not afraid to work hard, I could do what seemed impossible.

I'd been having trouble with long division, so she had asked me to do some problems on the board where she could watch me.

I walked reluctantly to the blackboard and wrote the numbers of the first problem, quite aware that many eyes were upon me. I carefully worked the problem through to its end, and with that I gained confidence. I quickly wrote the next problem and worked it through to its end. Then, number by number, I wrote the last and most difficult problem on the board. However, the more numbers I wrote in the divisor, the more prickly I felt.

I'll never get this one, and she knows it, I thought. I felt more and more frustrated as I studied all those digits. I panicked.

"Oh," I shouted angrily, "I hate this. I can't do it and you know it!" I slammed the chalk down into its tray and looked pleadingly at Mrs. Keller, who was teaching a younger child at the back of the room.

My teacher looked at me and spoke calmly but firmly.

"I know you can do it, Mary, so you stand right where you are and work the problem until you get the correct answer. Then you may go back to your desk."

I looked away from her and back at the board. I was angry and embarrassed to have been reprimanded when the other kids were watching. They were always watching everything in a one-room school. I felt my face getting hot, and thoughts were spinning in my head.

I just won't do this. I can't, anyway, so I won't, I told myself. She can't make me, either. I'll show her. I'll stand here all day.

And so I stood, it seemed, for hours looking at the black space before me with numbers everywhere.

Reason slowly replaced anger. I reached down and picked up the chalk. Think, I said to myself. She knows I can do it. I have to try.

As the minutes passed, I wrote the quotient numbers carefully into their proper places as I worked the problem to its conclusion. It came out even, so I knew it was right and I directed a big smile at the answer. I put the white chalk quietly into the wooden tray, closed my book, turned and walked slowly to my desk. I was very pleased, and goose bumps replaced the prickles I had felt earlier.

Now I know I can do just about anything if I want to, I thought, especially if I try really hard.

Another day, I was helping Jeanie Myers with her reading, and Mrs. Keller told me to let Jeanie read alone.

"But I like helping her," I argued.

"I want her to read alone," said our teacher.

I went to my desk and took out my book, *Little Women*, and slammed it on my desk.

She makes me so mad, I fumed to myself. I'm not helping anyone ever again. She'll be sorry for this. I can't do anything right in this old school.

I turned to page fifty-five and began reading so I wouldn't be so mad and make my stomach hurt. Recess came, and we went outside and played. I organized a great game of tag, and everyone giggled and shouted as they ran to and from each other taking turns being 'it'. I was always the organizer and the umpire for the games, and I made sure that everyone had equal chances. Nobody was left out or picked on. I remembered how horrible it felt to be the underdog at Mrs. Hardison's school, and I vowed it wouldn't happen on this playground if I could help it. I truly cared about every student, and I felt like their mother because I was the biggest. Ellen was the oldest, but she was my best friend, so she didn't care if I was in charge.

The day proceeded as usual, and at four o'clock, Mrs. Keller said we were dismissed. We put our books away and left the school. I didn't say good-bye to Mrs. Keller because I was still mad at her.

Maybe tomorrow I won't say good morning, either, I thought.

She's not going to boss me around like that. All my grades are in the nineties, and I know I can help anybody in that room. I bet I could even help my friend, Ellen, who's in seventh grade!

And so the days went by, and I didn't say hello or good-bye to Mrs. Keller. Finally, after a week of my obstinance, she asked me to stay after school.

"After school?" I asked.

"Yes, please, Mary," was all she said in her firm, kind voice.

When the students left their desks, they glanced back at me as they walked from the room. I thought about getting up and running out the back door, so I wouldn't have to hear what I knew had to be said to me. But I knew Mama and Daddy wouldn't like that, and I'd have all the adults mad at me. So I sat and waited, with prickles on my back, sweat on my face, knots in my stomach and twinges in my bottom.

I kept my eyes on Mrs. Keller as she came back into the room and sat in Ellen's desk beside me. She told me quietly and earnestly about authority figures and rules and regulations, about laws and enforcement, about obeying and rebelling, and about pleasant and mean dispositions. I knew what applied to me, and I felt like crying. She was one of my favorite people in my life, and I saw disappointment in her eyes and heard it in her soft voice.

"I'm so distressed with your attitude," she said. "You may leave now, and I hope tomorrow will be a better day for both of us."

She looked away from me, sighed, and rose from Ellen's desk, and her high heels tapped on the wood floor behind me. I felt so heavy when I moved from my seat, and I couldn't think of what to say. I didn't think "I'm sorry" was enough, but I looked at her and said it anyway.

She said, "Thank you," in her sweet voice and smiled, and I walked with head down out the door, wondering how I could face her tomorrow.

The next week, we got our report cards, and I knew mine was good. I quickly opened it and saw not a mark below ninety.

I'm really smart, I thought, probably the best in this school, and I felt so big and very important, proud as I could be. I'll probably be somebody great someday, I thought. Maybe I'll be a movie star!

I leaned to my right and whispered, "What'd you get, Ellen?"

"All ninety-threes and above," she said.

"Oh..h, g...ood," I stammered and looked back at my card.

"How about you?" she asked.

"Uhh—nineties," I mumbled.

"Good for you," she said. "You must have worked hard to figure out that long division, huh?"

"Yeah, I guessso. Did everybody in here get nineties?"

"Doesn't matter," said Ellen.

"No whispering, please," said Mrs. Keller.

As I looked back at my marks that didn't look so great after all, I wondered why Ellen would say it didn't matter. I turned the card to its back, and Mrs. Keller's handwriting said, "I'm happy to have Mary in school. She's a good student..."

Good? I'm better than just good, I thought.

"...but she needs to work on controlling her temper and her sulky moods."

Sulky? She doesn't like me at all, I pouted. I can tell. What's sulky? I've never even heard of that word.

I continued reading her comment. "She's a leader on the playground and a great asset to our school."

Well, that's a little better, but I don't have a temper and I'm not sulky, I told myself. I can't help it if *you* make me mad, and where did you get this fancy word, sulky, anyway.

I closed the report card and put it inside my *Little Women* book where I wouldn't have to look at it anymore. I am very distressed about this report, Mrs. Keller, I said to myself.

"....leave now, and do have a happy weekend with no home-work. Next week, we'll get ready for Halloween, and the week after that, we'll begin our lessons and decorations for Thanks-giving. Busy and happy times are approaching. I'm excited about them," she said.

I stood up, turned and smiled at Mrs. Keller. I said good-bye and have a nice time, even though I wanted to stick out my tongue at her.

When I walked into the afternoon sunshine, I saw that Jane had run on ahead of me with Jeanie and Joe Myers. She liked being with younger kids, and I didn't care because I didn't want to talk to anyone. I kicked a small stone and wondered how I could not have a temper and what the word sulky meant. I turned right onto the macadam road.

"I know what it means," I said to the stone as I gave it another kick. "It means you don't talk to somebody and you act like you're mad at them. Heck, that's what Mama does to me and to her husband after he yells at her a lot. I'd say they have tempers, and I'd say they sulk, too. Humph—I'm not the only one, so there, old stone, take that kick, too."

I wish Millie were here with me, I thought, so I could talk to her. What would she say about all this? I stopped walking and kicking, and I could hear Millie's voice.

"You know, Mary, that Mrs. Keller talked with you about all those 'portant things like rules and obeying and disposition. You have to try to be good, that's all."

And I talked to Millie. "You're right, little sister. I'll try to be good, that's all."

And this time when I said I'd try to be good, I really wanted to. Maybe it was because I suddenly remembered one of Miss Curtis' lessons: "...and if God never leaves us, we can let our conscience be our guide. Sometimes that's all we need to help us do right."

When I got home, I showed Mama my report card, and she said she was proud of me.

"But what about 'temper' and 'sulky'?" I asked.

"You can fix those," she said. "You're in the best school around. Let's go fix supper. Potatoes need peeling. How 'bout it?"

"Sure, I'll do it," I said. "And I won't leave one speck this time!"

CHAPTER 30

Sisters

When Jane knew I was sad about Mrs. Keller's comments on my report card, she tried to make me feel better.

"You want to see a bad report card?" she asked. "Look at mine, but don't tell anybody that you saw it." We were up in her room, and she took the card from under her pillow. "I put it under here, and every night, I ask God to take away those low grades, but He doesn't," she explained.

"God can't do that, Jane," I said. "He can only help you work hard and do better next time."

"How do you know that?"

"I went to Sunday school when I lived at the Tanners, and I learned a lot about the Bible and what God can do. Let me see your report card."

She handed it to me. I opened it and saw seventy in arithmetic and reading, but I saw eighty-five in handwriting and geography and ninety in science.

"This doesn't make sense," I said. "How could you get seventy in reading and eighty-five in geography? You have to read it to know it."

"But I like learning about other countries and how people live," she said. "It's just hard to read things that aren't interesting, like those paragraphs in the reading book. I have to answer questions that I don't understand."

"What does Mrs. Keller tell you?"

"She says I should think when I read. I don't know what to do. I hate school, and I always have. I like to be home taking care of Gordy and cooking and cleaning. I want to get married and have babies."

"I guess we want different things," I said. "We aren't much alike, are we?"

"No, but I like you, Mary. You're nice, and I'm glad to have a sister."

"Uh, uh, I'm not your sister. I'm Millie's sister, but I guess you and I can be 'welfare sisters'."

"That's right," said Jane.

"How about coming outside with me," I said, "and we'll practice jumping the barnyard gate."

"Oooooo, no," squealed Jane. "I hate smelly old barnyards. How do you stand it?"

"It's not bad. There are cow piles in there, and you know, Jane, Daddy takes all that out in the manure spreader, sprays it on the fields, and makes the corn and cabbage grow bigger."

"Yowee! You mean they grow in manure, and we're eating manure food? Oh, I'm gonna be sick."

"Quit being such a baby," I said. "It's the way it's supposed to be when you live on a farm. I'm going out and jump the fence. Wanna come with me?"

"No, I'll stay inside and help bake a pie for supper. Besides, it's too cold out, and it might snow."

"Boy, that's what I like, snow and more snow!" I said. "Are you sure you won't come with me?"

"I will, but just for a few minutes, because I get so cold I can't stand it."

"You must be sick," I said.

When we got to the barnyard, Jane thought she'd throw up from the smell, but I told her it would make her strong, so she stayed for an hour and we got pretty good at jumping. I showed her how to put her hands on the lower boards and raise her legs up and over the top board.

When Jane left, I kept running faster and faster up to the fence and hurtling myself over until I thought I was pretty good. My hands got cold because I couldn't grab the fence board very well in mittens, so I went into the horse barn to get warm.

"Hey, Polly," I called. "You in here?" I heard a whinny and walked over to her stall. I was afraid she'd kick me if I walked in behind her, so I stayed far back and talked to the large, white draft horse. I thought she was a real beauty, and I wished many times that I could climb on her back and ride her across the fields. But Daddy had told me she wasn't for riding, just for working.

Teddy R. was in the stall beside her, but he was just a quiet, old, brown workhorse compared to Polly. He was pretty nice, and I wasn't afraid to walk in his stall anytime. I just said, "Teddy R., I'm here," patted his rump and walked right in. But Dad—I felt like a baby calling him "Daddy" so I decided I'd call him "Dad"—told me that Polly was temperamental and I shouldn't go barging into her stall.

"She'll kick the daylights out of you, if she's in a bad mood," he said. But, I still loved her and daydreamed about getting in the saddle and going up and down the road. I wanted to take her to school and give the little ones a ride.

"Marreee. Come to supper." That was Mama. I liked her voice, even when she was calling so loud I could hear her across the field. She never made me feel afraid, and neither did Dad.

I do like living in this place, I thought, and I wonder if they'd let Millie live here, too. Think I'll ask.

"We've looked into that," said Mama, "but Mrs. Tanner wants Millie with her, and we've been told that Millie is happy, so there's nothing we can do."

"Well, I know Millie's not happy there, because I wasn't, and I know she'd be better with me," I argued. I wanted to say that Mr. Tanner did bad things to me, and I was afraid he'd hurt Millie the same way. But I thought Mama would think it was my fault or think that I was lying, so I didn't tell her, and I knew I'd never tell anyone.

"Mary, look at me," said Mama, and I looked through her glasses into her brown eyes.

"There's nothing we can do," she repeated, and then she turned, opened the oven and looked at the beef roast and potatoes.

Suddenly, I felt hungry and couldn't wait to have supper.

"Jane, did you bake a pie?" I asked.

"Yessiree, I did, and I'm not telling you what kind. But I will tell you it's your favorite!"

"Mmm, boy, cherry pie!"

"Is that your only favorite?" asked Jane.

"No."

"Well, then, you don't know what I baked," she said, putting her nose in the air, and turning into the dining room with a stack of plates for the table.

Supper never tasted better, I thought, as I scooped up a second helping of the beef, potatoes, peas, applesauce and bread and butter. When it was time for dessert, I thought I couldn't eat another bite, but that cherry pie smelled so delicious, I couldn't resist.

"Mmm, boy, Jane, you are a good cook," I said. "Can you show me how to make this?"

"Anytime," she said proudly. "It's so easy you won't believe it."

Later that night, I was in my room reading and decided it was time to get to the toilet and go to bed. As I reached the door to the back room, Jane ran up behind me.

"I'm first," she shouted. "I was heading there first, so get out of my way. I have to go real bad."

"Too bad," I said, feeling grouchy because I had just read in my *Little Women* book that Beth died.

Jane waited outside, sputtering about me being a mean person, so I took my good old time and pinched her arm when I passed her. A welfare sister truly was quite different than a real sister. I would never have pinched Millie.

"I would have pinched you back," Jane shouted, "but I have to go too bad. And I won't show you how to bake pies, either."

In my room, I closed the door and sat on my bed, and in a few minutes I heard Jane come up the stairs and slam her bedroom door.

I looked down at my book, which I had tossed on the yellow bedspread. "I hate you," I said, and threw it across the room. I undressed, put on my pajamas, and pulled the light string. Then I crawled into my bed between the flannel sheets and covered myself with the warm quilts. I quietly thought about how angry I had felt toward Jane. And it really wasn't her fault that I was so mean. It was the story that made me feel that way.

It was just too sad, I thought, and I sat up and looked at the window for moonlight, but there was none. My mind returned to the March family. They lost little Beth, I thought, and I've lost my sister. When would I ever see her again? Tears filled my eyes and spilled down my face. I cried for a long time, not for the sister in a story that was written years ago, but for the most special sister in the world who belonged to me.

CHAPTER 31

Holidays

At school, we decorated for Halloween with black cats and witches, orange pumpkins, black spiders and webs. All of them were cut out of construction paper or colored on white paper. We wrote poems, and we had a party with orange frosted cookies and root beer. We made costumes at home and wore them all day in school. I was a ghost, and Jane was a farmer wearing overalls and a straw hat. Ellen was a witch, with a black dress and hat and red lipstick streaks on her face. She had three teeth blackened so they looked like they were missing. She danced around the room carrying her broom and screeching, "I'm going to bake you in my oven."

Mrs. Keller came to school dressed like Mother Goose, and we chose her for the winner of the best costume contest. She said there wasn't any winner.

"You all look wonderful to me," she said, "so, honk, honk, honk!"

With Halloween over, Mrs. Keller said we'd have to go "double duty" on our lessons for two weeks, and then we'd discuss our plans for Thanksgiving and Christmas.

We agreed that recess and noon hour could be shortened by five or ten minutes so we could stay on the schedule Mrs. Keller had planned. Our little schoolhouse was quiet as we worked earnestly to meet our deadlines, and the only incentive we had, or needed, was the happy anticipation of holiday activities.

Finally, the day came when we heard Mrs. Keller say, "Now, let's talk about our plans for Thanksgiving. Would you like to put on a short play about the Pilgrims and Indians, or would you rather just decorate and save the plays for Christmas?"

"Yes, save the plays for Christmas," we said, "and we'll just fix up our school for Thanksgiving."

We took down the Halloween work and put up Thanksgiving things. Joey brought stalks of corn, and we put them in three corners of the room with several pumpkins. Ellen and I drew and painted a large cornucopia on ten sheets of construction paper taped together, and we put that on the front wall.

"That's our mural for the season," said Mrs. Keller, and we were very proud of it.

But, to me, the best holidays were my birthday and Christmas, and they had never been so wonderful as they were with Mrs. Keller and the Shays.

Mama Shay told me that my birthday was December fifth, and it happened to be Ellen's birthday, too. So her mother and my mama had a surprise birthday party for us with a cake and eleven candles that we blew out together. We each got lots of cards from the kids in school and Mrs. Keller, and our mothers gave us a scrapbook to hold the cards. Everybody sang first to Ellen and then to me, and that was the first time anyone had ever sung to me. Tears came to my eyes because I was so happy, but I swallowed ten times so I wouldn't cry.

Later that night, though, when Mama and I were finishing the supper dishes, I told her that I'd never gotten a card or a present or a cake for my birthday.

"Thank you, Mama, for this very good day."

"It was fun, wasn't it? And you deserved the celebration."

"So did Ellen," I said. "She's my best friend."

"She's very quiet," said Mama, "and that's good for you."

"But we can't be alike, can we?"

"No, we can't. We have to be ourselves, whoever that is," said Mama laughing.

"Is your school doing anything for Christmas?"

"Oh, yes, we are. There'll be a program on our last day before Christmas vacation, and I'm in two of the plays. The audience will get to sing Christmas carols with us. It's so much fun doing all these things, and Mrs. Keller is the best teacher in the world. I really think that's true."

"Dad and I know her very well, and we think she's the best. Not only is she a great teacher, she's a fine person."

I said goodnight and went to my room to work on my penmanship. Mrs. Keller had said I was getting a little sloppy with my writing, and it seemed pretty dumb to me to get a bad mark in that since it didn't take much of a brain to write well, just "attention and patience," as she had explained.

The next couple weeks at school were the busiest ever. We used up a tall stack of multicolored construction paper making Santas, elves, reindeer, manger scene and tree decorations. One afternoon when our lessons were finished, we went into the woods behind the school and cut down a small pine tree. We put it in a stand by the front window, and when the tree was decorated, we played records of our favorite carols. I thought that our school had to be the most festive in the land.

Mrs. Keller gave us our parts for several short plays that we would perform. I had to be a an old woman, who was bent over, wore glasses on her nose, walked with a cane and talked with crackles in her voice.

In another skit, I had to be "Miss Suitem" at the Bureau of Christmas Information.

There were three other plays and enough parts so that every kid had to learn lines. We did pretty well with them, but it helped to know that on the night of our performance, Mrs. Keller would stay behind the curtain and prompt us if we needed her.

That night finally arrived, and we thoroughly enjoyed showing off on the stage. I loved being the old woman and making people laugh. With my cane tapping, I hobbled across the floor, talking to myself. I had great difficulty, first, in finding my rocking chair, and then, in trying to sit without falling. And the more the audience laughed, the more I exaggerated my lack of agility. I liked hearing the applause and at the end of my act, I humbly bowed and smiled several times.

I hoped Dad and Mama were proud of me. They were there

with Gordy, and even though they weren't my real family, it could have been true because I certainly felt like their kid. Sometimes I wished I could have been, but only if Millie could have been, too.

At home, Jane and I helped Mama bake for the Christmas dinner. She made plum pudding a week before, put the soft mound in a muslin bag and hung it in the back room to cure.

Then, she told us she would invite the Shusters to eat with us on Christmas Eve.

Jane and I were delighted, because the Shusters had two welfare girls named Helen and Sarah Carson, and a boy and girl of their own.

What a time we had! We four girls played in the snow until supper was ready, and after we ate, we played Old Maid and Authors. There was no arguing among us on that special night, when we declared that we'd always be the best of friends.

"I have an idea," I shouted. "Let's ask Mama if we can go sledding in the dark."

"Hey, let's," said Helen, and we hurried to get permission.

"Not in the road, only in the fields," we were told. "Cars may not stop quickly enough, and you'd get run over."

We found the perfect field behind the Shuster's house and stayed out in the clear, cold moonlit night until we were called in at ten-thirty. By then, we were ready to say good-bye to each other, get into our warm beds, and think about Christmas Day.

I'd never had such a perfect Christmas morning! I got three presents, along with a stocking stuffed with fruit, nuts, gum, and Hershey bars. I opened one present, and it was a blue cardigan. The next was a plaid skirt to go with the sweater, and the third was the most beautiful doll, with a cloth body and porcelain head. I cried when I saw her dressed up in a long, blue dress with a green velvet cloak and black button shoes. I sat and stared at her through my tears, and I couldn't even say thank you for awhile. I looked at her dark curls and her blue eyes that opened and closed.

Her name will be Millie, I thought, as I held her up close on my shoulder, and I will love her always, very, very much.

"Thank you," I whispered, as I looked at Mama. "I love her."

And then I felt very sad when I thought about Millie, who would not get a pretty doll like this.

I looked at Mama and Dad sitting in their chairs by the tree. "Why can't Millie live here with me? Then she'd have a beautiful doll."

"Millie is happy with the Tanners, Mary," said Mama. "Don't talk about it anymore."

"I won't," I promised, but in my heart I knew I'd live with my sister someday, somehow. I'd make it happen, because I didn't like being away from her. Someday, I thought, I won't have to miss her because I'll be with her. I'll say my prayers every night and ask God to let us live together, and I know He will.

I hugged my new doll closer to me while the rest of the family oooed and ahhhed about their gifts.

"So come on, Mary," I heard Mama say, "I need some help in the kitchen with our Christmas dinner."

Christmas afternoon, I went sledding alone. While I was out in a pasture, a black and white collie dog came running up to me, and I was so scared I screamed. And when I did that, he sat down in front of me. I looked at him, and he looked at me, but I didn't dare move.

"Where'd you come from?" I said, barely above a whisper. He lay down in the snow with his paws out in front of him and kept looking at me. He turned his head a little to the side.

"What's your name?" I asked, feeling a little braver.

"Arf, arf," he answered.

"That's no name," I said, smiling at him. I held out my hand. "Come here."

He got up and walked toward me with his head down. I wasn't afraid anymore, so I reached out and patted his head, and he came alive. He jumped and barked and let his tongue hang out. He rolled in the snow and jumped all around me. I chased him and he ran, and then he chased me. I sat down and he came and sat beside me, so I put my arm around his neck, which was covered with long white hair.

"You look just like Lassie," I said, "but she's brown and white, and you're black and white." I stood up and pulled my sled behind me, and by my side was my new friend. When I got to the house, I dashed up the steps and into the kitchen.

"Hey, Dad," I called. "Look at this." I ran into the dining room where everyone was sitting. "There's a collie out here!" I shouted excitedly. "Come and see."

"OhmyGod," said Mama. "Can't be Shep! He's been gone for months!"

"Shep," I said. "He's a collie, not a shepherd."

Dad followed me to the kitchen door and looked out. "Yep, it's Shep all right." He opened the door and called, "Hey, Shep, whatcha doin', old boy? Didja come home, huh?"

Shep wagged and jumped all around, barking and yipping, and when Dad went out to him, the dog licked his hands and face and jumped around like he was crazy. Dad hugged him and told him he was an awful traitor for running away.

"This is my old dog, Shep, and there's not a better one in the county!" Dad told me.

"How old is he?" I asked, thinking he must be ancient.

"Oh, I'd say about three. Been gone for six months, but I guess somebody took good care of him."

Even though Dad had said it was his old dog, I think Shep liked me better than anybody. We were pals, and where I went around the farm, he went. I wanted him to sleep in my room, but he was allowed only in the kitchen and had to stay by the boarded-up back door. I didn't like to see him so confined inside, but I couldn't argue about rules that were made years ago. But on that Christmas Day, I thought Shep was almost as good a present as my Millie doll.

CHAPTER 32

Brown Eggs and Buttermilk

It seemed to me that the winter days dragged by, and I couldn't think of enough things to do to keep busy. So one day after school, I asked Mama if I could go to the barn and watch Dad milk the cows.

"Of course you can," she said. "Maybe he'll find something for you to do. He needs some help with the chores, and I'll just bet..."

I didn't need to hear anymore. I headed for the barn.

My first task in the cow barn was to clean the cows' udders so Dad wouldn't get dirt in the milk pail. I wanted to milk those cows in the worst way, but Dad said I was too young. How silly, I was eleven and getting bigger every day.

"But you could carry the pails to the milkhouse," he said.

"Well, don't fill them too full," I cautioned, standing behind Jessie, the only Jersey and my favorite cow. She turned her head to look at me when I called her name, so I walked up to her and put my arms around her neck. "You're the sweetest one," I whispered, so Dad wouldn't hear me and think I was foolish for loving a cow.

After a couple weeks of helping in the barn, I began taking care of the chickens, too. I happened to get home from school early one day, so I quickly changed into my dungarees, flannel shirt, pea coat and boots and ran to look for Dad. I found him in the granary filling two pails with chicken mash.

"Can I help with the chickens?" I asked excitedly.

"You can follow me and see how I do it," he said, and we left the building and walked to the largest hen house.

"Be quiet when you open the door," he cautioned. "You don't want to scare the chickens any more than necessary. Move slowly and quietly when you're anywhere near the hen houses. It's not good for them to get excited and go flying around."

"I'll just sing low," I said.

When he opened the door, and we walked inside, I lost my breath. "Whew, it stinks so bad."

"You'll get used to it," he said. "Here, hold this other pail so they won't eat from it. We'll take it to the next house. I already took care of the Rhode Island Reds in the small house."

"Oh, no," I said, "I like the red chickens the best. They're pretty. These white ones are ugly. What kind are they?"

"Leghorns, and they're the best layers."

I walked with him to the nests along the wall.

"Do they peck you?"

"Naw, you gotta be quicker than they are. They know if they peck me, I'll whack them across the room!"

I reached gingerly into a couple nests where the hens were sitting, and they didn't bother me, so I wasn't afraid anymore.

If they get sassy with me, I'll whack them, too, I thought.

As Dad was putting the latch on the outside door, he asked me if I thought I could take care of the hen houses for him.

"Sure," I answered. "I know everything to do."

"And when spring comes, you can clean them," he said. "I'll sell the hens and get new batches of chicks."

"Oh, boy, I can't wait to see all those babies. And you clean the chicken houses?"

"Yep, all three. I'll show you how, and it can be your job."

I walked behind him, placing my booted feet in the snow where his feet had been. And when he said, "It can be your job," I put my head up and moved my shoulders back and forth like he did when he walked.

Oh, wow, I thought, I'm a real farmer myself. I must be pretty important around here if I can help with milking and take care of all the chickens, too!

"Here, take these baskets of eggs up to the house, and then come back here and help me."

I hurried away. "Here are some eggs," I shouted, bursting into the kitchen.

"Thanks," said Mama, taking the baskets. "I see he separated the brown from the white. Good, I hate them mixed."

"Brown eggs are prettier, aren't they?" I said. "And I'd rather eat brown eggs. Are they more nutritious than the white ones?"

"I don't think there's any difference in food value, but the yolks might be a little darker yellow," said Mama.

"I just wish all the hens were Reds," I said, before I left.

I heard Mama say, "Brrrr, it's cold," before the door slammed behind me. And, instead of traveling the shoveled driveway, I ran through the banks of snow beyond the porch to get to the barn faster.

When the milking was finished, Dad handed me a half-full pail. He picked up two full ones, and we carried them to the house.

"Why are we saving these?" I asked.

"For drinking, and what's left after that is for butter."

"Butter! Wow!"

I followed him into the pantry where he lifted his pail almost over his head and poured the milk into a shiny metal bowl on a tall machine.

"What is this huge contraption?"

"It's a milk separator; separates the cream from the milk. We make butter with the cream. Keep some of it for ourselves and sell the rest."

"Are you going to make butter now?"

"No, Mama does that. She puts the cream in the electric churn. You watch next time, and you'll learn."

Late that night, on my way to the outhouse, I heard Mama and Dad arguing in their bedroom.

"I love kids. Why do you have to be so mean?"

"Don't need anymore, so just shut up and go to sleep."

She cried, and I hurried on so I wouldn't have to hear her crying and him cussing. He's mean to make her so sad, I thought.

The next morning when Jane and I came down to breakfast,

Mama had bacon, eggs, toast and milk on the table for us. Gordy was at his place eating a soft-fried egg on toast.

"Are these brown eggs, Mama?" I asked.

"Yes, they're always what I serve for breakfast. They make a plate look pretty, don't they?"

"I'll bet I could tell a brown one from a white one by the taste," I boasted.

Just then, Dad came in from the milking. He hung his coveralls on the pantry coat hooks, put on his good suede jacket and plaid hat, and went back outside without saying a word. I heard the Chevy engine start and the tires spin on the frozen snow.

"Where's he going?" I asked.

"Shh," said Jane, and whispered, "I'll tell you later."

"I wanna go in car wif Daddy," said Gordy.

"You can't go today," said Jane. "Maybe next time."

Later in the morning, when Jane and I were sledding, I asked her what happened to Mama and Dad.

"They fight bad," she said. "They've been good for a long time, though, probably 'cause you're here, and now they're mad at each other. They won't speak for several days, and then they'll be all right."

"He was awful mad," I said. "I heard them yelling when I went to the toilet last night, and Mama cried."

"He gets furious at Mama. She wants another baby, and he doesn't," explained Jane. "Every Saturday, he goes to town and drinks and comes back about milking time drunk as can be, and cussing about everything."

"Why doesn't Mama tell him not to drink?" I asked.

"Nobody tells Dad Shay what to do or what not to do. He can be mean sometimes, and I feel afraid of him, but he's good most of the time. When they're mad, though, don't talk. It will make them worse."

"I won't say a word," I promised. "Now, let's try the hill at the Shuster's. This one's no good."

When we reached the Shuster's field, Sarah and Helen were there, so we stayed until dinner time and asked them to come to our house for the afternoon.

But I didn't get to be with them because Mama made butter, and I wanted to watch. She poured the cream into a wooden churn.

"This one's electric, the lazy woman's way to make butter. I'll get it started, and you get a book to read and sit near it. When you hear it thumping, you'll know that the butter is made. Call me, and you and I will have some delicious, fresh buttermilk."

I followed instructions, and as I waited for the thumping, I began to think it would never happen. Round and round went the churn, and I could hear the liquid slushing against the wood. After reading several chapters of my book, I heard the long-awaited thumps and ran for Mama.

She was right about the buttermilk. I liked it better than fresh cow's milk, and I couldn't wait for the next churning.

By five o'clock, milking time, Dad hadn't come home, so I went to the barn, cleaned all the cows, and got the pails off the nails in the milkhouse. I placed my milking stool beside Jessie and began pulling on her teats, very gently. She turned to look at me with her large brown eyes and shook her head, losing part of her mouthful of hay.

"Whatsamatter, girl, think I can't milk you? Hhmph! You just wait. I'll show you!"

I squeezed the teats, right hand on the back one, left on the front one. Not much milk came out, so I squeezed harder and pulled down at the same time and more milk came out.

Hmm, I thought, it's like marching—left, right, left, right—except it's faster. I've got it! I'm actually milking!

"Oh, Jessie," I said excitedly, "you're such a nice girl. You helped me do this, didn't you? Here we go now, faster and faster, squeeze, pull, squeeze, pull."

I finished Jessie and went to the small Guernsey, the first one in the row of twelve. The only one that worried me was the nervous Holstein at the end. I hoped Dad would be here before I got to Spotty.

Cow number eight was Mildred, the largest Guernsey, and I had a pail half full of her milk when I heard Dad coming through the milkhouse singing, "For He's a Jolly Good Fellow."

He walked into the barn and shouted, "What the hell d'ya think yer doin'?"

As I knew it would, a stream of cursing followed. He scared me so with all his racket, I wanted to get away from him. But I wasn't going to leave because I had most of the work finished. I knew I had done nothing bad, but I felt that he had. I kept milking the big Guernsey, and remembering what Jane had told me, I didn't say a word.

He grabbed his milking stool and pail and went to Spotty.

Oh, boy, I thought, the poor cow will probably get whacked all over the place if she kicks him.

"Move over, ol' fool," he snarled. "Kick an' I'll break yer neck."

I guess Spotty was good, because I didn't hear him hitting her. Even though he sounded awful mean, like he could almost kill somebody, I wasn't afraid of him.

If he hurts the animals, I thought, I'll yell at him, and I won't care if he does hit me, he can't kill me.

When we went in to supper, he didn't say anything. He just ate and went to his bedroom. Mama talked to us like nothing had happened, and we three played rummy after Gordy went to bed.

On Saturday morning, the Mackinack Poultry Company truck came into the driveway and two crates, twenty-four dozen eggs each, were carried from our pantry to the truck. And several of the neighbors stopped by and bought five pounds of Mama's butter.

CHAPTER 33

Tantrums

The season of snow and work and wonderful play went on through April, 1945. I loved that winter of fox and geese and snow fort battles at school, of sledding and snow caves at home, and then farm chores and evening games of Old Maid, Rook, checkers and jigsaw puzzles. But beneath the fun and laughter, I felt an undercurrent of uneasiness at home.

Something will go *bang*, I thought, and then we'll have a free-for-all, and we'll beat up on each other until we're black and blue.

Talk of the war went on endlessly, both at school and at home. I didn't mind to hear Mrs. Keller talk because she was teaching history. But when Mama and Dad talked, they argued.

"Roosevelt doesn't know what the hell he's doing," Dad would shout.

"He's a good president," Mama would say. "I believe in him, and he will get us through."

"A lot you know," he'd say.

"I know as much as you. You've never been there."

"Oh, so you're throwing that in my face again, huh?"

Dad would spiel a line of loud cursing, barely taking a breath.

Mama would be quiet then and go back to reading or darning.

Jane and I didn't agree very often, either. She cheated when she played Old Maid and got mad if I beat her at checkers, which I did most of the time. Her problem was that she didn't take time to think about the moves. She just plunked the marbles any old place. But when I tried to help her, she got mad at me and told me I was a "know-it-all" and that ended the game.

As winter and the war went on, Mrs. Keller told us that President Roosevelt's health was failing.

"His Yalta trip in February was hard on him," she said. "But maybe with rest and care, he'll get stronger."

I was frightened when I heard that our President was sick. Who would take care of our people? I imagined the battles taking place in America.

We'll probably just all die, I reasoned, with no president. But we do have Vice President Harry Truman. I suppose he'll know what to do.

And that's what happened. On April 12, 1945, President Franklin Delano Roosevelt died of a brain hemorrhage, and Harry S. Truman became the thirty-third President of the United States. I hoped that the Shays would both like him and the way he ran the country so they wouldn't fight anymore. I saw President Truman's picture in the *Life* magazine Mrs. Keller brought to school, and he looked like a nice grandpa.

On May 7, Germany surrendered, and the war ended in Europe. We called it V-E Day. Truman was getting results and I felt encouraged about what he would do to make the Japanese surrender.

School was out in June, and I learned there were many things to do on the farm, including pulling weeds in the bean and cabbage fields. But before I did weeds, I had to clean chicken houses. And what an experience that was!

Dad had sold all the chickens and had cleaned the small houses, but he saved the big one for me.

"Why do I get the big one?" I asked.

"When you get in there to clean, you'll know why," he answered. "There's more breathing room. Here, you need this pitchfork, and I'll carry the shovel and broom."

"And you're going to show me, aren't you?" I asked, taking the fork. I was excited about doing something new.

"C'mon," he said. "I don't have much time. I have to plow."

The door and window of the hen house were open when we entered.

I hurried back out groaning. "Whew, I can't stand it in there. What's that terrible smell?"

"Won't hurt you, it's just ammonia."

"Why'd you put ammonia in there? I can't even breathe."

"Oh, you dummy. I didn't put it in there. It's from the chickens. They don't have a private bathroom, you know. Never mind, get in here and get busy. I need this building ready now. Got too many chicks in the little houses. I'll check later to see how you're doing."

Holding tight to the fork, I walked into the stinking place, which was a most difficult thing for me to do. But I couldn't argue with a man who might whack me with my own pitchfork. So, plunging it into the mess near my feet, I filled the fork, lifted it and dumped it in the waiting wheelbarrow. Thank goodness there was straw mixed with all that stuff, because it made it easier to get a good forkful. After two more quick dumps into the wheelbarrow, I went outside to breathe.

I continued in the same manner, pitch, pitch, go out and breathe, until I had cleaned the floor with the fork. Then I used the shovel to get what I'd missed, and last, I had to sweep to get what the shovel missed. I made fewer trips outside as my work progressed because the strength of the ammonia lessened. Eventually, I was going out only to empty the wheelbarrow in the manure pile behind the pigpen. It was difficult for me to decide which smelled worse, the pigpen or the chicken house. I decided it was the first because ammonia was stifling, while the pig odor was sickening.

I was greatly relieved when the dreadful task was finished, and I was proud of myself for staying with the job until it was done. Of course, to be honest with myself, I knew I had no choice but to finish. Dad would have stood over me, yelling and cussing, until I followed his orders. It was better to suffer through the experience without him. And now, the chicken house was perfect for the baby chicks, and the thought of those sweet, yellow fluff balls made me smile.

Dad seemed pleased with my work because he told me I could do all three chicken houses next year.

I had a retort, but kept it in my mind, because it wouldn't have been worth the price for being sassy.

The summer went on, and Mama and Dad listened closely to the radio every night at suppertime. We usually didn't have the radio on at mealtime, but things were happening with the war, and they seemed excited. I didn't care about listening to it, so when I finished eating, I excused myself and walked to the screen door.

"Can I come with you?" asked Jane.

"No," I said. "I want to play with Shep."

"You're a goof," shouted Jane.

"What's going on?" asked Mama.

"I don't want her with me," I said. "She's a pest." I stood on the porch beside Shep for a minute to hear what Mama would say.

"You stay here, Jane. I need help with the dishes."

"C'mon, Shep," I called. "Let's go look at the cabbages."

We ran to the field behind the cow barn. The plants were growing and so were the weeds. I knew what I'd be doing for the next couple weeks, since we had three fields of cabbage. That's how summer was: weeds, weeds, weeds. That's why I liked winter best.

The hotter the weather, the more Jane and I argued, and sometimes I hated her. She was a crybaby and just plain dumb. I didn't want to be anywhere near her. And one hot summer day in August, she pushed me too far.

I had been working all morning in the cabbage field on those ugly old weeds. My hands hurt from pulling the rough stems, and my face was beet red from the sun. I was so tired of weeds, I could have screamed. When Mama called, "Dinner, dinner," from the back porch, I ran to the house, delighted for the reprieve from the dirt and sun. I went into the kitchen and stopped at the sink, where I pumped water into the enamel basin and put my aching fingers into the coolness. Jane came and stood beside me, and when I reached for the Ivory soap, she stuck her hands into the basin. I ignored her presence and sudsed the dirt from my hands, rinsing them thoroughly around her hands. I took the towel from its hook and was drying my hands, when she grabbed the towel from me and snapped my legs with it.

That was it! She was asking for it! My face got hot, and it wasn't from the sun! I decided to take care of her this time!

"You dumb fool," I shouted, as I snatched the towel from her and snapped her legs quickly three times.

"Ouch, Mama, Mama, help me!" she screamed. "She hit me, she hit me. Mama!"

"Ya big baby," I yelled. "Cry for your Mama, I don't care."

Into the room came Mama on the run. "What's going on here, Mary?"

"I had the towel first," I shouted.

"She hit me, she hit me. Look at my legs," cried Jane. "Look at...all...the red marks. She did it."

I saw Mama glance at Jane's legs, and then she whirled around with her hand ready to swat me in the face, but instead she said, "Go to your room!"

"Go to my room?" I shouted. "She took the towel away from *me* and hit *me* first."

"Go to your room. Don't talk back. Go! Now!"

I saw her face turn redder and redder, but I didn't care what she did to me. The whole thing was unfair.

"All right," I screamed, "I'll go to my room, but it wasn't my fault. She's a dope, and I hate her, and you always take her side. She's a big, dopey crybaby."

I stomped through the kitchen and dining room, shouting as loud as I could, and when I reached the hall door, I opened it, went through and slammed it with all my might. I stomped through the hallway and up each step of the stairway, hoping Mama would hear how outraged I was and understand.

When I reached my room, I sat on my bed and sputtered at the great injustice that had just befallen me. I hated that Jane, and wished she'd go somewhere else to live.

I listened and heard a door slam, and then I heard

footsteps in the hall, and stomp, stomp, stomp, coming up the stairs. It was Mama. She was heavy and made a lot of noise when she walked the steps. She wasn't moving very fast, so maybe she wasn't too angry.

She came into my room with a yardstick in her hand. She had never hit me, so I was shocked. She came and stood before me, and looking into my eyes, she said, "Are...you...ever... going...to slam the door like that again?"

I did not answer, so she slapped the yardstick across my legs just below the hem of my shorts.

"Are you?" she asked.

I did not answer. She hit my legs again and they stung.

"Answer me," she said, holding the yardstick over me.

I said nothing, and I got a harder hit.

"I'm going to hit harder and harder until you answer."

Hit me forever, I thought, I'll never answer. And I looked at the red stripes on my tanned legs. I was proud of the marks, they were proof that I was pretty darn tough.

She struck again and again until my legs hurt so badly I couldn't stand it. I began to cry, and I answered, "No." She turned and walked out of the room.

She called me at six o'clock for supper, and I wondered how Dad had done the milking without me.

During supper, we heard on the radio that the Japanese had surrendered. World War II, for America, had begun December 7, 1941, and now it was Wednesday, August 14, 1945. It had consumed our thinking, our lives, and our very being, and now it was over! We shouted, "Hooray, it's over, it's over," and we were happy. But, it seemed to me that wartime had been fearful and dreadful, and I thought we should have been crying for those years of killing.

The shouts of joy continued in our house, and in a matter of five minutes, Helen and Sarah and Dot and Hank, carrying their little ones, came through our kitchen door cheering. We kids joined hands and skipped around in a circle. What a celebration we were having.

"Mary," said Mama. "You go to the toilet and go to your room for the night."

I was shocked! "The war is over," I pleaded. "Can't I..."

"Not another word. To your room, now!" she ordered.

It can't be true, I thought, as I went slowly through the kitchen and dining room. Without a sound I went to my room. I sat on my bed, wishing that she'd come to me and say, "It's all right. You may go out and play with the others."

But she didn't do that. I heard them outside playing ball and hide and seek, and I cried. And I wondered where God was. Had He left me because I had been bad? I didn't think so, because I felt that He'd be on my side and knew that Jane had provoked me when I had worked so hard all day in the hot sun. I told God I was sorry if I'd done something wrong. "And now, please help me," I pleaded.

Still feeling angry, I pulled the sheets and blankets off my bed. But I knew that wasn't the right thing to do, so I made my bed. After awhile, I sat on the floor beside the open screened window and called out to Helen. "I wish I could be there with all of you."

"So do I," she said. "What happened, anyway, Mary?"

Jane jumped in front of Helen. "You better get out of that window, Mary, and stop talking to us or I'll tell Mama."

I didn't feel like saying a word to Jane, and I knew if I didn't leave them alone, I'd be in double trouble, so I lay down on my bed and thought about the end of the war and me.

America's troubles were over, but mine were just beginning again. Mama and Dad would never like me. I just knew it. I thought I'd probably have to go live with someone else, but I didn't want to because I liked Mrs. Keller and my school friends. And I liked living with the Shays, too, except for Jane.

I felt sleepy. And since I wasn't happy right at the moment living with the Shays, I daydreamed about living in another home that God would help me find, somewhere with my sister.

CHAPTER 34

1946

What a year it was! I had turned twelve on December 5, 1945, and my world zoomed from a child's to an adult's. I could feel myself maturing by taking life more seriously at home and at school. I didn't think on childish things like paper dolls, easy jigsaw puzzles, and the Bobbsey twins. The only exception was the doll I had received the previous year. Millie wasn't a childish toy; she was a symbol of hope. The doll stayed on my bed with her head on my pillow. And every night, I picked her up and held her tight while I said my prayers, asking God to let Millie and me live together again.

I was in seventh grade at school, and my attitude had changed. I knew that I'd have to take lessons seriously if I wanted to amount to anything. If I worked just a little harder, I thought maybe I could make all A's with a B thrown in now and then. Math was the true challenge, but I liked it, especially when I'd struggle with a problem and then come up with the right answer. I loved seeing red check marks on my papers instead of a big red X. Pride became a nice, warm feeling, but one that I kept to myself. It wasn't nice to brag, I knew that. I didn't like to hear it coming from my mouth or anybody else's. That may have been because Mrs. Keller had given the class a lecture on the subject.

"Before you speak, stop and think," she had said, "about how you will make the other person feel." Yes, I was certainly growing up and learning important things about the adult world.

As the days of 1946 passed, my horizons widened and my life took on a new direction, all because of a wonderful experience. It wasn't the secondhand victory bike I got for Christmas, although that was a milestone. The bike could have been the high point, but my excitement about it diminished when Mama said the bicycle was mine for as long as I lived with them. I knew that the length of my stay with them would depend on Millie and where she lived. So, the ultimate happening that changed my life was the day Mama took me to see the movie *National Velvet!*

It was a rainy day in April. After Mama and I had finished the dinner dishes, and Jane had gone to take a nap because she felt sick to her stomach, Mama said to me, "Well, young lady, how would you like to see a movie?"

"A movie? Uh, oh, yes," I exclaimed, with dignity. After all, she had referred to me as young lady. And I knew I was.

"Where will we go? To the big city, Rochelle, or where?"

"To the theater on Main Street in Gallaway, our own little town," she said. "I'll ask Dad to take care of Gordy, so you and I can go."

When we arrived at the theater, where I'd never been, the usher told us we were a little late, and he'd have to show us in. As he led us to our seats near the back of the room, I heard the actors' voices, and I couldn't wait to sit down and watch. And once I sat, my eyes were focused straight ahead. I became the pretty black-haired girl who loved The Pie. The girl fainted, and everyone took care of her, so much attention. I couldn't imagine myself in that situation, where everyone would stand around looking down at me, making me the center of the family. That was nice, but I was too strong to faint like that.

I watched as Elizabeth Taylor cut off her long black hair so she could ride The Pie in the big race. It was all right with me that she cut it off because she looked better with short hair, like me.

When the movie ended, Mama said we'd stay and see the beginning, since we'd missed that part. We waited while the title and list of characters were shown, and then there was the girl again. But wait! Elizabeth Taylor had long hair now! How could that be? Ten minutes ago it was short. I sat watching and thinking. She was up there walking around the big stage with long hair, when ten minutes ago, she had cut it all off. I had been on the stage, too, at school, so I knew what it was like. But, hair just didn't grow that fast. I wanted to whisper and ask Mama how they did that trick. But, remembering what Mrs. Keller had said, that we should think before we talk, I didn't ask Mama about the hair. We watched more and more of the story, and then I knew! Those people were not on a huge stage. They were in a picture that went on and on, not like a photograph that I could hold in my hand, but like lots of photographs all joined together and shown one right after another very quickly. So, I deduced, no matter how many times we saw this story, it would always look the same. I was a little sad when I realized how a "movie" worked because I had thought beautiful Elizabeth Taylor was with us in real life.

Later, on the way home, Mama asked me how I'd liked the movie, and I said, "Just fine, thank you, and now I'd like to have a horse."

"A horse? You just got a bicycle for Christmas. Isn't that enough?"

"No. It's not really mine. It's yours. But I want a horse of my very own so I can love it and ride it just like Elizabeth Taylor loved her horse."

"I'm sorry," said Mama, "but I don't think your horse dream will ever come true."

We drove on in silence. Maybe Mama said something to me, but I didn't hear her. I was daydreaming about my own horse. Mine was white, like Polly, but her name was Winter, and I could ride her. And she and I were in my movie, but it wasn't about racing; it was about friendship. We were together, day after day, riding across the fields and down the cow lanes. She nuzzled me with her soft nose and ate sugar cubes from my hand. In the pasture, when she saw me coming to her fence, she ran to me and whinnied softly, a special hello just for me. When I walked in her stall in the barn, she turned her head around and shook it just a little, joking with me, as if to say,

"You here again?" I patted her rear and moved my hand along her belly and up her neck. Then I rubbed her nose, and she blew out through her mouth and gave that lip roll sound. Oh, how I loved my white horse, Winter, and she loved me.

Not only did I want a horse named Winter, I wanted to be an actress like Elizabeth Taylor. I knew I could faint like she did, and I could get all teary-eyed and cry if I had to. Tears came easy to my eyes if I thought about something sad or felt sorry for myself.

So, I practiced my fainting, not because I was weak and prissy, but just for the sake of acting. I remembered the scenes in *National Velvet.*

One hot, miserable summer day, I was throwing some grain to the chickens in the backyard when I felt a faint coming on. "Oh," I said, pretending everything was going around. "Oh." Staggering about, I dropped my grain bucket and raised my arm slowly and placed the back of my right hand on my forehead. "Oh," I groaned softly, and down I went, dramatically sprawling limply on the ground. I remained very still, eyes closed. I'd done a great job. It was a true, dead faint. But wait a minute. I felt something wet on my neck and the back of my head. I bolted upright and then stood up. Cautiously, I placed my hand on the back of my head. Chicken doo! Oh, how awful, how stinky. I hurried to the watering trough in the barnyard and dunked my head, hoping Dad wouldn't come around to see what I was doing and why!

I didn't do much thinking before my acting exercise, I decided. Now, I had a new rule in my adulthood. Think before you speak and think before you act!

Acting practice behind me, I went to supper that night and heard Dad say he wanted to raise more cabbage for more money.

"I'll need everyone's help to pull seedlings, so we're all going to Orange County tomorrow night. The neighbors, Dot, Hank, Helen and Sarah are going, too."

Tomorrow night came. The racks were placed on the back of the pickup, and the truck bed was almost full of kids. Dot and Hank brought their three nephews, Micky, Murray, and Butch, who was fourteen. All four of us girls were immediately

in love with Butch, but he talked to Sarah, so we knew he was
in love with her. Helen, Jane, and I didn't care about boys, and
Micky and Murray didn't care about girls, so we could all be
friends and just be ourselves. Shirley and Butch were looking
at each other and giggling, and their faces were red. I felt
embarrassed watching the two of them not being themselves.

Riding in the back of the old truck was too noisy for talking but just right for singing. We sang everything we could
remember, with the wind blowing some of the words back down
our throats.

Our whole gang was energized enough to get hundreds of
plants pulled well before dark. They were rolled carefully in
papers and placed at the back end of the truck, so we could
stand up near the cab and sing our way back home.

Early the next morning, I found myself on the right side of
the cabbage planter with Mama on the left. Our job was to get
a seedling into the planting row with each click of the planter.
The seats were nearly dragging on the ground, so it was easy to
whisk the tiny plants into the soil. It was great fun for me, but
as time went on, I became bothered by Dad, who was shouting
and cussing at Polly. She was moving too fast, and we were
missing places. Dad didn't want a space wasted, so the faster
Polly walked, the angrier he got, and when Polly heard him
shouting, she walked even faster. I was getting nervous. I remembered when Dad had lost his temper with me and hit me
with the milking hose. I wondered what he would do to poor
Polly, the sweetest horse I'd ever known.

Polly began prancing side to side, frightened by the noise.
Dad pulled the reins to stop her, jumped off the high seat of the
planter, and went to the apple tree where he broke off a branch.
All the time, he was yelling and cussing. His noise and actions
frightened me so badly that I couldn't say a word. And Mama
said nothing.

He ran over beside Polly and began hitting her over and
over again with the tree branch. I knew the feeling of a beating, so I began to cry for Polly, but I was still afraid to say
anything. The poor horse whinnied and pranced in her harness.
I couldn't stand it anymore. I didn't care if he hit me or what

he did to me. Polly couldn't save herself, and I could help her.

Off the planter I jumped and ran toward Dad. "Stop hitting her," I screamed.

Mama grabbed me by my shirt. "Get back over here with me," she shouted, and pulled me to the planter seat. "Sit down and be quiet. You'll be sorry if you interfere. He has to train the horse to walk slowly."

I sat with my head down and covered my ears so I wouldn't have to hear anything. In a couple minutes, Mama poked me with her elbow, so I uncovered my ears and looked up. Dad was getting back on his seat, and Polly moved slowly down the line. The planting was finished early in the afternoon, and Mama and I left the field to clean up.

The pain of seeing the horse beating, I knew, would never leave me, and I told Mama, without thinking first, that I would never help plant cabbage again. All she said was, "All right." What I didn't tell her was that I didn't think I'd ever forgive her husband, and even though I'd have to call him Dad, he would never again be "Dad" to me.

And so, after that day, while Mama and Dot planted cabbage with Dad, and because I wasn't needed anywhere in the house or outside, I went bike riding during the afternoons. And they were some of the best times I ever had. I rode over the familiar country roads, and when I got tired, I stopped to rest under a shade tree where I looked up to find faces in the slow-moving clouds.

When I passed mailboxes with familiar names, I'd stop and talk with the folks in the yard, and I made lots of friends.

In September, I went to my one-room country schoolhouse, and even though I was proud to be an eighth-grader, I missed my best friend, Ellen, who was now a freshman in the city high school.

In December, I was thirteen and a teenager, totally grown up as far as I was concerned. It seemed to me that Mrs. Keller had taught me so much, I probably knew about everything there was to know.

The 1946–47 school year ended, and I couldn't wait for high school to begin.

CHAPTER 35

New Horizons

High School—what a world! The ride on the bus was a thrill. The school building seemed huge compared to the one-room schoolhouses I had attended. Meeting many new teachers was a contrast to meeting one. A teacher for each subject, what an easy job they had having to learn just one thing and then teach it all their lives, so I thought. I decided I wouldn't want a job like that, I wanted to know everything!

I couldn't wait to get home with my books and show Mama. She said I'd be pretty busy for the next four years.

My days in high school were total pleasure. I did well in my classes and enjoyed new friends. When we had class elections, I became secretary of the freshman class, and I was happy to be so well-liked.

But, I wanted Millie to know about these days in high school—the new friends, the cute boys, the interesting subjects and nice teachers. And I wanted to tell her about the clothes these kids were wearing. I wanted some so I'd look like everybody else. That's what I'd tell Millie, I decided.

We had seen each other once in three years, and I still missed her. In fact, the missing became worse with these new, exciting days. I wanted to share them with the person I loved most.

The only reason we had seen each other was because I begged Mama, and I wrote letter after letter to Millie and Mrs.

Tanner. The Christmas of 1945, I got a letter from Mrs. Tanner.

What a letter! No mention of my coming for a visit, which meant it would not be all right since she said my sister was sick. She said she didn't remember my birthday, so that wasn't any different than when I lived with her.

After more letters between Christmas and Easter, Mrs. Tanner finally agreed to allow Millie to come to my house. Mr. Tanner would bring her and come to get her at the end of the day. The thought of seeing Mr. Tanner made my stomach churn, and I never stopped worrying about what he might be doing to Millie.

But it wasn't something I could mention to anyone, because I feared I'd be in a terrible mess with the adult world. They'd think me a liar if the terrible truth ever passed my lips, I thought, and then my life would be nothing, because nobody on earth would ever believe another word I said. I'd probably be called the Lying Louse of Gallaway County, and I really wouldn't be that at all. Everyone who called me that would be a liar. It was a terrible situation, and I had to save myself from it by keeping my mouth shut.

The day Millie came for a visit was one I'd never forget. I waited in the driveway, and when I saw the Tanner car, I cried. Millie jumped out and we squealed, hugged each other, and cried. I didn't even see the car because I was so close to Millie and my eyes were full of tears.

And when we stopped being sad, because we were so happy, we walked to my Shay walnut tree and sat under it so we could talk and no one would hear us. We talked about school, mothers, clothes, housework and barn work. But most of all, we talked about missing each other and wanting to be together.

"What can we do?" Millie asked, pulling on the stem of a buttercup.

"I don't know," I said, "but I'll think of something."

I looked at my sister holding the buttercup under her chin. "Do you like butter, Millie? The buttercup doesn't say you do."

"Of course I like butter, but where will we live, Mary?"

"Well, I don't want to live with the old Tanners, and the Shays don't want another kid, so maybe we could find another mother."

"Where will she be?"

"Millie, in this big world, there has to be another mother for us, and I'll find her, and we'll be together there. Just remember that and say it every night. And I'll probably even ask God to help me find the place for you and me," I said, standing up and reaching for Millie's hand. "And you could ask God to help us, too."

"I'll do it," said Millie, "just like this: God, help us live together again. Amen."

"That's right, Millie, and if we both pray, it will make our prayers stronger. I pray every night, either at my window where I can see the sky or in my bed, before I sleep."

"I prayed for you to come and see me, Mary, but you didn't."

"That's because Mrs. Tanner didn't want me with you, but we're together now, so your prayer was answered."

"What will we do now, Mary?"

"C'mon, let's go ride the bicycle."

"Me? Mary, I never rode a bicycle."

"Well, don't worry. I'll show you how, and I'm the best teacher you could have 'cause I'm about the best bike rider."

The lesson went well, I thought, but Millie didn't. She was riding down the gravel lane when the front wheel began to wiggle from side to side. Millie fell off and I ran, fast as lightning, to help her because I saw blood on her knee and hands and even her face. My stomach was sick and I felt awful seeing my sister hurt. She was crying as she crawled into the grass. I reached out to help her stand.

"Oh, Millie, it's all my fault. I'm so sorry. Can you walk? Let me help you. Oh, I hate that bicycle for hurting you. It's all my fault."

"No, Mary. It's not your fault. I just couldn't ride."

I helped Millie to the house and into the kitchen, where I got a cold cloth and held it on her cuts. I called for Mama to come and help. She came from her nap and took over the first-aid work.

When we went outside, my sister had gauze with Mercuro-chrome on the side of her left leg and knee, both palms and her forehead. She looked like an Indian with war paint, but I didn't laugh because I knew she was hurting. As I walked beside her holding her arm, she hobbled to the front porch and we decided to sit and color, if she could hold a crayon in her injured right hand. I was glad she stopped crying, but she said she'd fallen lots of times and had bandages just about everywhere, so I should not worry about her. Nevertheless, I babied her the rest of the afternoon and watched every move she made.

We had supper together and then waited in the driveway for the Tanner's black car. The ache inside me was terrible when I saw my little sister try to get in the car. How awful it was to send her back to Mrs. Tanner with so many injuries. I didn't feel like a good sister at all, but I didn't feel so bad that I gave up my dream of living with her. It would happen, I knew, but I'd never let her ride my bike again.

Autumn came, and the leaves were raked, apples picked, corn harvested and cabbage taken to the sauerkraut factory. I got skirts and sweaters for school and looked like every other girl there, right down to my new saddle shoes.

I was glad, too, that Jane and I now lived in two different worlds. It was easy being polite to her, but I avoided her most of the time and spent many hours studying. By the end of the first four months of high school, I had made all nineties and thought learning was a cinch.

During the Christmas holidays, Mama called me into the dining room, where she was knitting, and said she had some good news for me.

"Millie doesn't live with the Tanners anymore," she said. "She's living with the Harmons out on Murray Hill. Mrs. Harmon wants you to come and visit Millie. Do you want to go?"

I had to sit down. I was so excited, I couldn't talk. I thought about God, and I knew He had heard my prayers, and Millie's, too. I continued to stare out the window in front of me, and I barely heard Mama talking to me.

"Mary, Mary, do you want to go? You can if you would like."

"Yes, I have to go," I said, as I jumped up from my chair. "But I wish you had let Millie come here to live."

"I didn't have anything to do with it. Your own father knows the Harmons, and he wanted Millie to live with them. Now, you'd better pack your pajamas and toothbrush and your dungarees and flannel shirts so Dad can take you this afternoon."

"How long may I stay?" I asked.

"Until New Year's Day," said Mama, smiling at me.

I was upstairs, packed, and back down within fifteen minutes. I put on my hat, coat, mittens and boots and went out the door as I thanked Mama.

It seemed a long way from the Shays to the Harmons, and I was disappointed there were so many miles between us. But when I arrived, Millie was in the snow waiting. What happy hugging we did that day, and Millie couldn't wait for me to meet her new "mom".

Mrs. Harmon was a fine lady, and I liked her from the first hello.

She and I said we were happy to meet each other, and she took my bag of clothes. Since the day was sunny and bright, she said we should be outside.

"I'll call when supper's ready," she said from the back room.

Millie and I, along with ten-year-old Bonnie and five-year-old Ben, ran to the barn for sleds. For two joyful hours, we slid down every hill we could find.

After supper, we played Old Maid and dominoes until bedtime. What a Christmas holiday! The best present I could have received was to see my sister in a new home. It was a miracle!

When Millie and I were in her bedroom alone, I asked her how she got away from the Tanners.

"Our father came to visit me three times after you moved away, Mary, and the last time was a Sunday in October. He asked me how things were, and I told him that Dad Tanner did bad things to me, and I told him exactly what Mr. Tanner did. Our father was so angry, he swore he'd get me away from there. That's when he brought me to the Harmons, and I think our father told Miss Warring about Mr. Tanner, because she didn't try to take me back there."

I couldn't believe that my sister had been brave enough to tell on Mr. Tanner, but I was so happy she had. I told her about the things he had done to me, and it was good that I could finally talk with someone about my secret. It didn't seem as heavy anymore.

I told Millie that our father hadn't come to see me because the Shays didn't like him.

"But I think we'll both see him now, since the Harmons are his friends," I said, and Millie agreed.

I was sad to leave on New Year's, but I had talked with Mrs. Harmon and made future plans.

She was in the kitchen one morning, rolling out pie crust, and asked me if I'd like to help.

"Sure, I would," I said, and she handed me the rolling pin. I rolled out the rest of the crust, and when I picked it up to put it in the pie tin, it fell all to pieces. I thought she'd be aggravated with me, but she laughed. Then, I got to laughing so hard, I couldn't stop.

I don't know how we ever got the pie in the oven, but we did. And we were both covered down the front of us with flour. Mrs. Harmon said we looked like a couple of clowns.

She helped me mix a batch of oatmeal cookies, and we baked a yellow cake, along with the two apple pies. Every minute was fun. She was easy-going and full of laughter, and I felt very comfortable with her.

In the afternoon, I went to the living room and sat alone thinking. I thought I'd like to live with Mrs. Harmon, but I was sad to think about leaving the Shays. I would miss them very much. But I wanted to be with Millie, and I felt that this was the home where God must have wanted me because my sister was here.

It seemed that the puzzle would be all together if I could move to the Harmons.

I left the living room and went to talk with Mr. and Mrs. Harmon, who were alone in the sitting room.

"Could you take care of another kid?" I asked. "I want to

live here so I can be with my sister, and I want you to be my new parents."

There, that was easy. I waited for an answer.

"What do you think the Shays would say if you told them you wanted to leave?" Mrs. Harmon asked. "I'm sure they don't want you to leave."

"I would be sad to leave, but I would be sadder if I couldn't be here. Is it all right with you if I come to live here?"

"That would be fine with me. What about you, Hiram?"

"Doesn't matter," he said.

"I'll have to talk with the welfare lady," I said, "won't I?"

"If anything is done, you will have to do it, Mary," said Mrs. Harmon. "But, we will be happy to have you with us."

Back at the Shays, I pondered and worried and wondered and imagined.

I finally had everything clear in my mind. I decided not to say anything to the Shays until I first went to the welfare office and spoke with the social worker. If I got a yes there, then I thought I'd tell the Shays, but if I got a no, that would be the end of it.

The next trick was to find a way to the welfare office, and I knew I couldn't ask the Shays to drive me there. I had an hour at school before the bus came.

I talked with Miss Cranor, my new welfare lady, and explained to her what I wanted to do.

"But you have no good reason for leaving the Shays," she argued, "and you're doing so well. I hate to see you change homes and schools."

"I wish I didn't have to, Miss Cranor, but Millie and I have prayed and wished and wished and prayed for this. We know that we belong to each other, and we know that together we're our own family."

"I understand that, Mary, but how do you know you'll like living with the Harmons?"

"I know because my sister is there, and I like Mrs. Harmon more than any foster mother I've had. She's gentle and happy. I spent the week with her, and I noticed how much she loved the children and how well she and her husband got along.

There's just something about Mrs. Harmon that makes me feel that I'm like her. There's an invisible line that connects our thinking. I can't explain it any better."

"You must tell the Shays yourself," said Miss Cranor.

I had a feeling she thought I would be too afraid to tell them. I was afraid, but I could do it because I wasn't afraid enough to give up. And besides, God was in my corner. I could feel it!

CHAPTER 36

Bittersweet

The bus ride home was too short. I didn't have time to think about my approach to the Shays. I couldn't decide how I'd tell them my news.

Would I say, "I'm leaving," or "I have some news for you," or "I'm thinking of living with Millie. What do you think of that?" Well, that last question wouldn't do, I thought. I already knew what they'd think of that, or did I? Maybe they wouldn't mind. Maybe they'd be happy that I could be with Millie again. That was it! They'd be happy. No problem. I'll just tell them. Oh, no, I truly think they'll be angry and hate me. Oh, dear, there's the house. I have to get off this bus.

"Bye, you guys," I called, waving but not looking. "See you tomorrow." With a smile to the driver, I was off the bus. I walked up the driveway onto the porch and opened the screen door. Mama was in the kitchen mixing her special hot milk cake.

"Oh, Mary, I'm glad you're home. Dad is having some trouble with the milking machine and needs you to help him hand milk. He said he didn't know what he'd do without you." She poured the batter into the baking pan.

"I'll hurry," I said, and I ran through the hall and upstairs to change my clothes. Guess they won't find out tonight, I thought, not after hearing "he doesn't know what he'd do without me."

I was back on the bus the next morning, Friday, and doing

the same thinking I'd done on the way home the day before. That would change, I was sure, because I intended to use the weekend to work up my courage. Saturday afternoon. The perfect time, I thought. Miss Cranor had said she'd move me on a weekend, so it would be up to me which one.

If I told the Shays this weekend, I thought, I'd be taken the next. Oh, what a joyous thought, to be with Millie every day. It seemed like a dream. But, back to reality. There were things to take care of at school. I knew telling my new friends good-bye would hurt, but not as much as living three and a half years away from my sister.

I walked to the door of the dining room and saw Dad in his big chair reading a Zane Grey novel. Mama was in her rocking chair darning a pair of Dad's work socks. Gordy was taking a nap and Jane was in her room. It was the perfect time, quiet and peaceful.

"God, please help me," I whispered before I entered the room.

"I have something to tell you," I said nervously, pulling a chair from the table and turning it so I could sit and face them. My, oh my, I thought. This was the toughest thing I ever had to do.

Dad put down his book and looked my way. Mama kept her head down and said, "What is it, Mary?" as she pushed the needle through the heel of the gray wool sock.

I coughed to clear my throat, leaned back in my chair and looked down at my hands folded in my lap. Two more little coughs. It was much more difficult than I had thought it would be. Doubt ran through my mind as I thought that maybe I didn't have to do this now. Maybe it could wait another week. No, I knew I must think of Millie and how happy we would be.

"Mary?" Mama said. "What is it?" and I could hear the small pitch of anxiety in her voice.

"Well," I paused. Might as well get it out, I decided, quick, before I lost my nerve. I opened my mouth and the words fell out.

"I had a good time at the Harmon's with Millie during Christmas vacation, and I talked with Mrs. Harmon and asked her if she could take care of another kid. She said she could, and I told her I wanted to live there. She said it was up to me and she didn't want any part of it, and I said I'd take care of it all...."

"You want to leave us?" Mama said, as she poked the needle into the yarn and then dropped her work into her lap and stared at me.

I looked away from her, to Dad and saw him looking out the window.

"No...yes...well, I just want to live with Millie, that's all. You don't care, do you?"

"Of course we care," said Mama. "We've tried to give you a good home here, and you've seemed happy. You're doing well in school, and we thought we'd always have you, and you'd be like our own."

Her voice got shaky, and her lips quivered.

Oh, no, don't cry, I thought. But wait, I can't help it if she's thinking the wrong way.

"But I'm not your child," I said angrily. "I'm not anybody's child, and I will never be. I am my own child."

Dad turned from the window. "I can't get along without you. There's too much for me alone...I...." His voice was loud, and I knew he'd swear at me in a minute.

"I'm sorry I made you both mad at me, but I have to go live with my sister, and I will leave next Saturday." I stood and turned to leave.

"Wait," shouted Mama. "Come back here."

I stopped, but I did not turn around or move a step. I let the back of my head listen to her voice.

"All right. If that's the way you want it, fine. You can stay in your room the rest of the time you're here. Go to school, come and get your food and eat it in your room. You're so set on leaving, you can leave right now. Pack your clothes. And you cannot take the bicycle. Now, go."

I hurried down the hall and up to my room. And I was so angry, I got a big box of old clothes out of my closet. I put the clothes on the floor and went to my dresser to begin packing. I felt all mixed up inside, but mostly sad to think that someone who was supposed to care about me could be so mean. I also felt happy because I was really and truly going. I wondered if this was a dream. Just the thought made me throw the clothes faster into the box. I didn't want to wake up ever and find it not true. There was only one person who belonged to me, and I belonged to her, and neither of us loved anyone else like we loved each other. So, it didn't matter to me who was mad or not speaking or not caring. I was doing exactly what I had to do, what I had prayed so long and hard for, and I wasn't going to change my mind, no matter what kind of punishment I had to take. There was a storm raging in my head.

The next week was like being in jail. I would rather have had them hit me and get over their anger instead of carrying a grudge. But this time, when the Shays and Jane and Gordy didn't talk to me, I didn't care so much. I didn't want to talk to them, either, if they were sulky and childish. I knew what I was doing, and I wasn't about to change my mind, no matter what they did. She had hurt me the worst when she said I couldn't take the bicycle. I'd probably never have another one to ride, and I knew I probably never would have one of my own, even though it would always be a big wish of mine.

Riding a bike is the next best thing to riding a horse, I thought. The bike dream had seemed more realistic than my horse dream, but I supposed now they were equally impossible.

Monday, I left school to let Miss Cranor know that she should take me Saturday to my new home. I was sure, since I had chosen it myself, that it would be the best one ever.

As the week dragged on with the Shays, there were times when I wondered if I should just start out walking to the Harmon's. The jail-type existence was hard on me. I never did like having anyone mad, and I never wanted to hurt anyone if I could help it.

I knew I'd miss Shep and Polly, but there'd be other animals I could love just as well. And, I reminded myself, I'd be with my sister, which is the way life should be, sisters and brothers together. And that was another thing. Life was supposed to be mother and father and children living together. The books I read said so, movies I had seen said so, and even the Bible had said so. But, I hadn't read anything about parents taking care of their own children instead of leaving them on the street or allowing them to be mistreated by people the parents didn't even know. I was supposed to have parents loving me and making decisions for me. Even animals are better to their babies than my parents were to me.

This life of mine is quite lopsided and love-empty, I thought, but I'm not going to let anyone predict my future. I'll show them all that they might think they've got me down now, but I'm not giving up! God and I know what's right for me, and the whole world can be mad, but going to a new home to live with my sister is the right thing.

The more I thought about it, the more I was sure the Shays would come to me and tell me good-bye. I was wrong. Miss Cranor knocked on the front door at ten o'clock Saturday morning. I was waiting in the living room with my Millie doll in my arms and my two boxes of clothes, books and puzzles by the door. I asked Miss Cranor to wait while I went to the kitchen to tell Mama good-bye.

"I'm leaving now, Mama." Her back was to me as she stood at the stove, and I could smell the chocolate pudding she was stirring. I waited for her response, but there was nothing. I felt so heavy as I turned away and walked to the living room and out the front door away from my fifth home.

While we were riding to Murray Hill where the Harmons lived, Miss Cranor asked me if I was happy about my decision. I said I was happy about my decision but sad about the scene I'd just left in the kitchen with Mrs. Shay.

"I don't like to have people mad at me, Miss Cranor."

"They won't be angry forever," she said. "In time, they'll be friends with you."

I looked at Miss Cranor and smiled, thinking that what she said could never be true. Even though she'd never said she agreed with what I had done, I felt that she thought it was right. She talked so kindly to me, and I noticed a smile on her face as we rode along.

"Miss Cranor, thank you for taking me back to Millie," I said.

"You're welcome, Mary. I'm happy for you and your sister."

I took a long, deep breath, let it out with a sigh and leaned back against the car seat.

"I'm happy for us, too," I said. "But, you know, Miss Cranor, all of this reminds me of those games of hide and seek or kick the can, when I would try to think of a strategy for myself that would give me enough freedom to get to home base without getting caught. And that's how it is now. My struggles are over, and I'll be with my sister and the best mother a girl could have. And, do you know why I think she's the best for me, Miss Cranor? Because Mrs. Harmon and I have what you call a common bond. I believe we think alike and act alike. She seems to be just what I'd want my mother to be. Yessiree! When I walk in that door of the Harmon's house, I'll be home free.

E P I L O G U E

Through the years, my sister and I have remained very close, even though we have lived most of our adult years five hundred miles apart.

Mom Harmon was the best "mother" I had, and my happiest years were with her. During her years of foster care, she provided a happy home for thirty-two children.

My own mother died in 1991, and in her Will was the following statement: "I acknowledge that I have six children to whom I am leaving nothing, because they did not come to me in my time of need."